## Praise for *Tipping the Odds for the Entrepreneur*

Kevin Maki is a long-time student of entrepreneurial success. I have always been amazed by his ability to differentiate between great and mediocre businesses. I am proud of him for translating that knowledge into his own successful company. *Tipping the Odds for the Entrepreneur* is a joy to read because it provides valuable insights in an easy to read and entertaining format.

**Michael H. Davidson, MD, FACC, FACP, FNLA**; Chief Medical Officer, Radiant Research; Clinical Professor, Director of Preventive Cardiology and Vice Chair of Medicine University of Chicago Pritzker School of Medicine

As a scientist and budding entrepreneur, I was eager to read Kevin Maki's latest book, *Tipping the Odds for the Entrepreneur*. I was blown away at the depth of his experience and wisdom about the business world. Kevin leads the reader through simple, easily understood business and life principles that have stood the test of time. I am much more confident in my own prospects for success having this book as a guide.

**William S. Harris, PhD**, Founder and President OmegaQuant Analytics

If you are thinking of starting a business, read this book first. It is filled with good advice that will help keep the odds of success on your side.

**Anthony Curtis**, Founder and CEO Huntington Press & *The Las Vegas Advisor*

This book is a wonderful read for future entrepreneurs, seasoned entrepreneurs, and all business professionals. Something valuable can be learned by all who read it.

**Seattle Sutton, RN**, Founder and President
Seattle Sutton's Healthy Eating

Kevin Maki is the thinking man's entrepreneur. *Tipping the Odds for the Entrepreneur* is the perfect companion for the business person who wishes he or she had a trusted friend to provide perspective and practical guidance

**Roger Farley**, Founder and President
MTG Trading

If you are thinking of starting a business, this book is required reading. It is clearly written and well organized, with lots of stories to illustrate smart, practical advice.

**Stephen J. Vivian**, Partner
Prism Capital

Kevin gives expert advice from a personal and professional perspective. *Tipping the Odds for the Entrepreneur* is a valuable resource for anyone interested in starting a business.

**Annette Norwood**, Founder
Posh Hair Salon and Color Bar

This is a terrific book. It inspires with great story telling while teaching the entrepreneur what it really takes to keep your business competitive and moving forward.

**Rose Hanbury**, Founder
Night Light Designs

Kevin understands what it takes to be successful. I found *Tipping the Odds for the Entrepreneur* an exceptionally useful resource.

**Vlado Lenoch**, Managing Director
William Tell Banquets

*Tipping the Odds for the Entrepreneur* is general enough to apply to anyone starting any type of small business, but with good specifics and case studies on how to manage the details.

**David A Mark, PhD**, President
dmark consulting

# Tipping the Odds for the Entrepreneur

## Big Ideas on Success for the Small Business Owner

## Kevin C. Maki

**Provident Business Press**
Glen Ellyn, Illinois

**Publisher's Cataloging in Publications**
**Maki, Kevin C.**

Tipping the odds for the entrepreneur:  big ideas on success for the small business owner/Kevin C. Maki – 1st edition.

p.        cm.

Includes index.

LCCN-in-Publication Data
Maki, Kevin C., 1965-

ISBN-13: 978-0-9841417-0-8
ISBN-10: 0-9841417-0-7

  1.   Entrepreneurship    2. Small Business    3. Marketing

*Quantity discounts are available to companies and educational institutions for reselling, educational purposes, subscription incentives, gifts or fundraising campaigns.*

For more information, contact the publisher at Provident Business Press, 489 Taft Avenue, Glen Ellyn, Illinois, 60137; (630) 858-4400
Information@TippingTheOdds.com

**Other Books by Kevin C. Maki**

*Business and Investing*

*Beating the Dow with Rental Houses: How Small Investors Can Create Wealth and Income with Single-Family Rental Properties*

*How to be a Successful Value Investor in Single-Family Rental Properties (in press, 2010)*

*Medical/Scientific*

*Practical Lipid Management: Concepts and Controversies*
Co-Authored with Dr. Peter Toth

*Therapeutic Lipidology*
Co-Edited with Drs. Michael Davidson and Peter Toth

*This book is dedicated to the memories of Stanley and Zdenka Lenoch, who convinced me that I could achieve anything, as long as I was willing to pay the price in hard work and persistence.*

# Table of Contents

## Section 1 – The Big Ideas

## Chapter 5
## Avoiding Common Mistakes that Lead to Business Failure................................................................... 43

Lack of Direction
Insufficient Sales
Poor Quality
Greed and Impatience
Poor Cost Controls
Insufficient Working Capital

## Chapter 6
## Big Ideas about Marketing and Sales............... 57

The Four Elements of Marketing/Sales Performance
Generating Leads
Cost Effective Marketing
Narrow Your Focus (Avoid Blind Archery)
Internet Marketing
Test Small, Then Expand When You Determine What Works
A Few Percentage Points Can Make an Enormous Difference
The Importance of an Offer
Lead Conversion - Persuading People to Buy
The AIDA Formula in Advertising
Integrity in Advertising
Guarantees - Standing Behind Your Product or Service
Build Credibility with Testimonials
Use Press Releases to Help Make Potential Customers Aware of Your Business
Appear on Radio and Television Programs
Make the Process of Purchasing Easy and Convenient

## Chapter 6 (*Continued*)

## Chapter 7

## Chapter 8

**Chapter 9**

**Management that Promotes Employee Engagement and Enthusiasm**................................................... **99**

**Chapter 10**

**Leveraging Individual Strengths and Managing Around Weaknesses**................................................... **115**

**Chapter 12 (*Continued*)**
Learn to Communicate Well
On Being Happy

# Section 2 – Profiles of Entrepreneurs

*Section 1*

# The Big Ideas

*I have learned that if one advances confidently in the direction of his dreams, and endeavors to live the life he has imagined, he will meet with a success unexpected in common hours.*
— Henry David Thoreau

The first section of *Tipping the Odds for the Entrepreneur* covers some of the big ideas about success as a business owner that I have learned over more than 25 years of studying entrepreneurs, initially as an employee and later as a business owner and consultant. These experiences have led me to believe that entrepreneurial success is rarely a matter of luck. My experience has also convinced me that there is no such thing as a gene for entrepreneurship. With rare exceptions, success, or failure, results from learning and applying the knowledge and skills necessary to attract, serve and retain profitable customers. Application of these big ideas will – I am confident – help you to increase profits, enhance productivity and reduce management headaches.

*Chapter 1*

# Learning to be a Successful Entrepreneur

*Actions are seeds of fate. Seeds grow into destiny.*
                                              – Harry Truman

This book covers some of what I consider to be the most important ideas about succeeding as a business owner. I have learned these through personal experience as a business owner and manager, as well as more than 25 years of studying the strategies of successful and unsuccessful entrepreneurs. My experiences have convinced me that several key concepts and behaviors are central to running a profitable and satisfying business. I cannot promise that reading this book (or any other book) will provide you with all of the information needed to start and run a thriving business. However, I am sure that understanding these concepts will help you to avoid some of the most common errors made by small business owners. In addition to helping you avoid mistakes, this book aims to provide insights into success strategies used or described by:

1.  Small business owners I have admired;
2.  Managers of multibillion dollar companies such as Warren Buffett and Charlie Munger (Berkshire Hathaway), Jack Welch (General Electric), and Howard Schultz (Starbucks);

3.  Researchers and consultants who have studied businesses to identify traits and behaviors associated with success (and failure).

Understanding and applying these big ideas will – I am confident – help you to increase profits, enhance productivity and reduce management headaches. Charlie Munger, long-time business partner of legendary investor Warren Buffett, says "You have to learn all the big ideas in the key disciplines in a way that they're in a mental latticework in your head and you automatically use them for the rest of your life." If you thoroughly learn these big ideas about running a successful business (many of which are advocated by Buffett and Munger), you will find yourself automatically drawing on them for the rest of your life.

**Put the Odds on Your Side**
Statistics from the Internal Revenue Service and Small Business Administration show that there are roughly 27 million small businesses in the United States. Although the definition varies, a small business is often defined as one with fewer than 50 employees. Many small businesses are sole proprietorships with no employees, but, according to the US Bureau of Labor Statistics, small businesses still account for a large fraction of US jobs. Firms with fewer than 500 employees accounted for 55.8% of total US employment in 2005 and those with fewer than 50 employees accounted for 29.9%.

According to the Small Business Administration, there were an estimated 637,000 new business formations in 2007 and 560,000 business closures. Approximately 67% of new businesses survive at least two years, 44% survive at least four years and 31% survive at least seven years. It is difficult to determine what percentage of business closures are failures. Some are sold to larger organizations and some served their intended purpose, such as helping a parent to fund a child's education, and are closed because the original goal has been met. Regardless, it is clear that a majority of new businesses don't last five years and it is a good bet that a large proportion of these were unprofitable or marginally profitable before closing their doors.

Starting and running a business can be one of life's most rewarding activities, or, if done poorly, can result in enormous pain and suffering. I am a firm believer in success modeling. If you want to accomplish something, locate people who have already done so and study their methods. Find out what they did right and what mistakes were made along the way. Copy them, minus the mistakes. I was fortunate to spend time early in my life working for successful entrepreneurs. This experience provided a foundation for my views about entrepreneurship and convinced me that the knowledge and skills required to be a successful business owner can be learned and practiced effectively by nearly anyone with sufficient persistence and dedication.

**Luck is the Intersection of Preparation and Opportunity**
My investigations have led me to the conclusion that success is rarely a matter of luck. Luck may play a role in the short-term, but in the long-run the actions of the owner/manager will nearly always be the most important factor in the degree of success (or failure). A lucky amateur may knock out a top professional in the early rounds of the *World Series of Poker*, but professional players who have mastered the skills of successful play are able to earn six or seven-figure incomes year in and year out. In many respects entrepreneurs are like professional poker players in that, for both, luck nearly always takes a back seat to knowledge and skill in the long-run.

However, not everyone is cut out to be a business owner. I know very talented people who have either tried to run businesses and failed, or found that they did not enjoy the process. I have also known people who were successful as independent practitioners (e.g., consultants, accountants), who did poorly when they started adding employees. This book assumes that you either own a business or are convinced that owning a business is a good fit for your personal situation. The mechanics of starting a business will not be covered, since there are many good books that explain how to do so. Instead, the objective will be to provide insights into strategies and behaviors that have been used by other entrepreneurs to create and run successful enterprises. Most of the concepts covered apply to nearly any service or product business, whether a one-person, in-home operation or a company with dozens of employees in multiple offices. While the focus is on the small business owner, many of the ideas covered will also be useful to managers in larger organizations, especially those who have responsibility for a business unit that may function much like a small business.

**Learn from the Best**

I have learned a great deal from studying accomplished people. Among these, the most influential to me personally has been Warren Buffett. Mr. Buffett has been at or near the top of the Forbes 400 list of the world's wealthiest individuals for many years. He is well known as a highly skilled investor and Chairman of Berkshire Hathaway, a holding company with more than 200,000 employees that counts such iconic names as GEICO Insurance, Fruit of the Loom and Dairy Queen among its wholly owned subsidiaries. Since 1965 when he took over as Chairman of the company, at the time a struggling textile mill (which has since been closed), Berkshire Hathaway's book value has compounded at more than 20% annually, far exceeding the growth of American business in general, as represented by the Standard & Poor's 500 index.

Each year thousands of people, including my wife Cathy and me, make the trek to Omaha to attend the Berkshire Hathaway shareholders meeting. Warren Buffett and Charlie Munger (Buffett's longtime business partner and the Berkshire Hathaway Vice Chair) answer unscripted questions for six hours on topics ranging from current events, business, investing and how to succeed in business and life. Even though I have never had a face-to-face conversation with either, both Warren Buffett and Charlie Munger have played important roles in shaping my views about business and entrepreneurship. I am grateful to each for sharing their views and have included a full chapter (Chapter 12) on big ideas from Warren Buffet, Charlie Munger and Berkshire Hathaway.

Another individual of special note is the late Peter Drucker. He is credited with being the inventor of the discipline of professional management and the ideas and concepts that he outlined in his 39 books on the topic have influenced countless executives and business owners since the 1940s. I am continually amazed at how many useful concepts and strategies about business had their origins in the mind of Peter Drucker, including many of those promoted in recent business books by other authors.

No matter how helpful ideas from leaders of large companies and their advisors may be, the small business owner faces challenges that may seem far removed from those of running a Fortune 500 company. Rest assured that the topics covered in this book will have practical applications, whether you own a hair salon, sandwich shop, landscaping business, accounting firm or clothing store. I have included a mixture of real-world stories and examples from small and large companies, including my own, along with key points from research described by academics and business consultants such as Peter Drucker, Bain and Company and The Gallup Organization. The final section of the book profiles several entrepreneurs ranging from individuals who have just recently taken the plunge to start a new business to those who built successful family businesses that were sold to Berkshire Hathaway for hundreds of millions of dollars.

## My Life as an Entrepreneur

Warren Buffett often quotes results from a study he read years ago suggesting a relationship between entrepreneurial success and the age at which a person undertook his or her first business venture. Warren was buying six-packs of Coke for $0.25 and selling each for a nickel at a very early age. At the age of 14 he had earned enough money from activities such as delivering newspapers and operating used pinball machines to buy a farm. He did not grow corn or soybeans himself, but instead leased the land to farmers who did.

Like Warren, I delivered papers. I also cut lawns and shoveled snow. I worked in a Chinese restaurant for three years. By age 16 I was working at a small hotel. Over the 10 years I spent at that hotel, which grew from 97 to over 400 rooms during my tenure, I performed nearly every function at one time or another. I started as a general maintenance worker, was promoted to desk clerk, and ultimately Guest Service Manager. I performed the night audit on weekends for years, and at other times I was the weekend Housekeeping Supervisor. I cleaned rooms, bussed tables in the restaurant and banquet facilities, hauled garbage, acted as chauffeur and performed countless other tasks as needed.

The husband and wife who owned the hotel were immigrants from Eastern Europe who realized the American dream. They taught me more about running a successful business than I could have picked up in years of business school. Later I was fascinated to read academic studies that supported many of the principles that were second nature to me as a result of my years at the hotel. This experience also showed me that owning a successful business can be both lucrative and gratifying, and that doing so does not require an MBA from an Ivy League school. The owners' pride and satisfaction with each new addition or renovation to the hotel was palpable. Money was not their only motivation, but their enterprise was very profitable.

Owning a business allows you to surround yourself with people you like and respect. In our companies we work hard, but also have fun. I have been able to choose who I want to work with and walk away from those people (employees and clients) who don't fit into the culture we strive to maintain. To paraphrase Warren Buffett, "Working with people who make your stomach churn is like saving up sex for your old age; not a good idea."

While I remained interested in business, I chose to pursue education in a scientific field. I have a PhD in Epidemiology, which is the study of factors associated with diseases in human populations. Epidemiologists are sometimes referred to as medical detectives because they try to figure out what factors cause diseases with the ultimate aim of identifying strategies to more effectively prevent and treat them. In preparation for writing this book I have tried to apply my training as a "medical detective" to investigate the "causes" of business successes and failures with the goal of helping myself and other entrepreneurs to improve their odds for success.

I worked as a Research Health Scientist in the Department of Veterans Affairs for five years before leaving to join a private, for-profit clinical research organization. I ran the Human Nutrition and Metabolism Research Unit for 10 years in that company (actually a series of companies because of mergers and acquisitions) where I reached the levels of Senior Vice President and Chief Science Officer. During that time I met and married my wife, a nurse practitioner. Together, we started a family, as well as a side business buying and managing rental properties. This business allowed my wife Cathy to "retire" from nursing and work more flexible hours.

After 10 years of running a business unit for someone else, I decided to leave my job to start my own company. In 2004 I founded Provident Clinical Research & Consulting, Inc. with a partner who had been one of my staff members. Over the years I had developed relationships with clients who trusted me because I had been fanatical about our business unit providing great customer service and keeping promises. We had a consistent track record of delivering on time and within budget. Because of the hard won trust and confidence of many clients in the food and pharmaceutical industries, our new business had plenty of projects from its inception. Within two years, revenues had eclipsed the level that it had taken me 10 years to attain with my employer. Eventually, Cathy and I bought out our partner and the company has grown profitably. We now have three offices. Our other enterprise, the rental property business, has also continued to do well, even during the worst housing recession since the Great Depression.

As expected, the road has not been without potholes, but our main business success metrics – repeat business and profitability – have been highly satisfactory. Our lives are stressful at times, but I experience fewer frustrations and a greater sense of control as a business owner than was ever the case during my 25 years as an employee.

Because our businesses have done well and are staffed by competent and trustworthy people, I have been able to pursue additional activities, including writing textbooks and teaching. I have also started a scholarship fund to assist with educational goals for children of low-income families. With the publication of this book we are launching a new business to produce books and other information products aimed at helping individuals and entrepreneurs achieve their personal and business goals more quickly and with fewer errors. I get enormous satisfaction from helping others succeed and hope to live the ideal espoused by Ben Franklin of "doing well while doing good."

**We Welcome Your Feedback**
Golf coaches are fond of the expression "Practice doesn't make perfect, practice only makes permanent. Practice with feedback is what helps a player improve." If you find the information in this book helpful, or if you have suggestions for improvement, please visit our web site (www.TippingTheOdds.com) and let us know your thoughts. We are especially interested in hearing from entrepreneurs with stories about how they have applied concepts presented here and the results – favorable or otherwise. This feedback will be valuable in helping us to produce better products, including future editions of this book, and to identify where we can improve our offerings to make them more useful to our clients and customers.

*Chapter 2*

# Loyalty, the Key to Running a SLEEC Business

*Profit in business comes from repeat customers, customers that boast about your product or service, and that bring friends with them.*

— W. Edwards Deming

In his excellent books *The Loyalty Effect, Loyalty Rules!*, and *The Ultimate Question: Driving Good Profits and True Growth*, Fred Reichheld of Bain and Company outlines his research findings regarding what he terms the Loyalty Business Model. I stumbled across *The Loyalty Effect* at an airport bookstore. While reading it I could barely contain my excitement because the book provided a theoretical framework for many of the lessons I had learned during my years working at a hotel as a teenager and young adult. A theme I heard over and over was the importance of repeat business. It costs much more to obtain a new customer than it does to entice a happy customer to return. As a business owner, your job is to create and retain loyal customers/clients.

Fred Reichheld and his colleagues at Bain have studied many businesses in a variety of industries to assess what factors are associated with customer and employee loyalty. His years of investigation were launched by a curious finding in a Bain and Company study of the insurance industry. They noticed that there was a relationship between insurance company payroll expenses and profitability: higher payroll was associated with greater profits. This was unexpected and led the research team to ask why this might be the case. At first they thought that the companies with the higher payrolls must be hiring more qualified workers, such as those with prior experience or graduates from top schools. It turned out that this was not the explanation. The reason for the higher payroll was greater average employee tenure. In other words, the more profitable companies had lower employee turnover. Later studies across many industries showed that two factors were consistent predictors of profitability:

1. Low employee turnover,
2. Low customer defection.

Mr. Reichheld notes that, on average, US companies lose roughly half their customers in five years and half their employees in four. Those that do a better job of retaining employees and customers are consistently more profitable. He has shown that increasing customer retention by just 5% is associated with an average increase in pre-tax profits of roughly 50%. In addition, seasoned employees with high job satisfaction have 2-3 times the productivity of someone just starting with the company, suggesting that productivity grows more quickly than salary, leading to greater output per person in companies with low turnover. Not surprisingly, companies with employees who have high job satisfaction also tend to have high customer satisfaction.

**The SLEEC Business**
Reichheld's studies confirmed what I had seen in action while working in a family-owned hotel. I recently had lunch at that same hotel with a son of the original owners (he is profiled later in this book). He and his brother now own several hotels and the General Managers of two of their properties are individuals I worked with more than 18 years ago. I was surprised to walk in and recognize several staff members who I had known in the 1980s. They have obviously been successful at retaining some of their best employees. Fred Reichheld would not be surprised, as his research suggests that their ability to retain key staff members has contributed to their success.

Happy employees play a key role in creating happy, satisfied customers, generating a virtuous cycle. The purpose of a business is to get and keep customers. It is costly to obtain a new customer, so repeat business is typically more profitable than initial purchases. Happy customers will come back and purchase more frequently and in larger amounts whether your business is fast food, consulting or party baskets. They will also spread the word, helping to bring in new customers.

Rare is the business that has happy customers and unhappy employees. There is a strong relationship between employee satisfaction and customer satisfaction. Properly trained employees with a customer service orientation will go the extra mile to keep the customers and clients happy. In my experience with businesses large and small, there are few traffic jams on the extra mile. Employees who feel valued and who have received the proper training and encouragement will treat your customers or clients in a way that enhances loyalty. Employees who feel unappreciated and disgruntled will create customer experiences that destroy loyalty and profits.

I use the acronym SLEEC (which I pronounce "sleek") to remind our management team that everything we do must support our central goals. The components of SLEEC are:

S = Sales & Marketing
L = Loyal
E = Engaged
E = Employees &
C = Customers/Clients

**Sales and Marketing**
It has been said that "nothing" is the terrible thing that happens when you fail to promote your business. You can have the best service or product on the planet, but if you don't let potential customers know about it, sales will not materialize. I will cover this area in detail in later chapters, but the sales and marketing functions are intended to identify and contact people who may be

able to utilize your service or product and let them know about the advantages of your business. This not only applies to new customers, but also to current and prior customers. Repeat business is key to profitability.

## Engaged Customers and Employees

Loyal, engaged customers will purchase more often, in larger amounts and provide referrals. Loyal, engaged employees will produce more and be less likely to leave, lowering the extra expenses associated with recruitment, hiring and training staff. In our business, everything we do is aimed toward enhancing customer and employee loyalty and satisfaction. Our batting average is not perfect, but our numbers show that our employee turnover is far below our industry average and repeat customers account for more than 90% of our business.

## The Low Road and the High Road

Like the extra mile, traffic on the high road is sparse, but the high road is the surest route to long-term competitive advantage. Periodically Warren Buffett writes letters to the operating managers of the businesses within Berkshire Hathaway. A consistent theme of these letters is that Berkshire has benefitted substantially from its reputation for integrity and fairness. Each year at the annual meeting a film is shown that includes a clip of Warren testifying at a Senate hearing regarding the unethical and illegal activities in bond trading that resulted in the resignation of the Chairman of Salomon Brothers and to Mr. Buffett being named interim Chairman. In this clip he states that he has conveyed to all employees that should they lose money for the company, he will be understanding, but if they lose a shred of reputation for the company, he will be ruthless.

Customer and employee loyalty begins with trust. Trust must be earned and it results from consistently providing value and behaving with integrity. This involves more than a single-minded focus on financial results. Profits are the life-blood of a company, but the focus should be on creating long-term value through trust and loyalty rather than short-term profits. When money matters more than people, the result is often the low road where it is standard practice to take advantage of employees, vendors and customers to extract the maximum short-term profit rather than building long-term, profitable relationships that benefit all parties.

Common examples of this short-term mentality include fine print in contracts that leave the customer or vendor open to unpleasant surprises, such as a credit card that doubles the interest rate after one late payment. Airlines do this when they advertise flights after a certain number of frequent flyer miles have been accumulated, but then offer almost no seats for that number of miles. A call to the airline will frequently reveal that there are no seats available for, say 25,000 miles, but there are seats available for 40,000 miles. Should it be a surprise then that most major US airlines have struggled to maintain profitability?

**The Economics of Customer Loyalty**
Mr. Reichheld provides research to document both the value of repeat business and a model to illustrate why customer loyalty is so valuable. He cites several reasons for the enhanced profitability associated with repeat business, which include:

1. Initial customer acquisition costs;
2. Pricing power is enhanced with repeat business.
3. Satisfied repeat customers tend to make larger and more frequent purchases;
4. Working with a client or customer repeatedly leads to operational efficiencies;
5. Happy, satisfied customers provide recommendations and referrals.

**Initial Acquisition Costs**
To make an initial sale, it is necessary to identify a potential customer, qualify that customer to ensure that your product or service can meet his or her needs and that the customer really has the means to utilize your company. Your product or service must be pitched and information provided to counter objections and convince him or her of your advantages, relative to the competition, regarding time, price, quality (service and/or

product), convenience and risk (these will be discussed in more detail below).

Costs for initial acquisition are high. On the other hand, if you have previously made a sale to a customer who has been pleased with the results, and felt that he or she received good value for the money spent, it will typically be much less costly to make the next sale. A degree of trust has been established and the customer has already been identified and qualified. The cost to make a repeat sale is generally a fraction of that for an initial sale and the differential is usually larger when your product or service is complex or high-cost. It is much less expensive to do good work and keep your customers happy than it is to find new ones.

**Pricing Power is Often Greater for Repeat Business**
Once you have worked with a customer or client and he or she has felt that good value was received for the money spent, price tends to move to a lower rung in the hierarchy of factors driving the purchase decision (time, price, quality, convenience and risk). If there is high confidence that you will deliver good quality in the timeframe promised, the customer feels that he or she is taking less risk and will usually be less concerned about getting the lowest possible price. As Warren Buffett has said many times, "price is what you pay, value is what you get."

In our businesses we strive to provide excellent quality at a reasonable price. We are rarely the least expensive option, but our clients understand that we need to charge a bit more to be able to put the "best players on the field." In turn, our group is able to provide high quality and exceptional customer service. In the end, everybody wins. We make a fair profit and the client is left feeling that he or she received good value. In other words, we earn the trust necessary to be able to charge the prices necessary to maintain a high quality team that delivers results on time and within budget.

**Happy, Satisfied Customers Purchase More and More Often**
Customers who feel they have received good value will be more apt to come back and to think of your business for other types of

needs. The average size and frequency of sales both go up. In many businesses happy customers will tend to come back again and again. As long as neither party does something to undermine the trust that develops with a good working partnership, the relationship can continue to be a win for both parties.

## Working with a Client or Customer Repeatedly Leads to Efficiencies for Both Parties

In our business, it can take months to negotiate a first contract. Our average contract for conducting a clinical trial is in the hundreds of thousands of dollars and many issues must be resolved to both party's satisfaction in order to proceed. Companies differ in their requirements for billing and what information needs to be provided in periodic project updates. Documents and forms need to be developed that both parties approve. All of these tasks get easier with repetition, which leads to efficiencies on both sides. We often require 20-30% fewer hours for project management when working with repeat customers compared to a first-time customer.

## Happy Customers Provide Recommendations and Referrals

Customers who feel they received good value are much more likely to recommend your product or service to others. You have a powerful advantage compared to your competition when a satisfied customer recommends you. You can facilitate this by actively seeking referrals from satisfied customers, which will be discussed in more detail in the chapters on sales and marketing.

## SLEEC and Willingness to Walk Away from Bad Relationships

We use the SLEEC concepts as central guiding principles of our businesses. In all of our activities we strive to enhance the satisfaction and loyalty of our employees and clients. Murphy's Law tells us that we should expect that difficulties will arise along the way and we understand that our responses to problems in a project or with an employee are important signals about our commitment to increasing trust and loyalty.

You will undoubtedly find that a fraction of your employees and customers will account for most of your productivity and profits. These parties should be receiving the majority of your time and effort. You will also find that a fraction of your employees and customers will generate the great majority of your difficulties. It is not fair to your other employees and customers to spend so much time on these problem parties that the most productive get short-changed. Therefore, it is critical to be willing to walk away from relationships with toxic employees or customers. While this decision should never be taken lightly, you have to be willing to walk away from relationships from which you and your business are not receiving value. In later chapters I will cover how to identify those situations where walking away might be the best option.

**Detailed Strategies are Covered in Later Chapters**
This chapter has served as an overview of some of the guiding principles for running a SLEEC business. Later chapters will cover each of the elements of SLEEC in more detail with specific strategies to enhance sales/marketing efforts and to promote employee and customer engagement.

*Chapter 3*

# Attitudes and Habits of Successful Entrepreneurs

*When you do the things you need to do when you need to do them, the day will come when you can do the things you want to do when you want to do them.*

– Zig Ziglar

**Belief, Time Perspective and Integrity**
Over years of studying successful people, it gradually became apparent to me that three central themes described the most successful entrepreneurs:

1. Belief that their actions would lead to success in reaching their objectives. To paraphrase Henry Ford, if you believe you can or can't, either way you are probably right.
2. Long time perspective, that is, a willingness to delay gratification while working toward long-term goals;
3. Integrity.

Success requires continually taking actions to move toward your objectives, often in the face of obstacles and set-backs. Successful entrepreneurs believe that if they do the right things long enough, they will prevail. They are willing to delay gratification while obtaining the knowledge, skills and experience required to successfully launch and operate a business.

In the long-run, the world is mostly a fair place. If a person lives long enough, he or she is likely to get what he/she deserves. The most successful people build trust with customers, employees, other stakeholders and financial institutions. They tell the truth, keep their promises and treat people fairly. They deserve their success because it is not derived from lying, cheating or stealing, but rather from creating value for others for which they are fairly compensated.

**Know Your Personal Strengths and Weaknesses**
Some people have a good mirror. They look in and see themselves as others see them. These individuals are able to accurately assess their own talents and personal weaknesses. Such folks are lucky and few. Most of us have blind spots or distorted views. These may be obvious to others around us, but less so to ourselves.

It is a good idea to elicit feedback from your friends, family, colleagues, subordinates and superiors regarding your strengths and weaknesses. You should also give serious thought to those areas where you have been consistently successful and those where you have struggled. Think about the functions and tasks that will be required in your business. Those that will be critical for your success but are a poor match to your personal talents need to be dealt through outsourcing, delegating or partnering. The worst thing you can do is take on these tasks yourself and do them poorly or procrastinate, not getting them accomplished in a timely way.

As an example, I am an introvert and I would starve if I had to make cold calls to elicit business from new clients. I would find excuses, procrastinate and feel miserable until the business died of neglect. On the other hand, once a client has expressed an initial interest in our company, I am good at building rapport, making the case for our expertise and track record, and generally building trust and confidence. I compensate for my deficiency by employing sales professionals who can get potential clients to the table. I wish I didn't have to spend the money to do so, but I recognize that this is a critical element of the success of our company for which I am ill suited.

On the other hand, employees and colleagues have told me that I am good at mediating conflicts and helping people develop systems to prevent errors and work more effectively and efficiently. I agree that these are tasks for which I have aptitude. However, I find doing these things draining and unfulfilling. If I am not careful I will get sucked into spending far too much time helping people resolve conflicts and develop systems, causing me to burn out and lose enthusiasm. A key success principle is to identify which high-value activities you do best, that you also enjoy, so that you can engineer your business in such a way that you spend a majority of your time on these and less time on tasks you find personally unfulfilling, or that can be easily completed by a vendor, employee or partner.

**Have a Bias for Action**
The probability of success increases in proportion with the number of attempts. In business and personal life, many people suffer from analysis paralysis. They spend so much time deciding what to do, that they often wait much too long before taking action, resulting in lost opportunities. Successful people have a bias toward action. Simply stated, they try many things, abandon those that fail and keep those that work. They are also willing to take action when a careful analysis shows a high probability of success, even when those around them predict failure.

When it comes to starting a business, you should not wait for the stars to align. Like starting a family, there is never an ideal time. While you certainly want to have some contingency plans and a reasonable amount of start-up capital to get your business off the ground, there will never be an ideal time. There will always be things to worry about such as the economy, evolving markets and consumer trends, new technologies that might force a change in your business model, etc. If you are committed to the idea of starting a business, take some time to plan how to do so and then get moving. You may want to keep your full-time job and start your business on the side, take a part-time position to supplement your income during the start-up phase, or ensure that a spouse is able to work at a full-time job during the start-up phase to provide income and health insurance. However, many people end up perpetually in the planning stage and never make it to the doing stage.

## Behave Like an Optimist, Even if You Are Not

In her book *Breaking Murphy's Law, How Optimists Get What They Want from Life – and Pessimists Can Too*, Suzanne Segerstrom outlines a great deal of research showing that optimists are more likely to achieve their major life goals. The important question is why this is the case. No amount of positive thinking will make you successful without action to move you toward your goals.

She outlines some simple experiments with puzzles in which subjects were given a difficult, but solvable, test such as rearranging the letters YRIGCN into a word (the correct answer is CRYING). Most subjects did not get the correct answer because the task was difficult. Subjects were then given a second puzzle that was unsolvable, but told different things. At random, they were told:

1. Performance on the second test is related to anagram skill (creating a *negative* expectation because of failure on the first task); or
2. Performance on the second test is unrelated (*neutral - no positive or negative expectation*); or
3. Performance on the second task uses opposite skills, i.e., that people who do poorly on the first task tend to do well on the second task (*positive expectation*).

People in the neutral expectation group persisted 20% longer in trying to solve the unsolvable puzzle than people in the negative expectation group. People in the positive expectation group (optimists) persisted 50% longer.

In other experiments the opposite tack was taken. People were set up to do well in a task and then given instructions that created negative, neutral or positive expectations. For example, a positive expectation was created by telling people that good performance on the first task (on which nearly all did well) predicted good performance on the second. Again, a positive expectation resulted in persisting longer before giving up.

Optimism is a personality trait. Some people expect good things to happen and view setbacks as minor bumps in the road. Pessimists view the world through a darker lens. When they encounter a setback, they view it as insurmountable and are more likely to give up. The secret to the greater success of optimists appears to be mainly that they simply persist longer without giving up.

> Success seems to be largely a matter of hanging on after others have let go.
> –*William Feather*

Successful people are willing to persist in the face of temporary failure. All things being equal, the person who makes 20 attempts to achieve a goal has twice the probability of success than does the person who makes only 10. Colonel Sanders of Kentucky Fried Chicken fame approached over 1,000 restaurant owners trying to sell his method and recipe for fried chicken. Fortunately for him, he didn't stop after the 100th, 500th or 900th rejection. Thomas Edison performed more than 9,000 experiments on his way to success in developing the light bulb. He viewed each failed attempt as having successfully ruled out another unworkable approach, sort of succeeding by process of elimination.

Below is a quote that has been attributed to various people, including President Calvin Coolidge:

> Nothing can take the place of persistence.
> Talent will not; nothing is more common than
> unsuccessful men with talent. Genius will not;
> unrewarded genius is almost proverb.
> Education will not; the world is full of educated derelicts.

Persistence and determination alone are omnipotent.

I will add one caveat to the general rule about persistence. If you conclude that your original reasoning or assumptions about a business project or partnership were in error, don't keep trying to make a bad situation work out of ego or a desire to push on at all costs. Admit your mistake, ditch the effort and move on.

**Accept the Fact that it is Impossible to Please Everyone**
About 15 times per year I give talks. I have had the good fortune to speak to a wide array of audiences including medical professionals, scientists, investors and patients in various health-related programs such as weight loss clinics and cardiac rehabilitation. Speaker evaluation forms are often provided to those in the audience. These evaluation forms illustrate very clearly the folly of trying to make everyone happy. No matter how well I think my talk went and how many people give me EXCELLENT or ABOVE AVERAGE ratings, there are always one or two negative evaluations in the stack.

I have also experienced this with reviewers' comments after submitting articles to medical journals. My paper will often be sent to two or three experts in the field. It is not uncommon for one or two of these experts to find the paper to be valuable and recommend that it be published, while another expert in the same field will view the paper as badly flawed and not fit to line the bottom of a birdcage. It is not possible to submit a paper that is acceptable to everyone. Successful people develop skin a foot thick and don't incorporate these negative views into their self-image or let negative reviews stop them from trying again. If you believe in your idea and your reasoning, don't give up because someone else criticizes it.

History is full of examples of people who have been wildly successful, despite being told repeatedly that their ideas had no merit. One of my favorites comes from the publishing field. Vicky Lansky submitted her book *Feed Me! I'm Yours*, about making fresh baby food at home, to 49 publishers and received 49 rejections. Most people would have given up by that time, concluding that the idea was a dud. Fortunately, Vicky didn't accept the opinions of her 49 critics. She and her husband put up the money to have the book self-published. This was a good decision. *Feed Me! I'm Yours* has sold more than 2 million copies.

## Develop Discipline

Thomas Edison said "The successful person makes a habit of doing what the failing person doesn't like to do." Successful people dislike the same things that unsuccessful people dislike. The difference between the two is that the successful person accepts that doing difficult and unpleasant tasks will be necessary to achieve his or her objectives, then gets busy doing those things. If he or she doesn't have aptitude for what needs to get done, or has other high-value activities that take precedence, the successful entrepreneur makes sure that someone else is getting the necessary tasks completed.

Don't start a business unless you have passion for what you do. It will be difficult to stay motivated and disciplined if you don't. If you are motivated only by profits, ironically, you are not likely to experience long-term financial success. The most successful entrepreneurs have a passion for providing value to their customers and building a business that has a purpose beyond generating cash flow. Profits are the byproduct of a successful business. If you love what you do, you will find it much easier to exercise the discipline needed to get the job done and stick things out during downturns and after setbacks.

## Set Goals for Results and Activities

In the long-run, if you make a habit of doing the right things, good results will likely follow. In the short-term, anything can happen. The movie "21" is a loose adaptation of the great book *Bringing Down the House* by Ben Mezrich about a blackjack card counting team comprised of brainy students from the Massachusetts Institute of Technology. I have read that the team members would wish each other "good fluctuations" instead of "good luck" when they were going out to play. They knew that if they applied their card counting system consistently, they would have an advantage and would win in the long run. Along the way, they would have many losing days and weeks (negative fluctuations).

I know from years of experience that our company will win the contract for 50-60% of the bids we put out for a certain type of project (one of several types our company completes each year). Currently we would like to have roughly 12 new projects of this type per year, or about one per month. Given our long-term average, we should be putting out at least 24 bids each year to reach our target of 12 or more contracts. This means that we should be sending out at least two bids per month. If we do so, I am confident that we will win an average of 12 contracts per year. However, we could easily be awarded 8 or 16 without this being an indication of better or worse performance. In the short-term, fluctuations (luck, good or bad) will happen. Do not expect success to arrive in a straight line. Your results will ebb and flow. Like stock market returns, successful business results will often appear to be a random walk with an upward drift.

For this reason, I prefer to base our incentives on both activity and results. Both are important. I also like to set personal and company goals based on activity, as well as results. We know that when we get face-to-face with a client, we are asked to submit a proposal sometime over the next 12 months in 80% of the cases. Therefore, I set goals for the number of face-to-face meetings to complete, as well as the number of bids to submit, the number of contracts to be signed and the value of the contracts to be signed every year. If we do enough of the right activities (such as setting up face-to-face meetings), good results follow.

Too many entrepreneurs focus only on results, such as sales, contract value, etc. Without goals for activities, such as sales calls, face-to-face meetings, bids submitted and so forth, the business owner is simply reacting to results, which may be largely driven by luck in the short-term, rather than creating a process for obtaining those results. The expression, "what gets measured gets done" applies. Measure and manage both activities and results.

## Make Goals Challenging, But Realistic

Nothing is more de-motivating than continually failing to attain your goals. The ideal goals will cause you and your organization to stretch a bit beyond your comfort zone. However, goals that are too aggressive will tend to cause people to give up, feeling that they have no hope of reaching them.

I once worked for a company that set a ridiculous goal for the business unit that I managed. The financial goal was predicated on a very large project going forward that I knew had a good chance of delaying or cancelling. I went to senior management with the suggestion that we have a set of agreed-upon contingency goals that would be realistic should the large project not go off on time. I was told that if this happened it would be my responsibility to replace the lost revenue. Since that single project was going to represent more than 60% of the projected revenue for the year and require more than doubling the prior year's revenue, I knew the chances of achieving such a goal were almost entirely dependent on that single project. Not surprisingly, the big project was delayed indefinitely in February of that year. Since everyone understood that our business unit was essentially out of the running for a bonus that year, morale and motivation dropped precipitously. To this day, the logic of that decision by senior management, and their refusal to reverse it once the project actually delayed, eludes me.

While it is very satisfying to see the checkmarks adding up as you accomplish your goals, you should also recognize that you may not be able to get all of them done in the specified time frame. Don't beat yourself up if this happens. If you are able to achieve 80% of what you set out to do at the beginning of a year, celebrate your accomplishments and tack those goals you were not able to get to onto the next year's list of goals.

## Break Down Goals into Bite-Size Pieces

Per capita chocolate consumption in the US is about 10.4 lb. Few of us could eat this much in a day or a week, but eating a small amount at a time adds up. Big goals can be daunting and overwhelming. Successful entrepreneurs set short, intermediate and long-term goals. Big goals can be broken down into smaller steps and milestones, with each milestone having a projected date of completion. By breaking the process down to manageable steps, it is easier to get moving and stay moving toward the goal.

When one of our employees is feeling overwhelmed, I respond by saying, let's figure out how to get you back to "whelmed." (In a similar vein, I also say that our goal is to have a "gruntled" staff, which is, presumably, the opposite of disgruntled.) The strategy that is most often helpful is typically identifying one or two high priority steps for the person to focus on. Other items can be put aside or reassigned. Once these high-priority steps are completed, one or two more will be identified and so on.

Business and personal success author Brian Tracy is fond of the expression "By the yard, it's hard, but inch by inch, it's a cinch." A similar aphorism is that no matter how large the tree, if you take a few whacks at it each day with a sharp axe, it will eventually come down. I have taken this approach to writing books. When I set out to write a book, I usually set a goal of writing seven pages each week, i.e., one per day. This yields roughly 30 pages per month, 90 pages per quarter and 360 pages in a year (enough for 1-2 books, depending on the topic). If I get to the end of the week with fewer than seven pages written, I try to catch up. If circumstances prevent me from reaching my goal one week, I try to catch up the next. If I miss my 14 page goal over a two week period I no longer try to catch up because the task would start to seem overwhelming. Instead, I refocus my efforts on getting seven pages written the next week.

Most people have a distorted view of what they can accomplish in a given period of time. Studies of managers show that they consistently underestimate the time that will be required to complete a task. On the other hand, as a general rule, people underestimate what they can accomplish over longer periods such as a year or five years. The key to high achievement is to identify your most important goals, construct a plan for accomplishing each goal and make some progress each day toward executing your plan. Progress may seem frustratingly slow at first, but slow, steady progress will eventually get you there. If you consistently undertake the right activities, good results will follow.

**Reward Your Staff and Yourself for Achieving Goals**
Human beings are designed to respond to positive reinforcement. Therefore, it is important to create positive reinforcement for yourself and your staff when goals are met. Don't underestimate the power of praise and public recognition of individual contributions as a way to keep staff morale and productivity up. Remember Jack Welch's advice about keeping productive employees: reward performance with money, recognition and training (MRT). Those who make the most progress toward achieving agreed upon goals should receive the most MRT.

You shouldn't forget to reward yourself for achieving milestones. Rewards can range from something small, like a massage or night out for you and your significant other, to larger items such as a new car or a vacation. I sometimes reward myself for finishing a book chapter by taking time off to see a movie or read a book for a few hours on a weekday afternoon. Doing so feels like a well-deserved break which also serves to recharge my batteries.

**Remember the SMART Formula for Goal Setting**
Successful entrepreneurs tend to be highly goal oriented. When setting goals for yourself, managers and employees, using the acronym SMART can be a helpful tool. Ideally, goals should be:

> S = specific
> M = measurable
> A = achievable
> R = relevant
> T = time bound

*Specific* – The goal should be specific regarding what is to be accomplished and by whom.

*Measurable* – There should be no ambiguity about what constitutes success. Fuzzy goals lead to fuzzy results. Numerically quantifiable results are preferable where possible.

*Achievable* – Goals will tend to motivate toward action if they are realistic, but de-motivate when they are too difficult or too easy. It is okay to stretch, but stretching too far tends to be counter-productive.

*Relevant* – Goals should be instrumental to the mission of the organization. Employees and managers should always be clear on why each goal is important to the success of the company.

*Time-bound* – It has often been said that the difference between goals and dreams is a timeline.

### Create a Simple Business Plan Each Year

I advocate putting together a business plan each year. Unlike the MBA types who will spend weeks or months doing this, my business plans are simple and can fit on a couple sheets of paper. I don't want to give the impression that this will take the place of a traditional business plan, particularly if you are trying to attract investors. However, I suspect that most small business owners never put together a formal business plan. My process is simple and constitutes what I think is the most important part of putting a business plan together: establishing goals and a plan to achieve each goal.

I lay out our major goals for the year, usually about 5 and never more than 10. I then list the main steps that will be required to accomplish each goal. Usually this constitutes 4-6 steps per goal. I then rank the goals in order of importance and get busy on the most important goal. I may have someone else start working on goal #2.

When working on a specific project, I will break the major steps into smaller steps, each with its own steps and deadlines. If the project starts to get off track, I will know early in the process so that I can adjust my assumptions or reevaluate the timeline. This way I am not caught by surprise when delays occur or the results are otherwise not as originally planned.

As an example of this process, one major goal for 2008 was for our company to open a new clinic in the Chicago area. Our major goals were as follows:

1.  Identify and hire a Site Director (operating manager) by the end of the first quarter or Q1.
2.  Find and lease a location with the right characteristics by mid-Q2.
3.  Identify inaugural clinic project by end Q2.
4.  Hire key staff (physicians, study coordinators, lab personnel) by end Q2.
5.  Train key staff by mid-Q3.
6.  Open clinic by end Q3.

Of course, each of the steps above had many sub-steps and not all could be completed in order, as some had to be done in parallel. Regardless, by identifying milestones and putting a date to each, we were able to track our progress. I am happy to report that our clinic opened during the first week of the third quarter of 2008.

I have read studies showing that small business owners who put together a business plan are much more likely to succeed than those who do not. Yet, it has also been reported that few of the entrepreneurs who put business plans together actually look at them during the course of a year. My guess is that the effectiveness of a business plan is not related to some magical powers it exerts from the drawer where it is filed soon after completion, but rather from the process of thinking about goals, and the steps required to accomplish them.

**Make Continual Learning a High Priority for You and Your Staff**

We are living in an information age. Those who have invested the most time and effort in building knowledge and skills will have a major advantage. This is true whether your business is financial consulting, fast food, auto mechanics, accounting or plumbing. Entrepreneurs who study and learn more will have a competitive advantage over those who invest less in learning. A 2007 National Endowment for the Arts study (Research Report #47) on reading in the US concluded that both reading ability and the habit of regular reading have declined markedly in recent years. According to this report and others, reading correlates with almost every measurement of positive personal and social behavior surveyed and is associated (not surprisingly) with both academic and economic success.

Brian Tracy has said that when he advocates investing more in staff training and education to small business owners, someone inevitably asks the question: "What if people leave my company after we have spent so much upgrading their knowledge and skills?" His response is: "On the other hand, what if you don't invest in training and education and they stay?"

If you spend 30-45 minutes per day reading on topics in your field, you will complete the equivalent of about one book per week, or 50 books per year. This will put you miles ahead of your competition. In addition to reading, I recommend turning your car into a mobile university. Listen to audio programs instead of the radio. When I had a daily commute of 45-60 minutes each way, I listened to books on tape or compact disc and finished 2-3 per week. Charlie Munger, Vice Chair of Berkshire Hathaway, says that when he was a practicing attorney he always sold the best hour of each day to himself. In other words, he worked on upgrading his knowledge and skills for at least one hour.

Another useful way to learn is to make a point of seeking out and interacting with successful entrepreneurs. Study their methods, ask questions, learn their best practices and share your own. If you interact with successful people, you will tend to move in their direction. Their success reinforces your belief in your own ability to succeed.

A corollary to this idea is to avoid negative people, low-achievement types and those lacking integrity. Their attitudes and habits are likely to rub off on you. To paraphrase Brian Tracy again, you will never soar with the eagles if you continue to scratch with the turkeys.

## Make a Habit of Saving for the Future

If you lack the discipline to save money, you likely lack the discipline to operate a successful business. According to Thomas Stanley, author of the books *The Millionaire Next Door* and *The Millionaire Mind*, self-made millionaires save an average of 15% of their incomes. They don't start doing this once they are rich, they are rich, at least in part, because they have consistently saved and invested a substantial fraction of their incomes. As a business owner it is especially important to maintain the habit of saving. When times are good you should save more. When you hit lean times, which are inevitable, you may need to cut back on what you save, but don't cut it back to zero. Maintain the habit of paying yourself first. Aim for saving at least 15% of your income, but work hard to avoid putting away less than 5% in any year. If you consistently save and build your reserves, both for your business and for your retirement, you will feel more confident and likely be willing to take more prudent risks knowing that you have a financial cushion.

## Set a Good Example

Peter Drucker was fond of the expression "A fish rots from the head." If you, as the head of your company, do not commit yourself to living the values and behaviors that you expect of your employees, you will lack moral authority. Just as you will tend to move in the direction of those you associate with, employees will tend to move in the direction of their leaders.

*Chapter 4*

# The PARETO Principle - Using 80/20 Thinking to Achieve More with Less Effort

*If you don't design your own life plan, chances are you'll fall into someone else's. And guess what they might have planned for you? Not much.*

— Jim Rohn

The PARETO Principle, or 80/20 rule, is so critical to business success that I thought it deserved its own chapter. The 19th century economist Vilfredo Pareto discovered a consistent pattern when studying wealth and income in Europe. He found that approximately 80% of the wealth and income were concentrated in the hands of roughly 20% of individuals. This type of imbalance seems to occur under nearly any economic system and structure for taxation.

As outlined in Richard Koch's books *The 80/20 Principle* and *The 80/20 Individual*, investigations over the next 100 years showed that the PARETO Principle applied in many other situations. The central concept is that there is often an imbalance between inputs and outputs. A large percentage of the results can be accounted for by a fraction of the inputs. Thus, 80% of profits may be generated by 20% of products sold or 20% of clients. It should be noted that 80/20 is used as a shorthand way to express this concept, but the numbers don't always sum to 100 and the input side of the equation is not always 20%. So, for example, 10% of customers may account for 65% of profits.

This principle has enormous implications for business. Since roughly 20% of entrepreneurs will account for 80% of business success, studying actions and strategies of the top 20% will yield the best results. Also, the top 20% of employees will generate 80% of productivity and the bottom 20% will generate 80% of the headaches and actually drain productivity from the organization. The top 20% of customers will often generate 80% of the profits, so working harder to get more business from these few, or to identify their characteristics in order to attract more of this type of customer or client will usually be more productive than less focused efforts.

The Marmon Group is a conglomerate consisting of 125 business units in manufacturing and service sectors with over $7 billion in annual revenues. The company was formed in 1953 when Jay and Robert Pritzker acquired an ailing manufacturing company called Colson Corporation. The Pritzker family is best known for their ownership of the Hyatt Hotel chain. In 2008 Warren Buffett's Berkshire Hathaway acquired a 60% interest in The Marmon Group. The current CEO is John D. Nichols and the following is from an interview with Mr. Nichols by Ross Foti for *Forward Online*.

> **Question: How have you tried to impart your own values without disrupting Robert Pritzker's best practices already in place?**
>
> **Answer:** While we use many of the same management techniques, the organization was changed to build on the fundamental culture Bob had established. As a testament to our success, we have had virtually no management turnover. [*Authors note: take notice that low turnover among key individuals is a trait common to successful companies, as discussed in Chapter 2.*]

For 35 years, I've been developing a set of thinking processes, based on PARETO analysis, or 80/20, in which people analyze what they're really good at and identify customers they can serve really well and their core competency products in order to determine how to simplify all of their business activities.

Mr. Nichols has formally adopted the PARETO Principle as a guiding tenet for managing this diverse group of businesses. You will almost certainly find that your business will profit from adopting similar methods.

## The 80/20 Principle and Your Staff (The Vital Few)

Joseph Moses Juran, one of the pioneers in the Quality Control movement of the post-World War II era, referred to this as the Rule of the Vital Few. Most quality issues could be cheaply and effectively remedied by focusing on the "vital few" causes while ignoring the "trivial many". Identification and nurturing of the vital few among your staff will pay large dividends. One of the most brilliant ideas implemented under Jack Welch at General Electric was the 20/70/10 system of categorizing employees, which has its roots in the PARETO Principle. Under this merit-based system, the top 20% of employees, based on performance appraisals, were lavished with MRT - money, recognition and training. For the middle 70%, the group was subdivided into top and bottom halves. Rewards were proportionate to ranking and employee management was based on trying to move a person up the scale toward a higher ranking.

The most controversial aspect of this 20/70/10 system was the handling of the bottom 10%. These individuals were not making the grade. Under the GE system, the bottom 10% were explicitly told that they were in this class and given one year to find a new position outside the company. This strategy made room for more productive people, allowing the organization to constantly upgrade and maintain high productivity.

You may be wondering how the system above squares with the concept of maintaining low employee turnover. I do not see these concepts as being in conflict. In our company we do not trim the bottom 10% each year *per se*, but we do actively seek to identify and retain the top performers and eliminate those individuals who do not perform or who create a toxic environment. I like to say that we have high turnover in the first six months and low turnover thereafter. By rewarding top performers while eliminating the underperformers and the people who are chronically dissatisfied, despite reasonable efforts to meet their needs, we create and maintain a culture of teamwork and productivity. This enhances profits, which are shared in proportion to performance.

**The 80/20 Principle and Your Customers/Clients**
Segmenting your staff will help you to focus your time, energy and resources on the vital few who really drive results. Segmenting your customers will have a similar effect. In most companies, a small percentage of customers are responsible for a large majority of the profits. Many businesses make the mistake of focusing their sales and marketing efforts mainly on bringing in new customers rather than working to sell more and more often to existing customers, particularly the best customers (the top 20%).

If you also take the time to analyze and understand the profitability of your customers, you may discover that some are unprofitable. In our business we are very reluctant to take new business from clients that we believe have low potential for providing more than one project. Our analyses show that first projects have marginal or even negative profitability, so we have to charge a premium price to even consider such clients. On the other hand, for clients that have high potential for repeat business, we will often discount the first project as a way of getting our foot in the door and having the opportunity to show our stuff.

If your business is like most, you may discover that 80% or more of your profits are coming from customers with certain characteristics. For example, if you are an accountant, you may find that nearly all of your profits come from working with clients who are business owners that have 5 to 20 employees. Other types of clients such as non-business owners or business owners with larger companies may be only marginally profitable.  If this is the case, you might want to focus your efforts on bringing in more clients that fit this profile and perhaps reducing the number of existing clients that do not meet this profile if you find them to be unprofitable.  When this is the case, it is often desirable to refer such clients to another provider who is a better fit for their needs.

## The 80/20 Principle and Your Products and Services

Just as a fraction of your customers may account for a majority of your profits, you might also find that a fraction of your products or services account for most of your profits.  I recently met the owner of a landscaping company.  He told me that he used to provide residential and non-residential landscaping, but found that a larger portion of his profits came from non-residential clients.  In particular, he found that churches in suburban neighborhoods were excellent clients.  They paid on time and were less demanding than many other non-residential customers such as small office parks.  He found that he would make more money with fewer hassles if he marketed to a wider geographic area with a focus on churches.  Once he made a sale to at least one church in a community (an anchor client for that community), he would market to other businesses in the area to spread the travel time over more clients.  He also found that many of his warmer season non-residential clients would use his snow removal services in the winter, whereas few residential clients would do so.

Eventually he stopped doing residential landscaping altogether.  The result was that his business became much more profitable with fewer headaches.  Had he not taken the time to segment his clients by customer type and analyze the contribution of each to his bottom line, he would likely still be trying to bring in more residential customers and spending much less of his valuable time and resources marketing to the most profitable segments.

## The 80/20 Principle and Time Management

Owning a business can be all consuming.  It is easy to fall into the trap of becoming the Fire Marshal for your company so that you spend most of your time putting out fires.  Often this is not the highest and best use of your time.  As the owner of the company, if you spend all of your time working "in the business" it is hard to devote enough time to working "on the business."

You should identify three types of activities and ensure that most of your time (about 80%) is spent on those. These are:

1. High value tasks that you can perform better than anyone else that are key to the success of the business;
2. Activities you find enjoyable and fulfilling; and
3. Strategic planning.

### High Value Tasks

In our business I have found that I am better than anyone else at talking with new clients about the technical aspects of planning a research project. We have capable scientists working for our company who can sometimes play that role, particularly if the project under consideration is similar to work we have done in the past. However, we tend to get the best results when I am involved at the early stages. Since this translates into more sales, I spend a good deal of my time on that activity.

### Activities You Find Enjoyable and Fulfilling

If you fall into the trap of spending too much of your time tending to activities that need to be done, but that you find draining and unfulfilling, you will soon find yourself burnt out and dissatisfied. Engineer your work life so that you get to do things you enjoy and are good at. Psychologist Mihály Csíkszentmihályi uses the term *flow* to describe activities in which the person loses track of time because he or she is so engaged in the task at hand. Flow is defined as the mental state in which the person is fully immersed in what he or she is doing by a feeling of energized focus, full involvement, and success in the process of the activity.

Artists may experience flow when painting. I often experience flow when writing or analyzing data from a clinical study. After engaging in activity that creates flow, one tends to have a pleasant sense of accomplishment bordering on euphoria. If you do not deliberately engineer your daily activities to allow time to engage in those activities that you enjoy, the demands imposed by customers, employees and the other day-to-day realities of running a business will almost certainly crowd out those items that create flow for you.

### *Strategic Planning*
As the owner of a business, you also need to spend time thinking about the big picture and strategic planning. In order to do this, you must set aside time to analyze metrics such as profit by type of customer, results from marketing efforts, etc. That doesn't mean that you need to generate the numbers yourself. You can have someone else do that if you prefer and spend your time analyzing and interpreting the results. To reiterate, you need to devote time to working "on the business," which is hard to do if all of your time is spent "in the business."

You need a steady stream of ideas about how to improve your business. These can come from reading, listening to audio programs, attending seminars, meeting with other business owners, etc. In the classic book *Think and Grow Rich*, Napoleon Hill outlines the concept of the Mastermind Group. This is a group of individuals who have similar interests (such as small business owners) and meet regularly, sometimes in person and in other cases by telephone or through other media. Usually groups of four to eight work best. These individuals share ideas and provide support for one another. This is a great method for getting new ideas for improving your business while helping others to improve theirs.

You should also actively seek ideas from your employees. Have periodic brainstorming sessions where key staff members are given two or three topics to think about and then spend time with them discussing their ideas. Ray Kroc, who acquired the rights to franchise McDonald's from the McDonald brothers, got the ideas for the Egg McMuffin and Filet-O-Fish sandwiches from franchise operators. While franchise operators are not exactly employees, the concept is the same. These ideas have translated into millions of dollars of additional profit for the company over the years.

*Chapter 5*

# Avoiding Common Mistakes that Lead to Business Failure

*Shallow men believe in luck. Strong men believe in cause and effect.*

– Ralph Waldo Emerson

Accounting and consulting firms have performed autopsies on thousands of failed businesses to identify traits that predict failure. In the book *The Way to Wealth: Success Strategies of the Wealthy Entrepreneur*, Brian Tracy outlines seven of these:

1. Lack of direction
2. Insufficient sales
3. Poor quality
4. Impatience
5. Greed and impatience
6. Poor cost control
7. Insufficient working capital

**Lack of Direction**
Many entrepreneurs launch a business without specific goals and metrics for assessing their progress toward those goals. I often repeat the phrases:

- What gets measured gets done; and
- You can only manage what you measure.

A business plan is simply a method for formalizing your goals, timelines for achieving them, and strategies for accomplishing each of the steps required to reach these goals. If you are vague about what you want to accomplish and in what timeline, it is difficult to get all of the necessary parties aligned to move the business in that direction. Fuzzy goals lead to fuzzy outcomes. Specific, measurable goals with timelines for major and minor milestones will allow you gauge your progress and make course corrections when necessary.

An element of your direction should be your competitive advantage relative to your competition. Why should customers or clients choose you instead of them? The factors on which sales decisions are made are time, price, product and service quality, convenience and risk. Your business must have an advantage in one or more of these in order to convince a customer to choose you. You should be explicit about what you want your advantage to be and how you plan to accomplish this. You then need to communicate this clearly to your employees and customers. That is the only way that your customers and employees will know what you are promising to deliver and the only way your employees will know what is expected of them in order to deliver on those promises.

A hotel chain used to run ads with the motto "No surprises". In other words, guests could expect a clean comfortable room and friendly, helpful staff. We often tell our customers that we hope that when they work with us they will experience "No surprises…except good ones". Our goal is to under-promise and over-deliver, never the reverse.

**Insufficient Sales**
This may seem self-evident, but insufficient sales will lead to the failure of a business. Nevertheless, I have watched in horror as many businesses failed because they did not put sufficient resources into marketing and sales.

A friend opened a business that provided a high quality product at a very reasonable price. She put a great deal of effort into making her retail shop attractive and producing a great product. Regardless, in less than two years she closed the doors, leaving her and her husband with a large debt and lost income from the two plus years that she did not have an outside job while she tried to make a go of her business. I am convinced that she would have been a success if she had put adequate time and effort into marketing.

Everybody listens to their favorite station WIIFM (What's in it for me?), so you have to give people a reason to seek out your business. Good marketing will get the attention of potential customers, generate interest and desire and move them to action, which may be either contacting you or actually making a purchase. This is sometimes referred to as AIDA formula: Attention, Interest, Desire and Action.

Offering something for free, or at a significant discount, works to get people through the door for many types of businesses (literally for a traditional bricks and mortar business, figuratively for an internet business). This could be a free or discounted trial of a product or service, or it might simply be information, e.g., "Visit our web site to download our free booklet *10 Mistakes to Avoid when Selecting an Accountant for Your Small Business*."

Once you make an initial contact or sale, you have to keep reminding the customer about your product or service and its advantages. A customer database is critical. Regular contact through e-mail, the postal service and even telephone contact is essential to developing and maintaining the relationship with your customers. Far too many businesses fail to even collect contact information from their customers. How can you develop and nurture a relationship with someone who you can't even get in touch with? Think about how many businesses you have contact with in a typical week. How many of them collect your contact information and contact you regularly?

Holidays and birthdays are great opportunities to contact your customers to make offers. For example, a restaurant might offer a free entrée during the month of a customer's birthday. Often, the person will show up with at least one other person, perhaps even with the whole family. Giving away an $16 entrée might generate $100 or more in sales and leave the customer with a very favorable feeling about restaurant. This or other similar strategies that have been tested to assess their cost effectiveness are easy to implement, but much too rarely used.

When sales are slumping, too many business owners cut back on marketing and sales efforts. This is a bit like cutting off your leg to lose weight; the number on the scale may go down, but it leaves you handicapped. Too often the result is a death spiral of fewer sales leading to cuts in sales and marketing, which further reduces sales, and so on until the business folds. It is very difficult to cut costs to achieve profitability. The key to success is to always keep the cash register ringing. Any loss of sales momentum should be responded to with massive action rather than hope and prayer. Paraphrasing Warren Buffett again:

> Like the Lord, the market [or marketplace] helps those who help themselves. Unlike the Lord, the market does not forgive those who know not what they do.

**Poor Quality**
People will generally return to make repeat purchases if they feel they have received good value. Clever marketing may help to drive initial purchases, but customers will only come back for more if they were happy with the transaction. Be sure that you fulfill the promises made during your marketing and sales process.

Price and quality are related. You need to deliver an experience that is consistent with the positioning of your business. Service that might be acceptable at a budget hotel chain would not be acceptable at the Four Seasons or the Ritz Carlton. Wal-Mart customers have different expectations from those at Nordstrom or Saks. People will remember the unexpected in either direction.

Unexpectedly good service will leave an impression, as will unexpectedly bad service.

In his book *The No BS Guide to Ruthless Management of People and Profits*, marketing and business consultant Dan Kennedy describes the "million dollar bathroom" at the dental office of one of his clients. The ladies room has five kinds of scented soaps, freshly laundered towels, perfumes, potpourri, and is more like what one would expect to find at an exclusive spa than at a dentist's office. This practitioner has positioned himself as an "upscale" dentist whose patients feel pampered when they visit his office. The restrooms are emblematic of this positioning. His patients are willing to pay more for this pampering, just as the guest at the Ritz Carlton is willing to pay more for a night's stay than would be the case at a Hampton Inn. When a new patient visits, he or she is treated like royalty and is likely to remember the experience favorably. It would be difficult to accomplish this through actual dentistry, so it must be accomplished through the overall ambiance and patient experience. The exceptional is remembered and contributes to the sense of value the customer perceives – good or bad.

I recommend that you avoid positioning your business as a low cost provider. No matter how low your prices, there is almost certainly someone who will figure out a way to sell cheaper than you. If you cater to customers that use price as their main criterion for selection, they are less apt to have loyalty to your business when someone down the street starts to sell at a lower price.

In my own business I tell employees that we want to be the Costco of clinical research, not the Wal-Mart or the Saks of clinical research. We cannot be the low-cost provider because the services we deliver are complex and we need to have the best players on the field to deliver good results. In order to attract talent we need to compete with much larger companies for employees and pay accordingly. We invest in our people, but work very hard to keep other costs low. This allows us to deliver good service at a reasonable price. Our clients are like Costco customers. They want good quality and are willing to pay for that, but they also want good value. Our very high rate of repeat customers suggests that we are succeeding in that realm.

## Greed and Impatience

I will reiterate that price and expectation are related and interact to determine whether the customer feels that he or she received good value. Small business owners who try to charge too much for the quality of product or service they deliver will soon find themselves struggling.

As discussed previously, many customers will be willing to pay more if they trust that they will receive good value. Trust is built over time through favorable interactions. In my business, I have some clients with whom I have been working for 15 years. In some cases these individuals have followed me through various mergers and name changes. A large percentage followed me when I left my employer and started my own company. In addition, it is not uncommon for us to continue to work with a client as he or she moves through two, three, four or more positions in different companies. These are people with whom we have developed mutual trust and loyalty.

In general it is better to price a bit low at first in order to increase the number of customers and build trust. Prices can be raised later, after relationships have been developed with a group of customers. If you are delivering good value, they will be willing to pay more.

Another way that impatience and greed can cause a business to fail is by driving the owner to take too much risk. Concepts need to be tested and proven before they are rolled out on a large scale. This is true with advertising, as well as opening new locations, renting space, hiring employees, etc. There will be inevitable peaks and valleys. Too many business owners obtain additional space and staff and make other long-term commitments during peak times, then find themselves struggling during a recession or soft market because their costs are too high and cannot be reduced or reduced quickly enough. Too much growth too quickly can lead to a deterioration of quality and customer service. It is much better to have steady, sustainable growth. Of course, some businesses are more scalable than others, so sustainable growth for a sandwich shop franchise may be quite different than that for a law firm.

Peter Lynch of the Fidelity Family of mutual funds tells a story of an upscale sandwich shop that he invested in for the Fidelity Magellan mutual fund. He describes this as being among the investments for which the value of all of the shares he bought would not buy him a Hershey bar today. The company had a successful operation across the street from the Fidelity offices in Boston. They went public and raised funds that were used to open several new stores at once. Unfortunately, the concept (upscale fast food), which had been such a hit in Boston, didn't do well elsewhere. If the company had been more cautious, opening just one store in a new area and waiting for it to be successful before opening more, it might have been able to find its niche (e.g., financial districts in large cities) and prosper. Instead, the red ink from the opening of too many stores in rapid succession proved too much to overcome and the company filed for bankruptcy protection.

In his book *Why the Mighty Fall*, Jim Collins (who is also the author or co-author of the classics *Built to Last* and *Good to Great*) describes the results of his study of previously great large businesses that experienced significant declines. One might expect that this would occur because management rested on its laurels after experiencing a long stretch of good performance, failing to innovate and invest adequately in Research and Development. In fact, his results show just the opposite. The companies in his study were more likely to falter because they were too ambitious, trying to achieve too much in too little time and taking on excessive risk in the process. The lesson applies for small business owners as well. Sustainable growth tends to be steady and deliberate, not outpacing the rate at which systems and personnel can be developed to maintain efficiencies, cost controls, good execution and excellent customer service.

## Poor Cost Controls

As alluded to above, poor cost control increases risk. If you do not have good systems to track costs, you will find all sorts of ways that expenses creep up. Small leaks can sink your company's financial ship. Watch expenses such as telephone and internet service, office supplies, etc. They may increase with inflation (some technologies actually go down in price over time) and as you add employees, but if you watch closely you will almost certainly find that there are areas in which significant savings can be realized.

Elicit suggestions from your staff on how costs might be reduced. When you get an idea that saves you money, reward that person with a bonus to show your appreciation. I know of two cases where employees made suggestions that reduced costs by $250,000 per year or more. In one case an employee suggestion lowered cost and added productivity in a way that added over $1 million in revenue. He got a pat on the back and some recognition as "employee of the month", but no money. If that happened in my company, I would be sure that he also received a check linked directly to that suggestion.

Overhead walks on two legs. In most companies the employees are the biggest expense, both in terms of funds paid out and intangibles such as time required for proper care and (emotional) feeding, potential liability, insurance, etc. While you never want to understaff in such a way that quality suffers, overstaffing is worse. Be skeptical of claims that head count must be increased. Look for ways to use outsourcing and vendors to get the job done with few people. I like the philosophy at Nucor Steel where the stated goal is to have a team of 5, work them like 10, and pay them like 8 (my paraphrasing). In other words, put together highly productive teams that generate higher than average output, but also get paid well above average amounts.

Shop around for better rates for commodity services, but reward good performance by your vendors with continued business. If a vendor that has been providing good service gets too expensive, work with them toward a mutually acceptable price, but don't try to squeeze out every last dime.  More often than not, this will result in a deterioration of service.  Instead, work toward a fair price at which you feel you are receiving good value.

Be slow to make long-term commitments such as leases or contracts for advertising.  If you have a significant amount of space being used for storage, think about how that might be accomplished more inexpensively.

Above all, know the numbers and be sure that your key people know the numbers.  Understand where your money is going.  Discuss your expectations with the staff.  Don't accept expense reports that just show the total for a meal.  Get the details.  If I see an expense report showing dinner that included four glasses of wine at $8.85 per glass, I will approve it the first time, but talk with the employee about what I expect in the future so there are no misunderstandings.  I don't like to set rigid guidelines (breakfast in Bloomington, Indiana for an employee might cost $7, but breakfast in a downtown San Francisco hotel might be $25).  However, most people know what is and is not reasonable.  Some will push the envelope and keep doing so until you stop them.  We stop them early.

I had one employee who had a distorted view of what our company should pay for during travel.  She worked remotely in another city and would come to the office every six weeks or so.  Her first expense report showed five meals per day.  Not four snacks and dinner, five full meals, all at expensive restaurants.  Her food for one day totaled something like $240 (no clients, just her).  I sat her down and explained that this was far above what we expect.  I generally avoid rigid guidelines, but was forced to give her a daily food number above which we would not reimburse.  She charged the maximum every single day of travel and complained about how restrictive we were.  Eventually I fired her.  She clearly did not fit our culture.

I encourage our staff to stop at Starbucks and happily pay for a cocktail or two with dinner.  I don't require people to stay in budget hotels.  If people have to travel for business, I want them to feel comfortable while doing so.  However, our culture emphasizes keeping costs under control, so I see very little abuse of my trust.  The people who do abuse that trust don't last long.

**Insufficient Working Capital**

It is a common myth that large amounts of money are needed to start a business.  A recent article in the Chicago Tribune indicated that 70% of businesses are started with less than $25,000 in capital, mostly from savings and other sources of personal assets such as home equity.  If you are starting from scratch, it may be possible to keep a job and start your new business on the side.  If you have a spouse with a job, this may provide income and benefits such as health insurance during the start-up phase.

My company was started with $10,000 in capital from each of two partners.  We went without salaries for a few months, but paid back the start-up capital and began taking salaries within a short time.  However, we started with a proven track record in the business and clients with whom we already had relationships and earned trust.  We had to be in a position to go without incomes for a period of time, which we could because of savings, working spouses and, in my case, a rental property business.  There are several good books about starting a business and finding the capital to do so (see the Resources section at the end of the book).  Therefore, I will not go into more detail about the start-up phase and will instead focus on the growing to mature business phases.

Cash flow is king.  Without cash flow, your business will die.  It is possible to have profits without enough cash flow and be unable to keep the doors open.  Conversely, it is possible to have accounting losses while generating a great deal of cash flow.  Don't confuse accounting profits with cash flow.

It is critical to manage cash, which involves several steps.  First, you must have sales.  Second, you must collect money owed, either at the time of the sale or in a reasonable period after completing the work.  Third, you must manage your costs.  Fourth, you should have back-up plans to avoid disaster during cash flow crunches.

I have already discussed the importance of keeping the cash register ringing, so I won't belabor the point about maintaining sales momentum. For some types of businesses payment for work completed is traditionally provided after the fact. For example, landscaping, house painting and accounting services are often paid for, at least in part, after the work has been completed.

Our company has several business units. One of them is involved in providing clinical trial services to pharmaceutical companies. The payment terms that are customary in that business are truly bizarre. I have seen research centers go out of business because they sign contracts that have them doing work for which they do not get paid for months.

In our company we live with such terms to an extent, but are very aggressive about negotiating contract terms that keep us cash flow positive. Fortunately, we have other business units that work in the reverse fashion. We collect funds up-front and invoice as we go for work completed, always maintaining a client "credit balance". This has helped us to manage around the horrible contract terms we sometimes agree to in other parts of our business.

In one case we signed a contract with milestone payments. Our assumptions turned out to be off-target and it took us much longer to reach the third milestone (out of four) than anticipated. In the meantime we kept incurring expenses, including money we had to pay out to vendors. Eventually we got to the point where we were $600,000 out of pocket. I asked our bank to increase our line of credit temporarily, explaining the situation and showing them the contract, which was with a large, multinational company (i.e., not a poor credit risk). The bank delayed and delayed approving my request. While waiting, we hit the third milestone and fired off an invoice immediately. The bank approved our increase in credit line the same day a $750,000 payment hit our account.

The story above illustrates some important points. First, the time to get credit is when you don't need it. A banker is someone who will give you an umbrella on a sunny day, but ask for it back when clouds appear. Second, I should never have agreed to such terms. Even if I had, I should have gone back to renegotiate them as soon as I realized that we would be significantly out of pocket. I knew that doing so would be an enormous hassle, so I procrastinated. Dumb! I did not allow for Murphy in the contract assumptions. You will always have two business partners, whether you like it or not: Murphy (as in Murphy's Law) and Uncle Sam (the tax authorities). We averted disaster, but should not have gotten ourselves into that position at all. I will not make those mistakes again.

Some companies will try to slow-pay you. Large companies generate huge amounts of interest on "float," the money they owe to vendors. The contract may say that you are to be paid in 30 days, but some companies will try to stretch that out to 45 or 60 days. Sometimes this is intentional, other times it just reflects inefficiencies in their systems, such as requiring multiple signatures to authorize payment. If you find your company being slow-paid, put systems in place to remedy the situation or negotiate for more money up-front to avoid this problem. Make sure that calls or e-mails are going out quickly if you do not receive payment. Be courteous and professional, but ask for the money you are owed.

If you find yourself in a cash flow crunch, take action. Don't do what I did in the example above and just hope that things will work out. Take action to:

1. Get invoices out quickly,
2. Collect money from those who owe and are overdue,
3. Renegotiate contract terms if necessary,
4. Use secondary or tertiary sources of credit you have secured ahead of time (before you needed it),
5. Minimize expenses (e.g., reduce hours for employees who volunteer to do so).

We try very hard to staff in such a way that downsizings will not be necessary. In more than 25 years of running businesses and business units, I have only had to institute reductions in force (layoffs) three times.  In one instance one of our business units hired staff based on projections that were not realistic.  I had failed to put sufficient systems into place to prevent this from happening, which was a costly seminar for me in the school of hard knocks.

When layoffs are necessary, it is best not to procrastinate.  However, it is preferable to avoid them whenever possible.  Repeated cycles of staffing up and then downsizing will erode morale and loyalty.  If you have good marketing and sales processes in place and are conservative about hiring (work your teams of 5 like 10 and pay them like 8), layoffs should only be necessary in extraordinary circumstances.  However, all employees should be held accountable for performance.  Those who perform well should be rewarded with money, recognition and training.  Those who are not making the grade after receiving proper training, feedback and encouragement should be terminated.  There is no point in continually paying someone who is not producing for your business and it is not necessary to wait for a cash flow crunch to terminate a poor performer.  It may be painful to do so, but you will usually find that this actually improves morale because other staff members resent someone who is not pulling his or her weight.  In addition, the terminated employee will have an opportunity to find a position that is a better fit for him or her.

*Chapter 6*

# Big Ideas about Marketing and Sales

*The only difference between successful people and unsuccessful people is extraordinary determination.*
                                                    − Mary Kay Ash

At its core, the purpose of a business is to obtain and keep profitable customers. Profit may not be the only motive, but it is as necessary as blood is to a human body. Customers provide that profit by purchasing the goods and/or services of the business.

> Our only job security comes from satisfied customers. Unsatisfied customers can fire us at any time.
>                                                    − *Sam Walton*

Marketing and sales are the processes through which potential customers are made aware of what your business has to offer and are then persuaded to buy. This includes bringing in new customers and making additional sales to prior customers.

In my experience, inadequate attention to sales and marketing is the most common reason for failure of new businesses. Furthermore, many established businesses don't reach their potential because they devote insufficient resources to these functions or perform them poorly.

**The Four Elements of Marketing/Sales Performance**
There are four basic elements to the sales process are:

1. Lead generation;
2. Lead conversion;
3. Initial sale;
4. Residual customer value due to:
    a. Repeat sales;
    b. Referrals.

In order to increase sales you must alter one or more of these factors. In other words, you will need to increase the number of leads, the percentage of leads that are converted to sales, the size of the initial sale, or the residual value of customers to whom you have already made a sale. Residual value can be increased by selling more and more often to existing customers and leveraging your relationships with them by obtaining a greater number of referrals and recommendations for other potential customers from them.

The remainder of this chapter will be devoted to concepts related to lead generation and obtaining the initial sale. The next chapter will cover ways to increase the residual value of your existing customers.

**Generating Leads**
Lead generation is the process of getting potential customers to express an interest in your product or service. For some products or services this may mean simply visiting your store or web site. For complex sales, a lead may be in the form of a telephone call or e-mail message expressing an interest in learning more.

You must let potential customers know that you exist. As obvious as this sounds, far too many businesses do an inadequate job. They seem to think that if they open doors the customers will beat a path to their door. The methods used for lead generation vary widely by business, but some basic principles are universal. You must have systems for reaching out to potential customers to let them know your business exists and the benefits of what you have to offer.  This might be through advertising in newspapers, trade journals, on the internet, sales materials sent out via direct mail, calls made by sales people, or any other media through which you get out your message.

If you find methods that are cost-effective for bringing in leads that convert to sales, the law of averages says that, given fixed response and conversion rates, the more prospects who are contacted, the greater the number of sales.  Many times business owners will find one method of generating leads that works a bit better than another and will stop using the old method.  This may be a mistake.  The better approach might be to use both methods, as long as the number of sales justifies the expense.  Marketing consultant Dan Kennedy tells a story about a doctor who consistently added 30 new patients a month to his practice.  When asked how he did this month after month he replied that he knew of no method to add 30 patients per month, but he did know 30 methods to add one per month and used them all.

**Cost Effective Marketing**
The key point about contacting potential customers is that you must find a way to do so cost-effectively.  The only way to know that your marketing is cost-effective is to set up systems to track your responses so that you know where they come from and can assess the return on investment for each marketing dollar spent.  This will allow you to test various elements to see where you get an acceptable return.  By using 80/20 analysis, you will be able to assess where you are getting the bulk of your results and which efforts are not providing adequate returns.  You can then do more of what works well and stop doing what doesn't provide an acceptable return.

The elements of your marketing include medium or media used (e.g., web site, newspaper, direct mail, e-mail, flyer, radio, etc.), what the ad says (headline, ad copy, offer, etc.) and how the message is delivered.  For example, a radio ad might be delivered by you (the owner), an actor, or by a spokesperson with a recognizable name and voice.  If you religiously track your response from each method you employ, you will be able to analyze the cost per lead generated.  By altering one element at a time, you will be able to assess important factors that determine your response, such as one headline vs. another, a script read by you as the owner vs. one read by a celebrity spokesperson, etc.

Your analysis should not stop there.  You should also track the cost per sale.  Some methods may generate many leads but few sales (unqualified or poor quality leads that are not a good fit for what you have to offer).  Others might generate few leads but have a high conversion rate to sales (high quality leads).  Still others might generate a few leads and a few large sales that make the advertising very cost-effective.  The only way to know is to measure the response and analyze the results.

Several years ago the company I worked for obtained a large project that involved recruiting 270 post-menopausal women to participate in a clinical trial over about 3 months.  We expected to have to field about 5,000 telephone calls (leads) and schedule about 900 appointments (qualified lead) to identify 270 women who were qualified and interested in participation.  Although not a perfect analogy, each subject who entered the treatment period could be thought of as a "sale."

Because we knew we would have to generate a large volume of calls, we tried several approaches at once, including newspaper, radio and television ads.  For each caller we asked where the person had heard about our study and tracked the results.  One of the things we tried was a television ad during the *Oprah* show.  Even though this was the most expensive form of advertising, it turned out to be much more cost effective than newspaper or radio ads.  We were able to generate three statistics that were used to compare results:

- Cost per telephone call (lead);
- Cost per initial screening visit (qualified lead);
- Cost per subject entered into the treatment period (sale).

In this case, advertising on Oprah won hands down on all three statistics.  In other cases, we have found that the three statistics don't jive. In most cases the third (cost per sale, or more accurately, cost per dollar of sales) is the most important. However, in some instances this may not be the case. For example, when we recently opened a new clinic we were interested in quickly growing our database of people interested in participating in clinical research trials. We knew that if someone came in for one study but did not qualify, we would likely be able to find another down the road that would be a good fit. Therefore, the second statistic (cost per qualified lead) took on greater importance.

**Narrow Your Focus (Avoid Blind Archery)**
A great deal of money is wasted each year on advertising that is not targeted to an audience that has greater than average likelihood of being receptive to the message. For example, the owner of a sporting goods store that focuses mainly on hunting, fishing and camping might advertise in a local newspaper. However, only a fraction of the readers are likely to be interested in hunting, fishing or camping. Also, the paper may cover a large area, whereas the owner might know from experience that most of his or her customers come from a 15 mile radius. Marketing consultants Dan Kennedy and Joe Polish refer to this type of non-targeted marketing as blind archery. That is marketing to a general audience for which there is no reason to believe that they, as a group, have a particular need or desire for what you are selling.

A better strategy might be to rent a mailing list. For example, a sales letter or advertising flyer might be sent to subscribers to hunting and fishing magazines within certain zip codes that are relatively close to the store. A good list broker can help to guide you through the process of evaluating lists and combinations of lists. By combining lists, it might be possible to identify a group that has very high potential. There are dozens of magazines and other publications that target people interested in fishing, hunting or camping. A mailing to individuals who subscribe to more than one of the most popular publications might be an excellent candidate. For example the list of all subscribers to both *Field and Stream* and *Fly Fisherman* might be a better prospect than a subscriber to either publication alone. By experimenting with lists and combinations of lists on a small scale, it may be possible to identify groups with a much higher than average response rate, which will improve the cost-effectiveness of your marketing efforts.

Although magazine and newsletter subscribers are often a good starting place, there are many other ways to identify groups that may be predisposed to have a need or desire for your product or service. Other examples of identifiable target groups include organization members; registrants for particular meetings or conventions; people who have made specific types of purchases (e.g., recent purchasers from a particular store's catalog); people who have specific conditions (e.g., diabetes, asthma); small business owners, people with particular characteristics such as those who recently bought or sold a house, got married or divorced, had a child or had a family member die, etc.

I recently co-authored a textbook and co-edited another. One is targeted toward primary care health professionals such as family practice and internal medicine doctors, nurse practitioners and physician assistants. The other is intended for a much more narrow audience of individuals who are interested in taking exams to become board certified Lipidologists or Clinical Lipid Specialists.

For the more general book, there are many groups and organizations that might be good candidates for mailings such as members of the American Academy of Family Physicians and the Preventive Cardiovascular Nurses Association because the book is likely to appeal to substantial proportions of these groups. For the more specific book, a mailing to American Academy of Family Physicians members would probably provide a poor return because only a small fraction of family practice physicians are interested in becoming board certified Lipidologists. On the other hand, a mailing to individuals who have taken or are planning to take a review course for the Lipidology board certification exam would likely be excellent candidates to purchase this book.

**Internet Marketing**
On the internet it might make sense to purchase an ad on a web site that caters to people who might be good candidates. Popular web sites and blogs have ads for related services. As an example, financial web sites such as MarketWatch and Yahoo Finance have ads for financial services companies. The internet has made it possible to reach much larger groups of pre-disposed individuals than was practical just a few years ago. Today, many customers will find you if your business has a web site they can locate by doing a search on Google, Bing, Yahoo, etc. For this reason, one of the most critical elements of marketing is your web site and search engine optimization. I am not an expert in this regard, but have included several references in the recommended resources section at the end of the book that cover this, as well as other strategies such as marketing your business on FaceBook, MySpace and Twitter.

**Test Small, Then Expand When You Determine What Works**
By starting on a small scale and testing different lists or strategies, it may be possible to find one or a few that work substantially better than others because you have been able to identify a particularly receptive group. It is not uncommon to see differences of several-fold in response rates. In our business we once completed two mailings within a short time of one another to two unrelated lists. I assumed that one of the lists would be better than the other, but I was not prepared for how different they turned out to be. The mailings were designed to get people to call one of our clinics to participate in a cholesterol screening program. For the better mailing we received calls from more than 6% of the individuals we mailed to and for the other the response was only 0.25%. In other words, the responses differed by a factor of 24!

**A Few Percentage Points Can Make an Enormous Difference**
Let's use some numbers to illustrate how different our results were for these two mailings. We will assume that it cost $1.00 total for each postcard we mailed (list cost plus mailing piece

creation plus postage). We will also assume that the first year value of each person who makes an appointment and actually comes into our clinic is $750.

If we mailed 2,000 postcards to each list, our results would be as follows (note that we are ignoring the small number of returned postcards due to people having moved, died, etc.).

**A comparison of results from mailings to two lists, one with a 0.25% response rate and one with a 6.2% response rate (see text above for assumptions).**

| Variable | List 1 (Poor List) | List 2 (Good List) |
|---|---|---|
| Initial Cost (One Mailing) | $2,000.00 | $2,000.00 |
| Calls (Leads) Generated | 5 | 62 |
| Appointments Completed | 2 | 25 |
| First Year's Sales | $1,500.00 | $18,750.00 |
| Sales per $ Spent | $0.75 | $9.38 |

With the first list, we would not even generate $1 in sales for each dollar spent on advertising. This is not a strategy that will lead to long-term success. With the second list we would make $9.38 in sales for every dollar invested in the first year alone, or a net of $8.38 after paying advertising expenses. With a 15% net profit margin on sales, that translates into $1.26 in first year net profit for each dollar spent on advertising.

Because our relationship would likely last longer than a year and the value of a customer tends to grow with time, the numbers above do not fully capture the profit, but do represent a useful starting point for analysis. With those kinds of numbers, we would want to mail to many more names from that list if they were available. We would also want to complete second, third, fourth, and possibly more, mailings to that same list until the results were no longer profitable.

**The Importance of an Offer**
In the book *Getting Everything You Can Out of All You've Got*, Jay Abraham describes a strategy that has worked well for a heating and cooling company. In the spring and autumn months the owner would run ads and send mailings offering a heating (autumn) or cooling (spring) system check-up. He offered this at a low price that offered great value. In fact, the price was so low that it did not cover his cost of completing the check-up.

How could this business owner offer a price so low that it didn't cover his costs? He knew that this was a profitable strategy because he had tested it and found it to offer a good return. It worked for two reasons. First, in a certain percentage of cases he would find problems that required repairs, which could be done at full retail price. Second, it gave him an opportunity to start a relationship with a new customer, or reinforce a relationship with an existing customer. The customer recognized that he or she was getting excellent value for the price, so was left with a good feeling about the relationship. As part of the service, a sticker or magnet was placed on the furnace or air conditioning unit and the customer was provided other materials so that he or she would know who to call in the event of a problem. Eventually, the owner of the business knew that the customer was likely to have a problem and that he would get the call when that occurred.

Everyone listens to the station WII-FM (What's in it for me?), so you must give people a reason to get in touch with your business. Usually this is in the form of an offer, that is, something of value that your business offers to induce potential customers to contact you. This might be a free quote, such as that offered by the GEICO gecko on their television commercials; "A 15-minute call might save you 15% on your auto insurance." The offer could be a 20% discount on your first order, or information such as a free special report. For example, Fisher Investments offers free reports such as *Ken Fisher's Stock Market Outlook* and a *The Eight Biggest Mistakes Investors Make and How to Avoid Them* to induce people to contact their firm.  This allows them to collect contact information from prospects in order to start a relationship. You need to make a compelling offer in order to get people to raise their hands to let you know they might be interested in making a purchase.  If they never raise their hands, you never get a relationship started.

**Lead Conversion - Persuading People to Buy**
This is not a book on the specifics of selling or on writing good copy for advertisements.  The Resources section at the end of the book contains information that you may find useful in this regard. However, I will mention a few basics that are essential to understand and recommend two books as starting points for obtaining a better understanding of this process:  *The Psychology of Selling* by Brian Tracy and *The Ultimate Marketing Plan* by Dan Kennedy.

I should mention that some of Mr. Kennedy's methods and viewpoints make me uncomfortable.  I believe that his books are some of the best and most clearly written available on the subject of marketing for the small business owner.  I have also read academically oriented texts that say many of the same things, but in a less clear and interesting manner.  Although I don't agree with all of Mr. Kennedy's viewpoints, I generally find his materials to be of tremendous value.  I have probably learned more about marketing from his books and other materials than any other individual.  In addition to the books listed above, his book *No BS Business Success* on the mindsets and habits of successful entrepreneurs is a classic.

Having said that, I find that much of his marketing turns me off personally.  Many of his seminars and audio programs have titles such as *Renegade Millionaire Wealth Attraction*; *$10 Million Secrets* and *XXX Rated Sales*.  Mr. Kennedy has been very successful, so I am in no position to criticize his approach.  It is simply not my style.  If you are not familiar with his work, I recommend starting with the recommendations above.  I will leave it to the reader to decide how he or she feels about his style.

Persuading people to buy is where the process of marketing hands off to the process of selling. Selling is a personal act where you, or your representative, discuss the merits of your product or service and your value proposition with the potential customer. Selling is largely about listening and helping the prospect to understand why your product or service is a good fit for meeting his or her needs and desires. Buyers want to pay the lowest price possible for a comfortable solution. The cheapest solution is often not the most comfortable, particularly when purchasing a service where the consequences of errors can be substantial. Nobody with common sense will simply take the low bid when hiring an attorney to handle a complex legal matter, or an architect to create plans for a building costing tens of millions of dollars.

The sales process should be consultative. The job of the salesperson is to ask questions in order to evaluate the prospect's objectives and convey to him or her the merits of your product or service with regard to the basic elements that drive purchase decisions: time, price, quality, convenience and risk. The most effective sales people spend more time listening than talking. They ask questions in order to develop a thorough understanding of the customer's needs and areas of concern. They then provide information to help the customer understand how and why your solution is a good option. In general, the more complex and expensive the purchase, the greater the time and effort will be required. For a simple purchase, like buying a book, the customer may require no consultation. For more complex sales, the time and effort devoted to direct contact is usually substantial.

My wife and I operate a clinical research and consulting company. The bulk of the sales of our research business are for designing and conducting clinical trials from concept through interpretation and communication of the results in a report or scientific journal. The average contract is in the hundreds of thousands of dollars and we generally have at least one project each year with a contract value greater than $1 million. The decision makers who hire us are putting their reputations on the line along with us. Serious errors on such a project can bring scrutiny and criticism to the person who hired us, damaging his or her career, so we often need to spend quite a lot of time explaining our experiences and processes, as well as the advantages and disadvantages of the particular methods and study design we are advocating. This is necessary to raise the comfort level of the prospect to the point where he or she is confident enough in us to commit to a six- or seven-figure expenditure.

## The AIDA Formula in Advertising

Much of what is done in advertising is formulaic, and for good reason; the basic concepts that worked 20, 30 or 40 years ago still apply today. We have a number of new media today such as e-mail, internet banner ads, blogs, podcasts, etc. However, the same principles apply. One such formula is known as AIDA, which stands for:

- Attention
- Interest
- Desire
- Action

Any advertising you employ, whether it is a space ad, a sales letter or other form should follow this sequence. In order to get your piece read you must first get the reader's attention. This is usually done with a headline. The purpose of the headline is to get attention and drive enough interest to get the reader to continue reading the copy below the headline.

The copy should enhance interest and generate desire. Desire is generated by emphasis on the benefits the customer will enjoy if he or she uses your product or service. The GEICO gecko emphasizes saving 15% on your car insurance. Ads for Trump properties emphasize luxurious living. Recently, ads for cars have been emphasizing fuel efficiency and the money that will be saved on gasoline purchases.

Many marketing experts recommend that you include a reason to act now. This is the reason that you see so many statements such as "For a Limited Time," "Seating Limited," "While Quantities Last," "Limit Two Per Customer," etc. in advertising. Their argument has merit. People will naturally tend toward inaction and procrastination. Your ad must help to motivate a strong enough desire to overcome this inertia and take action to either make a purchase or contact your business to express interest. On the other hand, I personally hate the feeling that I am being manipulated to purchase rather than persuaded with logic and an offer of value. Our businesses have always tended toward a no-pressure approach to marketing and sales. We hold ourselves out as experts with valuable services that are available to those who feel we are a good fit for their needs. Our sales might be higher if we were to follow the lead of the marketing experts who tell us to generate a sense of urgency to act, but we feel more comfortable using a no-pressure approach. As I mentioned earlier, our results thus far have been highly satisfactory.

I recommend that you spend some time looking through magazines to locate ads that have been running for a long time. Advertising is expensive, so if an ad has been running for an extended period, you can be certain that it has produced a good return for the advertiser. Study the headlines and the copy to see how the elements of the AIDA formula have been applied. Unlike many corporate secrets, advertising is available to the public, so you can use other successful ads as success models for your own. This beats learning about advertising through trial and error.

**Integrity in Advertising**
A central theme throughout this book has been integrity. Every action you take either builds or destroys trust. It is perfectly acceptable to emphasize benefits in your advertising, but you should not mislead. Do not engage in the type of "Get Rich Quick" or "Lose Weight Fast with Little or No Effort" types of advertising that is so common today, particularly in late night infomercials. Your goal is to use advertising to generate customers with whom you can have a long-term relationship. This will not happen if you mislead them or if you over-promise and under-deliver.

Maintain high quality products and services so that you can feel good about the benefits that you truly deliver to your customers or clients. If you feel confident that you are delivering good value, your enthusiasm will show to your staff and customers.

**Guarantees - Standing Behind Your Product or Service**
If you are selling a product, your sales will almost certainly be enhanced by offering a strong guarantee. If you offer a full, money-back guarantee in the first 30 days if not satisfied, that is good. A full money-back guarantee if not satisfied in the first 90 days is better, one year is better than that. If you will pay shipping and handling for returns, that further supports that you are willing to stand behind your product. Offering such a guarantee will generally increase returns, but also increase sales to a greater extent, so the net result is usually positive. If you have a high quality product that offers good value, your returns will be low. If you do not maintain good quality, your returns will be high and your return policy will be the least of your problems.

I recently had an interaction with a company that will prevent me from ever doing business with them again. My wife and I bought a high-tech bed through the internet. When the bed arrived it had a defect and did not work properly. We called the company and were told that they would not allow us to return the bed for a refund or exchange it for a new one. They would send us replacement parts so that we could fix it ourselves. The last thing we wanted to do was fix a bed that never worked properly. We received the parts and fixed the bed. All told, this caused us to expend several hours of our time between phone calls and repairs and we had the inconvenience of a bed that did not work properly for several weeks while this was being straightened out. That will be our last purchase from the company.

I also had an experience where I purchased a low-end telephone from a national electronics chain store. This purchase was made in December, but the telephone never worked properly. It buzzed loudly in the earpiece during calls. I bought a better telephone elsewhere and put this one aside to return, which I got around to doing sometime in February. I was told that I could only return the product within 30 days for a refund and that since it had been more than 30 days I could only obtain store credit. I did not want store credit and stated that I thought they should provide a refund since the product never worked properly. The manager was called over and he told me in a very condescending tone that the return policy is clearly printed on the back of the receipt and that all he was willing to do was to give me store credit. I left the defective telephone and receipt on the counter and walked out. When I got home I went to the company's web site and sent a complaint through their customer service system. Adding insult to injury, I received no reply of any sort. To this day, several years later, I make a point of avoiding this store and have given my employees strict instructions not to spend any company money at that chain. I have been watching the company's earnings growth and stock price since this incident. Not surprisingly, both have been poor.

For service businesses, offering a guarantee is a bit trickier. Sometimes they make sense, other times there are too many factors outside your control as a business owner that could result in the client not being satisfied. If a guarantee is not feasible, the main way to keep customers happy is to ask them how they would rate the service and whether there is anything that could have been done differently. If a customer is dissatisfied, talk to him or her and try to find a win-win solution.

### Build Credibility with Testimonials

No matter what you say about your company, it will not be as powerful as something positive expressed by one of your happy customers or clients. Make an effort to obtain testimonials from happy customers or clients. One way to do so is to ask people to complete a customer satisfaction survey after a purchase or completion of a project. Include a comments section.

Obtain their permission to use these comments in your advertising. This last point is important for two reasons. First, you want to be able to provide specifics about the individual who made the comments, including at least a first name and city where the person lives. Second, if you are ever challenged, you need to show documentation that the testimonials used are real. It is fraud to advertise using made up testimonials.

## Use Press Releases to Help Make Potential Customers Aware of Your Business

If you have an interesting story or announcement about your business, you can often get newspapers, radio stations, television stations and other media to pick up the information by issuing a press release written like a news story. If the article or news segment mentions your contact information, this can be a very effective way to promote your business. Like testimonials, the fact that a third party reporter is providing information about your business adds credibility to the message.

## Appear on Radio and Television Programs

Our company occasionally runs studies to test interventions that are of interest to the public. On several occasions we have contacted local news outlets about these studies and, as a result, I have been interviewed by newspaper or television reporters about clinical trials for which we were seeking volunteers, generating considerable interest in our studies. In addition, it is often possible to obtain video or audio recordings of these interviews that can be posted on your web site.

I am not an expert on obtaining press coverage, but in my somewhat limited experience, the process is relatively simple. Some businesses hire public relations specialists to help them facilitate the process. Several of the books on marketing in the recommended resources appendix at the end of this book contain sections on using press releases to obtain media coverage.

## Make the Process of Purchasing Easy and Convenient

I am a busy person with low tolerance for long or complex processes when I am attempting to buy something. On numerous occasions I have aborted a purchase because the shopping cart on the web site was frustrating to use or a telephone call to the business resulted in a seemingly never-ending electronic tree that kept me from talking to someone who could take my order.

In one case my wife and I wanted to buy a new Honda automobile. We have had other Honda vehicles with which we were very happy. This would have been the easiest sale the dealership made that year. We knew what we wanted and planned to just go to the dealership and write a check. We showed up at a local dealership on a busy day and waited, and waited, and waited for someone to help us. We flagged down several employees and emphasized that we just wanted to write a check and buy a car. After a while we walked out. The sales manager ran out of the door to talk to us in the parking lot. I told him that he had missed an opportunity. We drove a few miles to another Honda dealership, were waited on promptly, and drove home a vehicle that afternoon. We were already happy with the Honda brand and no selling was required, only some way for us to give the dealership our money. Which of the two dealerships we visited do you think sells more cars? Which dealership do you think we will go to when we get our next Honda?

Don't have a "user hostile" system for purchasing. Make sure the process is as easy and convenient as possible. It is tragic to have all of the time, money and effort expended to generate a qualified lead lost when the customer gets frustrated with the process of trying to give you money and aborts a sale. In particular, if you sell through a web site, test the process. Be sure that the instructions are simple and clear. Don't irritate your customers with complicated or difficult processes.

In our business we work with large food and pharmaceutical companies. As soon as we are awarded a project we ask to receive a contract template for review or we provide the client with one of our contract templates to review so that we do not get to the point of starting a project and get hung up on contract issues. The earlier these can be resolved the better. We have also worked hard to make our own template contract language simple and reasonable, which cuts down on questions and long, complicated negotiations.

**You Can Only Sell What People Want, Not What You Think They Need**

I once worked for a company that had three business units. Senior management was obsessed with tying the services of all three units together as an integrated package. They felt that the process would be more efficient for us and our clients and that our company would realize higher margins if we sold the entire package rather than the individual services in a piecemeal fashion. This was a great concept except for one minor issue…it didn't work. The companies we were trying to sell to were not organized in such a way that this was feasible. A better strategy would have been to focus on making each business unit as strong as possible and using the trust and credibility earned through good performance as leverage to get introductions for members of the other business units. Senior management's failure to recognize this early and change course contributed to financial difficulties that ultimately forced the sale of the company to a larger competitor.

It may be true that you have a better solution than what your customers are accustomed to, but you may not be able to sell the idea or product in any volume until the marketplace is receptive to varying from the traditional way of doing things. This is often true with new technologies. The adoption curve is shallow at first, as only a few early adopters try out the new product. A successful product will show much more rapid growth as it moves from early adopters into the mainstream. However, many products never make the transition and either remain niche solutions or fall by the wayside as other methods are adopted on a larger scale. There is nothing wrong with being a pioneer, as long as you recognize that such a strategy is a high risk approach (some pioneers end up with arrows in their backs).

Most successful small business owners do not have a better mousetrap. Tapping in to a pre-existing market is almost always easier than creating a new one. Most successful entrepreneurs enter traditional businesses and are successful because they are better than their competition in one or more of the elements on which people make buying decisions: time, price, quality (of the product and/or service), convenience and risk. They gradually build a base of satisfied customers from whom they have earned trust and loyalty through good marketing and sales efforts, coupled with good service and execution.

**Don't Sell Anything You Don't Believe In Personally**
One cautionary note is that there are times when there is great
demand for products or services that are not in the customers' best
interests. My advice is to never sell anything that you don't
believe in, even if you could do so profitably.

A few years ago I wrote a book about buying and managing rental
properties called *Beating the Dow with Rental Houses*. During
normal times, I believe that someone willing to put in the time and
effort to buy at good prices, carefully select tenants and provide
them with good service can earn good returns without taking
excessive risk by investing and managing single family rental
properties. My wife and I have done so and I felt that I had useful
information to share with others with similar interests.

A couple of years after publication, the housing market took off
and prices rose to unprecedented levels. The demand for books
on investment real estate had never been higher. I probably could
have sold a lot of books during that period. However, I
understood that the high prices were not being driven by
fundamental factors and that the market was largely being driven
by poor lending practices. I was fairly sure that the speculative
bubble would eventually pop and housing prices would fall to a
level more consistent with long-term averages, although I have to
admit that I underestimated both the size of the bubble at its peak
and the magnitude of the subsequent decline. One thing I did
know was that during the bubble it was nearly impossible to buy a
house that would provide enough rental income to provide a good
long-term return.

I didn't want to encourage anyone to get into the rental real estate
business during this crazy period because I knew the risks were
unusually high, so I stopped selling the book. As I write this in
2009, prices have come back down considerably and (for those
who can obtain financing) I again feel comfortable that
conservative, long-term investors can do well with rental houses.
For that reason we will start selling *Beating the Dow with Rental
Houses* again soon.

**Regularly Review the Five P's of Your Marketing**

It is useful to periodically evaluate your company's performance on each of the five P's of marketing. While there are some variations, the five P's of marketing that I use include:

1. *Price* – the objective is to select a price at which customers feel they are getting good value.
2. *Positioning* – the expectations you set for your customers, which helps to determine what prices they will be willing to pay and the quality of product or service anticipated (expectations are different for customers at a Holiday Inn compared to a the Ritz Carlton).
3. *Promotion* – your company's marketing efforts to communicate the features and benefits of your product.
4. *People* – every interaction with any person representing your company is marketing and each interaction will either enhance or diminish that customer's relationship with your business. Are your people consistently presenting your business in a favorable light through their appearances and actions?
5. *Packaging* – how and where your product or service is presented to customers is exceptionally important. This includes all aspects of presentation, including the information you offer on your web site, the cleanliness of your place or places of business (including the restrooms), and the dress and appearance of your employees.

Price, positioning, people and promotion are covered elsewhere, so I will focus my commentary here on a few important concepts about packaging. As stated above, every interaction a customer or potential customer has with your company will either *enhance* or *diminish* the relationship that individual has with your business. First impressions are lasting and you never get a second chance to make a first impression. Therefore, you should give a great deal of thought to packaging, which I broadly define as all of the ways your products and/or services are presented to potential customers.

Think about the experience a customer or potential customer has when he or she encounters your business, both in person, as with a retail location, and in advertising materials, including your web site. Are all of these consistent with the image you would like to portray? Are your employees reinforcing this image through their appearance and demeanor? Is the image you are projecting consistent with the tastes of your target customers?

In a city where our company once had an office there are two restaurants within a short distance of one another in the main town square. One targets mostly college students and the other is a more elegant restaurant, targeting more affluent diners. These establishments could not be more different, but both are successful, partly because each provides an atmosphere and overall experience consistent with the tastes of their respective target customers.

No matter what field you are in, insufficient attention to cleanliness will negatively impact your customers' perceptions of your business. Every employee should be trained to notice and correct cleanliness issues and managers should be held accountable for ensuring that all areas accessed by customers are maintained to a high standard. I am continually amazed at how many businesses allow bits of trash such as paper cups, cigarettes, straws and wrappers blow around in their parking lots for days or weeks. I regularly go into restrooms in various types of retail establishments and find that all of the paper towels have been used, or that the trash containers are overflowing, or some obvious and foul-smelling mess has not been cleaned for hours. I often find that promotional displays and decorations are covered with a thick layer of dust, suggesting that they may not have been cleaned since the Carter Administration.

Attention to cleanliness helps your business to project an image of competence and attention to detail. Customers will feel more comfortable and confident in your company's products and services if you keep things neat and clean. Ray Kroc, legendary former CEO of McDonald's, understood this. He was obsessed with product consistency, service and cleanliness. He required his store managers to keep not only the premises clean, but to also take responsibility for picking up trash from the ground for entire city block on which the restaurant was located.

**Study Other Businesses Inside and Outside of Your Industry**
Many aspects of other businesses are difficult to evaluate directly because they require obtaining information that is not readily available to non-insiders. However, packaging used by other businesses is often relatively easy to observe directly by simply visiting the establishment if it is a retail operation or viewing marketing materials on the company's web site, printed advertising, etc. It pays to study the methods employed by other businesses, including the competitors in your own field, as well as those in other businesses.

In his book *No BS Business Success*, Dan Kennedy points out that the drive-up service window was first used by banks, but was later employed profitably by other industries such as fast food restaurants (about 70% of McDonald's sales are at the drive-through window), dry cleaners, pharmacies and others. Two of my favorite examples are drive-through wedding chapels in Las Vegas and a drive-up window for the purchase of bull semen by cattle ranchers.

Paul Orfalea, founder of Kinko's copy shops and author of the book *Copy This*, met a convenience store owner who told him that his overall sales had jumped by 50% when he had started staying open 24 hours a day, even though his overnight foot traffic was light. By being open all the time, customers didn't have to worry about whether or not the store would be open when they needed something. In addition, by being open when the competition was not, they had the opportunity to develop relationships with customers who they might not otherwise have had the chance to serve. In Kinko's case, this included students and small business owners who often needed work done during off-hours. As a result of staying open overnight and developing new relationships, sales increased, not only at night, but also during daytime hours at Kinko's stores that switched to a 24-hour format. In 2003, McDonald's started experimenting with a 24-hour format in some of their stores.  Just as Paul Orfalea would have predicted, same-store sales increased in the stores with the new format.  Ironically, since FedEx acquired Kinko's, they have discontinued the 24-hour format in many locations.

These examples illustrate the point that creativity in business is often a matter of legally "stealing" the best ideas from other businesses.  To quote Oscar Wilde, "Talent borrows, genius steals."

## Chapter 7

# Maximizing Lifetime Customer Value

*You can't build a reputation on what you are going to do.*
— Henry Ford

### The Initial Contact is Just the Start of the Relationship

A very common mistake that small business owners make is not working hard at maintaining and deepening their relationships with their customers and potential customers after an initial contact. Think about how many businesses you come in contact with during a typical week? How many of these have asked you for your information so that they can maintain their relationship with you? Have you had a service provided in your home such as plumbing, heating or air conditioning work, painting, remodeling, carpet cleaning, etc.? How many of these vendors have stayed in touch through mail or e-mail on a regular basis? These businesses have your contact information, but if they are like most, they wait for you to contact them the next time you need their help.

I have a challenge for you. Ask your friends and colleagues for recommendations for any of these services. See how many can recall who they have used. At least half will say that they have used such a service within the last year, but fewer than half of them will be able to remember the name of the company that provided the service, even if they were very happy with the work (if they were unhappy they will be more likely to remember).

## Maintain Top of Mind Status

A good portion of success in business comes from maintaining "top of mind" status. You want to be the first business that people think of when the need or desire for your product or service arises. If you don't keep in touch with your customers and potential customers regularly, someone else is likely to be in that top of mind position when the need or desire arises, and that company will get the call.

There are many ways to stay in touch with your customers and potential customers. There are several very good books that cover this topic in detail, so I will not do so here. I will mention a few effective strategies.

One of the simplest strategies is to send a thank you of some sort after a sale, particularly a first sale. For regular customers, you should be sure to send an acknowledgement at least once a year thanking the customers for their business. This might be connected with an offer such as a coupon, but does not have to be to make the gesture meaningful. In our rental property business we send gifts to all of our tenants at least once each year and have often been told that we are the only landlords who have ever done so. If our small gifts get even one tenant to decide to stay rather than move at the end of a lease, the gifts will more than pay for themselves.

Another strategy is to send out a short newsletter on a regular basis. This is a bit costly and time consuming, particularly if you include information of value such as a feature article. Nevertheless, the return on investment is nearly always positive and the cost can be minimized by using e-mail as a method of delivery. In our business we have a newsletter that goes out once per quarter. It should be more often, probably once a month (this is an opportunity for you to learn from my mistakes). Every time we send out the newsletter, we get calls from people asking us to bid on projects. Since our average project sale is in excess of $350,000 the cost and time required are miniscule relative to the benefit.

Nightingale-Conant is a private company headquartered in the Chicago area that sells self-improvement audio programs. If you ever contact them or buy a program, be prepared to receive offers from them several times a week in the mail. I have made a number of purchases from them over the years, sometimes with stretches of as long as 18 months between purchases. Nevertheless, without fail, I receive sales letters in the mail at least once each week. They also have a newsletter and a quote of the day feature that I receive via e-mail. I am not likely to forget their name any time soon. I am quite sure that they have tested these strategies thoroughly and found them to provide more than one dollar in profits for every dollar spent.

For certain types of business, particularly consultants, attorneys, investment advisors, accountants and others who are selling their knowledge and expertise, a blog or new articles posted regularly on a web site is an excellent way to give your customers a reason to visit and take an active part in maintaining their relationship with you. These will also help to draw new people who are interested in these topics to your web site, acting as a low-cost method of advertising. An e-mail announcement can go out each time a new article is posted.

**Rewards for Repeat Purchases**
Businesses often use rewards programs to encourage customer loyalty. Many work well, although some can become problematic and annoy customers, like airline programs with expiring miles and ever shifting rules to obtain reward flights.

I recently went to a fast food restaurant and ordered a breakfast meal. With my meal I received a card that can be stamped with each purchase of a breakfast meal, amounting to a "buy three, get the fourth free" offer. This can be a very effective strategy when offering a new product or for a service that will be used regularly, such as dry cleaning. An example might be to provide a card that offers 50% off (maximum value $25) on the fifth dry cleaning order.

**Develop Systems for Obtaining Referrals**

Happy customers will recommend your business to their friends, colleagues and relatives. However, you should not simply allow this to occur by happenstance. There are ways that you can facilitate this process.

Northwestern Mutual has used a referral-based selling system as a cornerstone of their approach, which helped them to become the one of the top selling life insurance companies in the US. They earned the highest customer satisfaction score in the 2008 University of Michigan's American Customer Satisfaction Index survey.

My wife and I have Northwestern life insurance policies. This came about because my former boss had given my name when his agent asked him for referrals. He had been pleased with the service he had received from this agent and was happy to provide my name. I was at the beginning of my professional career and just about to get married, so the timing was very good. Every six months this agent meets with me and, without fail, asks if I can give him the names of one or two people who he might contact, using my name as a way to turn a "cold call" into a "warm call." Since I have been pleased with this agent's no-pressure, consultative sales approach, I have been more than willing to provide referrals, even though I would never have done so without a bit of prompting.

In addition to simply asking, you can offer a reward for referrals. Health clubs and other businesses that sell memberships often have "refer a friend" programs. I belong to a health club and referred my assistant. When she joined, the health club gave me a $100 gift certificate. In our rental property business we offer tenants an incentive to refer other tenants to us. We have found that good tenants usually provide good referrals. Recently, we had a tenant who moved out of one of our houses after having lived there for several years. They referred a friend who moved in a few days after the prior tenants moved out, allowing us to avoid any vacancy. Since our properties generally rent for between

$1,000 and $1,600 per month, saving even one month of vacancy is a substantial benefit.

## Exchange Referrals with Vendors
If you have received good value from a vendor, be sure to recommend that business to others. After providing one or more referrals, you should not be shy about asking if there is anyone that vendor works with who might benefit from your product or service.

This process can be taken a step further in some cases by providing endorsements. For example, you might be willing to send a letter to all of your customers recommending the product or service of the vendor while his or her business may do the same for yours. Of course, this is only a good idea if you have high confidence that the vendor will treat your customers well. You don't want your company's reputation damaged by recommending someone who does not share your commitment to quality.

## Exchange Referrals with Related Businesses
Our company provides consulting and clinical research services for food and pharmaceutical clients. Over the years we have had occasion to work with consultants and other professionals who serve the same types of clients, but with a different focus. We have been able to provide a number of referrals to these firms and vice versa. We make a point to stay in touch with our contacts at these companies in order to exchange leads.

## Rekindle Relationships with Former Customers
If you track customer purchases, you will be able to not only identify the most and least profitable customer segments (80/20 analysis), but also identify former customers who have stopped buying from you. This represents an opportunity to rekindle your relationship and obtain important feedback at the same time.

Former customers can be contacted directly by telephone or indirectly through a letter or e-mail. The letter can state something along the lines of the following. I have used an office supply store as an example:

Dear Ms. Eckerly:

I was recently reviewing our accounts and realized that you have not made a purchase from us in the last year (or whatever timeframe is appropriate). We value your business and are wondering whether we have done something that left you less than fully satisfied.

In order to learn how we might serve you better, we have included a short customer feedback survey, along with a $5 gift card for Starbucks (enjoy a latte on us). Please be frank in your assessment, as the only way we can improve our service is "practice with feedback." In addition, this letter will entitle you to 10% off of your next order. Just mention offer code GEB-0908 to obtain your savings.

Thank you for your business. We hope to be able to serve you again in the future.

Best regards,


John M. Doe
Customer Service Manager
Gizmo's Office Supply Depot

Such a letter will often bring a substantial fraction of lost customers back to the business and will provide useful feedback for improving your systems. Many times a single bad experience with one employee will be enough to turn a customer away. If no attempt is made to investigate why customers have defected, there is no opportunity to get them back.

## Respond Quickly and "Make Things Right" if You Learn of a Problem

I try to bring in lunch or take the staff in our office out for lunch regularly. At least once a month we will take a group out to a restaurant. After one such event I noticed on the credit card statement that the total differed from what my receipt showed. I asked my assistant to call the restaurant to let them know. Although the discrepancy was small, the carbon copy of the receipt showed very clearly what the total should have been, which made me think that the restaurant might have a dishonest server.

Sure enough, she spoke to the manager who informed us that the server had been terminated. The manager followed up with a letter of apology and included a gift certificate for $25. The letter stated that our feedback was appreciated and that many customers would have simply stopped coming to the restaurant. I took our staff to that restaurant the next time we went out, spent far more than $25, and have remained loyal customers. The letter of apology was appreciated and we not only have continued to patronize, but have recommended the restaurant to others, often telling the story of the great service we received from that manager when doing so. The service at the restaurant in general has improved recently, which I suspect is due to the influence of the customer service oriented manager from whom we received the letter. An unhappy customer can frequently be converted to a raving fan if the situation is handled correctly, as this episode illustrates.

**Your Database is an Enormously Valuable Asset**
The discussion above makes it clear that the database of people with whom your business has made contact and started relationships (including customers/clients, vendors and related businesses) is an enormously valuable asset. Too many entrepreneurs spend all or nearly all of their marketing efforts on attempting to start more new relationships, rather than nurturing and maximizing the value of those they have already started. It costs as much as seven times more to make a sale to a stranger than it does to make a sale to someone with whom you have already transacted. If you come recommended by one of your happy customers, or by someone from another business that has earned the buyer's trust, you will enter the sales process with a running start. When recommended by a third party you are

walking through the door (literally or figuratively) with credibility, rather than having to earn that from scratch.

I have no universal answer for the question of how much of your marketing budget and resources should be spent on nurturing old relationships as opposed to starting new ones. Both are important. However, from talking with other business owners, I have the impression that most give existing relationships short shrift and are leaving profits on the table by doing so.

*Chapter 8*

# Managing Your Business in a Way that Builds Customer Equity

*To try and fail is at least to learn. To fail to try is to suffer the loss of what might have been.*

– Benjamin Franklin

By now you should be able to recite the factors on which customers make buying decisions: time, price, service/product quality, convenience and risk. When you build a relationship with a customer built on trust, you become the low-risk option. If the customer feels that he or she is getting good value, there is no reason to try the competition. Saving a few dollars with a competitor will generally not be worth the risk of having a bad experience. This is a form of customer equity that has tremendous value. Every interaction with a customer or client will either build or destroy equity. Building equity does not happen by chance. You must manage your business in a way that does so.

## Set Your Customers' Expectations and Then Meet or Exceed Them

In every interaction with a customer there is a certain expectation. Your job is to define your value proposition for your customer; in other words, what he or she should expect, and then meet or exceed those expectations. Wal-Mart's value proposition is "everyday low prices". Their customers expect to find prices lower than are available from other retailers, but they do not expect exceptional service. They might not be willing to accept rude or indifferent service, but they also don't expect the same level of service that is anticipated at Nordstrom's. Wal-Mart's value proposition revolves around price and customers understand that low price comes with certain trade-offs regarding service and atmosphere. Wal-Mart can maintain this competitive advantage because of their scale, which allows them to negotiate very low wholesale purchase prices. Being the low-price provider is rarely the best value proposition for a small business because there is almost always someone who will eventually try to undercut your prices.

McDonald's value proposition is fast food, with the emphasis on fast. A majority of McDonald's daily sales occur at the drive-through window and the company has worked hard to make the process move quickly. Amazon's value proposition is the convenience of a very large selection and shopping from any place with a computer that has internet access. Customers have to wait longer to obtain their merchandise than they might if they went to a bricks and mortar store, so, unlike McDonald's, speed is not their value proposition, although they do allow customers to pay more to obtain their purchases more quickly. Nevertheless, customers do expect to receive their purchases after a reasonable wait and will become frustrated and unhappy if their orders do not arrive in the expected timeframe.

Some companies such as McKinsey (business consulting) or Goldman Sachs (investment banking) have developed reputations as being among the top providers in their fields. Their clients are willing to pay more because of their stellar reputations, which, in the minds of their customers, makes them low-risk providers.

The businesses described above have each set expectations for their customers. Your job as a business owner is to define your expectations, and then consistently meet or exceed these, so that your customers feel they are receiving good value. Your marketing and sales process will help to define your implied promises and your operations will determine how well you deliver on those promises.

A few years ago my wife and I obtained bids from several painting companies to paint the inside of our home. We selected a company that was not the cheapest, but was owned by an individual who lived in the neighborhood. From the start, we were disappointed with the service. They told us they would start the job in two weeks. The specified date arrived and they did not show up. We called and were told that they had run over on another job and could not start yet. This would have been fine had they simply let us know so that we could plan. When the painters showed up, they did the job with reasonable quality, but annoyed us in a number of ways. They drank cans of soda from our refrigerator without asking permission, watched our television all day while painting, and smoked cigarettes on our driveway which were stubbed out and left for us to pick up. We were told that the job would take one week. In fact, it took considerably longer, partly because the people who were actually doing the painting appeared to be working at about half-speed, suggesting that the owner of the company was not holding his staff accountable for performance. Once they started we were never told when they would be done. Each day we had to guess based on what progress had been made. All told, the painting took two full weeks, including Saturdays. We would have been much happier paying more if it had meant not having our lives disrupted for this length of time.

We happen to own a number of rental houses. Had that company met our expectations, or even communicated along the way to reset our expectations, we would have probably hired them over and over for painting jobs on our rental units (as we have subsequently done with another company). They overpromised and underperformed, destroying any equity they had built up with us when we selected them over the other bidders.

### Obtain Customer Feedback
In the example above, we were never asked for our opinion during or after the job. Thus, the owner of that business not only destroyed all of his equity with us, but also missed an opportunity to find out that we were unhappy and potentially earn back our

trust. Don't make this mistake. While it may not be practical to obtain feedback from every customer after every transaction, you should, at the very least, obtain feedback from a representative sample periodically.

I don't recommend long surveys because many people will not take the time to fill these out. If you keep your customer satisfaction survey simple and convenient, more people will take the time to complete it, providing a more representative sample. In addition, you will be more likely to take the time to tabulate and analyze the results of a simple survey than one that is long and complex. You can always use a more involved survey periodically or select a smaller subset to receive such a survey.

Fred Reichheld makes a compelling case for asking at least one question, which may be enough by itself in many cases. What is this question?

*How likely would you be to recommend [your company name] to a friend or colleague? Please circle your answer below.*

|  0   1   2   3   4   5   6   7   8   9   10 |

Not Likely                                      Extremely
At All                                            Likely

**Comments or Suggestions:**

_____

_____

_____

_____

_____

Research results from Bain and Company suggest that only scores of 9 or 10 are adequate. Reichheld and colleagues define customers who provide scores in this range as *promoters*. Those who provide ratings of 7 or 8 are *passively satisfied* customers and those at 6 or below are *detractors*.

Their studies showed that promoters accounted for more than 80% of referrals, whereas detractors were responsible for 80% of negative word of mouth comments (80/20 strikes again). Your goals should be to maximize the number of promoters and move the passively satisfied into the promoter category. Some of the detractors are worth working on to see if they can be moved up the scale. On the other hand, some need to be "fired" because they are probably responsible for a large proportion of the headaches that you and your staff deal with. They may simply be poor fits for your business.

Pay particular attention to comments and suggestions. For positive comments, ask the customer for permission to use his or her statement as a testimonial. For negative comments, assess whether this is an opportunity to salvage a damaged relationship. In some cases the answer will be yes and in others the negative comments may be a sign that the customer is a poor fit for your company. If the relationship is worth salvaging, have a system for follow-up. Apologize for not meeting the customer's expectations and see if you can somehow make up for this disappointment. In many cases just showing that you care about his or her satisfaction will be enough to obtain repeat business.

Customer feedback will provide valuable insights to help you improve. It may help you to identify a problem employee or ways to improve your systems to reduce customer frustration.

**Communication is Key to Avoiding Unpleasant Surprises**
Warren Buffett once said that the secret to a happy marriage is low expectations. I am not suggesting that you try to set low expectations for your customers, but rather that you should have systems to communicate in such a way that the customer is not surprised in a negative way.

In our business we typically put together two to four bids per month for clinical trial projects. This is an involved and time consuming process that often includes collecting bids for subcontracted services.  Our default timeline for providing a bid is one to two weeks.  However, we always ask the client when he or she would ideally like to receive the bid.  In some cases we are told that four weeks is fine because the bid is needed to prepare for a specific meeting, or the key decision maker will not look at the bid until he or she returns from vacation.  In other cases we are told that it would be very helpful to have the bid back in a few days.  By asking the question, we are able to establish a timeline that is workable for both parties.

**Make Your Values and Expectations Clear**
One of the best business books I have ever read is *Winning* by Jack and Suzy Welch.  They recommend explicitly endorsing very specific and understandable values that will help guide employee behavior.  They offer as an example a list of values and behaviors that were prepared by CEOs Jamie Dimon and Bill Harrison when Bank One and JP Morgan Chase banks merged.  Some of these are listed below:

- Give customers a good, fair deal.  Great customer relationships take time.  Do not try to maximize short-term profits at the expense of building enduring relationships.
- Never let profit center conflicts get in the way of doing what is right for the customer.
- Always look for ways to make it easier to do business with us.
- Don't forget to say thank you.

In the employee handbook for our company we state that the well being of our study subjects should always be our primary concern.  When interacting with individuals who are participating in, or being screened for a study, we recommend that staff treat that person in the manner that one would want if the person was a parent or other close relative.

If there is ever a dispute about how a study subject has been treated, the standard we hold our staff to is whether or not the subject was treated as the employee would want his or her mother or father treated. This usually ends the discussion quickly.

## Have an Energizing Mission Statement

A mission statement conveys what you hope to accomplish if your business is successful, i.e., your vision. At Microsoft, the mission statement in the 1980s and 1990s was "A computer on every desk and in every home", which I like a lot better than their current mission statement: "At Microsoft, our mission and values are to help people and businesses throughout the world to realize their full potential" (www.Microsoft.com, accessed August 2008). The former is very clear and objective. In fact, their mission has become a reality in the US and many parts of the world.

In our business, we have tried to convey that what we do has implications beyond simply making a profit, which we hope will help our employees to recognize that they are making meaningful contribution to society each day.

> At Provident, our mission is to advance the science of chronic disease prevention by designing and conducting clinical trials. In doing so, we hope to contribute to the development of safe and effective ways to help people live longer, healthier lives.

## Provide Training on Customer Service

Several years ago McDonald's went through a tough period. Their restaurants had deteriorated in both service and cleanliness. Add to that a price war with Wendy's and Burger King during an economic slowdown, as well as expenses associated with a program of tearing down and rebuilding older stores, and McDonald's showed its first quarterly loss in company history.

A new CEO took over and made customer service and cleanliness training top priorities. Howard Schultz recently did the same thing when he retook the CEO position at Starbucks. In both cases, I saw noticeable improvements, which prompted me to buy stock. It is too early to report the results from my recent

Starbucks purchase, but McDonald's stock has nearly quadrupled in the period between 2003 and 2008.

If you don't provide explicit instructions for staff on how they interact with your customers, you are not likely to get good results. Many young people today have never been exposed to good customer service and are baffled when criticized for behavior that they thought was perfectly acceptable. You must follow this training with ongoing feedback and accountability. Also, remember that the way you interact with your employees will be reflected in the way they interact with your customers. If you treat your employees poorly, you can be certain that they will do the same with your customers.

**Accountability**
The only way to be certain you are achieving your goals for customer service is to set up systems, measure compliance, and hold people accountable when the systems are not followed. Often this will mean using checklists to ensure that all steps are completed. It also means providing ongoing feedback, since new behaviors do not become habits until they are practiced for some time. Without continuous corrective feedback, people tend to slip back to their old habits. Also, be sure to provide lots of positive feedback for behavior that is consistent with the training. Catch people "doing something right" and acknowledge this. The more public the positive feedback, the better.

Our company has two individuals who handle the bulk of our accounting functions. Both are smart and competent, but nearly every month I would get a financial statement, then a week or so later would find out that some entry had been neglected, resulting in a need to generate a revised statement. My solution was to request that a checklist be created, but I made the mistake of not reviewing the checklist to ensure that it had enough detail. For example, the checklist said Check Payroll Entries. However, it turned out that this was insufficient detail because they continued to fail to enter partial weeks of payroll. Later, we revised the checklist to state:

---

1. Calculate number days of payroll for the month.
2. Enter number of days of payroll here _____ .
3. Ensure that all days have been entered.

Another example is that we require that each study subject receive a Thank You card after completing a clinical trial. However, we discovered that some staff members were consistently completing this step while others were not. We have subsequently instituted a policy in which a photocopy of the card is entered into the subject's chart. A quality check is performed on each chart before it goes into long-term storage so that we can catch it when this step has been missed. Employees who consistently fail to send a Thank You card will be told that this is unacceptable, while those who complete this task as intended will be acknowledged for their consistent performance.

You need ways to objectively measure compliance with your systems. What gets measured gets done, and what gets measured can be managed. However, you also need methods to assess and document how well people are adhering to the values you have articulated. These assessments will, by necessity, be somewhat subjective. However, it is no less important to hold people accountable for upholding your company's stated values than for easily measurable behaviors such as punctuality or sending Thank You cards. Performance appraisals will be covered in detail in the next chapter.

**Empower Your Staff to Make it Right for the Customer**
At Starbucks, their training emphasizes going to great lengths to ensure that the customer has a great experience. If a customer orders a drink, leaves the store and comes back a few minutes later, ordering the same drink, the barista (clerk) will ask what happened. Frequently the answer is that the customer dropped his or her drink. When this happens, the clerk will tell the customer that the replacement is on the house.

The Starbucks approach mirrors that advocated by Steve Wynn in a speech he gave to his staff just before the opening of a new property in Las Vegas (either Wynn or Bellagio, I can't remember which) that was filmed and shown on the Charlie Rose show. In his talk, Wynn told the staff that they needed to be his eyes and ears. They needed to do whatever was necessary to make it right for the customer. If a room service order is botched, take it off the bill. He wants his staff to put themselves in the customer's shoes and do what they would want done if the situation were reversed.

Of course, this concept can be taken too far. You can't have your staff giving away freebies to every other customer. You need to track how much of this goes on to ensure that it is being used as intended – to build relationships with customers – or you will find yourself with no profit margin. Staff members who abuse your commitment to making right for the customer by giving away freebies to their friends and relatives or otherwise abusing the system need to be identified and removed.

Warren Buffett says that you want people with integrity, energy and intelligence working in your business. However, if an employee lacks integrity, the other two attributes will kill you. If you have a dishonest staff member, you should hope that he or she will also be lazy and not too bright, which will limit the damage that can be done before the person is terminated. You want your honest staff members to direct their energy and intelligence toward doing everything they can to build equity with your customers through both word and deed.

*Chapter 9*

# Management that Promotes Employee Engagement and Enthusiasm

*We have committed the Golden Rule to memory; let us now commit it to life.*

— Edwin Markham

After Jack and Suzy Welch published their excellent book *Winning*, they went on a massive tour, speaking to business groups and at business schools in the United States and all over the world. Between their book tour and their weekly column in *Business Week*, they have answered thousands of questions from managers and entrepreneurs. Their follow-up book *Winning: The Answers* includes responses to questions on topics that were not addressed in *Winning*, as well as others that expand and clarify material that was covered in their prior book.

One of the most interesting questions was: *Which three measurements would you say give the best sense of a company's health*? Their answer was that there are three key indicators that really work:

1. Employee engagement;
2. Customer satisfaction;
3. Cash flow.

I was very pleasantly surprised to read this response because it mirrors almost exactly the SLEEC (Sales/Marketing; Loyal, Engaged Employees and Customers) model that I have been promoting for several years. Note also that, like me, they advocate measuring employee engagement and customer satisfaction. Without quantifying your company's performance on these metrics, it is nearly impossible to determine where (and why) you are doing well or poorly, and how performance might be improved. Clearly, Jack and Suzy Welch are brilliant – not just because they agree with me, but I confess that my assessment may not be totally unbiased!

Customer satisfaction and cash flow management have been covered in previous chapters. The current chapter will provide an overview of some big ideas about managing your business in a way that promotes employee engagement and enthusiasm.

Engaged and enthusiastic employees are more productive, stay with the company longer, and business units with higher proportions of engaged employees are more profitable. High employee engagement is also associated with high customer satisfaction. Supervisors and managers drive employee engagement, although some people will never be engaged. While you cannot change your employees' inherent characteristics – some are persistently bitter and angry, no matter what you do – you can manage your company in a way that meets some basic human needs and therefore promotes greater employee engagement and enthusiasm.

This chapter is far too limited a space to do more than provide a broad overview of some key concepts. I encourage the reader to familiarize him or herself with the work done by two organizations that have, for decades, been studying employee engagement and its relationship to business outcomes.

### The Gallup Organization
When people hear about a Gallup poll, many think of election-related opinion polls that are so often reported on news programs. What is less well known outside of the business community is that

The Gallup Organization has a business unit called Gallup Consulting which has conducted interviews and surveys of literally millions of employees and managers. They have developed objective methods to evaluate employee engagement and provided compelling research-based evidence to support their assertion that managers can be taught skills that will help them to create a culture that encourages engagement. They have also shown that business units and companies that have high levels of employee engagement are more likely to have better outcomes, including lower employee turnover, enhanced customer satisfaction and greater profitability. I strongly recommend *First, Break All the Rules: What the World's Greatest Managers Do Differently* by Marcus Buckingham and Curt Coffman (who have both since left Gallup), as well as other books published by them and their Gallup colleagues.

**Sirota Survey Intelligence**
Another group that has long been involved in the study of employee morale and attitudes is Sirota Survey Intelligence. Their model for organizational effectiveness is outlined in the excellent book *The Enthusiastic Employee: How Companies Profit by Giving Workers What they Want.*

**Different Approaches, Similar Findings**
Although the Gallup and Sirota organizations took somewhat different approaches to studying employee engagement and its influence on business outcomes, their findings are remarkably consistent. Both have developed and validated tools for assessing employee engagement and reasons for its presence or absence. In addition, both have provided compelling research results supporting the view that employee engagement predicts business outcomes and, importantly, that interventions aimed at enhancing engagement improve business outcomes.

**Employee Engagement in Practice**
My career has afforded me the opportunity to observe and interact with managers and employees from dozens of business units. One company I worked at for 10 years underwent five mergers or acquisitions while I was there, including an initial buyout of the

small company I worked for, acquisition of the acquirer by another company, a spinoff of our business unit to another firm, and eventual acquisition of that company by yet another firm. Throughout, I was responsible for running a business unit, but over time became part of the senior management team that interacted with the heads of many other business units, where I was able to closely observe many managers in the same basic business endeavor. I saw how those that were most effective at maintaining employee engagement were – not coincidentally – also the most successful financially.

During my years as a hotel Guest Services Manager I developed many good habits from the successful couple who owned the hotel. I knew that these methods were effective, but had no empirical evidence to back up my viewpoints. Reading the book *First, Break All the Rules* that summarized key results from surveys and interviews with tens of thousands of employees and managers produced a number of "aha" moments for me and validated the effectiveness of much of what I had learned at the hotel, and used in my own business unit with good results. Sadly, my arguments for wider application of these concepts went largely ignored. I eventually tired of trying to change the management styles and cultures of my employers and launched my own company.

**The Spectrum of Employee Enthusiasm and Engagement**
In this book I will use the terms employee enthusiasm and engagement interchangeably. Both are expressions of employee morale and commitment to their employer's organization. Engagement is a continuous variable, but when doing research it is often helpful to use categories, which helps one to more easily describe the characteristics of an organization. Sirota uses four broad categories to describe employee morale:

1. Enthusiasm
2. Satisfaction
3. Neutrality
4. Anger

As a business owner, your job is to create a culture where employee needs are being met. To the degree that you are successful, you will have a higher prevalence of enthusiasm and satisfaction and lower prevalence of anger and neutrality. The extreme categories are particularly important. Enthusiastic employees are more productive and act as champions for your values and mission. In contrast, just a few angry employees can spread negativity like a cancer and do serious damage to your organization. If such individuals do not respond to reasonable efforts to get them on-board with the company's mission and values, they need to be removed. However, removing angry employees will not help if you are running an organization with a culture that doesn't promote satisfaction and enthusiasm. One of the key responsibilities that you and any managers you may employ is to create a culture that meets employee needs, which will help them to reach their potential to perform. Management expert Peter Drucker used to say "a fish rots from the head." If a company's leaders (owner and managers) fail to meet employee needs, the owner may find that angry employees are a renewable resource.

**Three Major Goals**
Although individuals may vary widely in personality traits, talents, knowledge and skills, David Sirota and colleagues assert that there are three major sets of goals that are most important to people at work. Since these arise from basic human needs, they do not change over time and apply across cultures. Their research supports the view that business units operated in a way that aligns with these goals have higher worker morale and performance. In order of importance, the three goals are:

1. Equity;
2. Achievement;
3. Camaraderie.

Regular evaluation of employee satisfaction in a way that provides feedback to management on their performance in these areas is critical in order to ensure that these needs are being met. I sometimes use the term "team spirit" in place of camaraderie, which allows me to use the acronym EATS (Equity, Achievement, Team Spirit) to help remember the categories.

## Equity
This is the degree to which employees feel fairly treated. Greater equity ratings are recognized by companies where employees feel that management truly cares about their well-being, treats them with respect, and provides compensation and benefits that are at least in line with industry norms.

One indicator of respect is that employee opinions are elicited and taken into account when establishing systems and policies. Praise and recognition for good performance builds a sense of equity. In contrast, equity is destroyed when management doesn't provide recognition to individuals and teams who perform well and when poor performers are tolerated without consequences.

Equity is also eroded when management treats employees as replaceable parts in the business. Several years ago American Airlines' management made a major blunder that eroded equity. After the terrorist attacks of 2001 the airline negotiated concessions from its unions that were agreed to in a spirit of working together to ensure the survival of the airline. Shortly after new contracts were signed it was revealed that key executives were to receive large bonuses that had not been disclosed during negotiations with the unions. While there is an argument for doing this in order to retain talent who might be able to earn more in a less troubled industry, the union employees viewed this as a violation of the spirit of shared sacrifice for the good of the company and the uproar resulted in the resignation of the CEO.

Employees generally understand that when sales are down because of an industry slowdown or a general recession, it is not possible to maintain the same level of staffing that was the case during good economic times. As I write this, the US economy is in a recession and a "credit crunch." Sales of our business are down compared to the previous year. We have responded by asking for volunteers to reduce their hours.

Since we are very happy with the teams we have in place at our business units, we want to do everything in our power to retain these employees, whose knowledge and experience represent valuable assets to the company. My wife and I have taken pay cuts, which illustrates that we are sharing in the pain. Employee loyalty is enhanced when the owners are observed enduring short-term pain in order to maintain valued staff members. Layoffs were necessary at one of our business units because delayed and cancelled projects resulting from the economic downturn made doing so unavoidable. However, the remaining staff knew that we had done so as a last resort.

In more normal economic times, a sense of being fairly treated among employees arises from day-to-day interactions with the company's owners and managers. One of the most important things that managers can do is share credit for successes and own blame for failures. They can also give a fair hearing when employees are frustrated and work in a constructive way to lessen frustrations.

Offering a certain amount of flexibility can also enhance employee equity. In our company we have a number of employees who work part-time, unconventional hours or who work primarily from home. This helps many of our staff members to accommodate childcare issues or coordinate with spouses' schedules. Such arrangements can be tricky to manage because not all positions lend themselves to being performed in unconventional ways. Sometimes such arrangements can create resentment among others who would like to do so, but cannot.

In particular, for employees who want to spend part or all of their work week at a home office, we have a candid conversation before starting in which we discuss the fact that this added convenience for the employee comes at a cost to the company because it is more difficult to manage and communicate with someone who is not in the office every day. We lay out expectations regarding how productivity will be evaluated and what we expect in return. As an example, by necessity, I often have to communicate with our home office workers outside of normal business hours.  When I need to discuss an issue with an employee who is in the office, I simply walk over to that person's work space and have a chat.  With someone who works at home, I may call and get voicemail.  When the person calls back, I might be on a conference call.  A home office will not work if the telephone and computer are turned off at 5:00 pm.  Of course, it is not fair to expect staff members to be available 24/7, but some greater flexibility is required on the part of the employee in return for the privilege of working at home.

In summary, one way to view the influence of management on employee equity is to think of it in terms of trust.  Just as customer equity is developed through acting and communicating in a way that earns their trust (telling the truth, under-promising and over-delivering, etc.), employee trust and equity are earned when management communicates frequently with candor and behaves in a way that leads staff members to believe that management cares about their well-being and wants to see them succeed.

### Achievement
No matter what level, employees generally need to feel challenged by the work they are doing and regularly have the opportunity to upgrade their knowledge and skills.  They will generally feel energized in an environment that allows them to perform well in terms of resources, training, direction and authority.  They want to be doing work about which they can feel pride and to be recognized for good performance, which reinforces their sense of achievement.

Allowing people to do what they are good at and enjoy doing – in other words, engineering jobs so that they allow individuals to utilize their strengths – helps to keep people engaged.  Beyond that, however, it is critically necessary to provide ongoing encouragement and praise.  I have had employees literally work all night to meet a deadline.  This has, of course, elicited extreme expressions of gratitude.  However, few would be willing to go so far down the road of the extra mile without receiving ongoing expressions of appreciation, recognition and praise for work well-done.  Money (raises and bonuses) is a type of recognition. Additional training such as attending conferences, seminars, workshops, etc. can also be a form of recognition and can be positioned as such.  By obtaining knowledge and learning new skills, employees are better equipped to take on more responsibilities and more ambitious projects.  In turn, this helps to keep staff members challenged and maintains an ongoing sense of personal growth.

## Camaraderie (Team Spirit)

One of the most neglected areas in management relates to camaraderie.  Human beings spend a large percentage of their time in the workplace and need to feel a sense of teamwork and community.  Low ratings on camaraderie will result when employees experience incompetence or lack of cooperation, whether from management or co-workers.  Having friendships at the office has been associated with greater engagement.  The most productive business units are characterized by groups of people who agree with the company's mission and values, enjoy interacting with one another, and report a spirit of teamwork and cooperation both within and across business units.

A particularly good way to enhance camaraderie is to encourage mentoring relationships between junior and more senior staff members, as long as the senior staff member is enthusiastic about doing so.  Don't try to force anyone into a mentoring role that he or she doesn't want.  If both parties are enthusiastic about this kind of arrangement, it can be very fulfilling for both.

One of the most common questions I have been asked by managers and entrepreneurs relates to dealing with individuals who are good producers but who don't get along well with others in the organization.  I have heard this described in terms such as, "she gets a lot done, but has sharp elbows" or, "he always delivers on time, but he leaves a wake behind him."

On more than one occasion I made the mistake of promoting an individual who was a good performer, but who did not do well with regard to our values about teamwork.  To paraphrase Jack

Welch, business is a game. The manager who wins will be the one who gets the best players on the field and gets them playing well together. Over the years I have come to the conclusion that both are equally important – individual performance and true embrace of the value of teamwork. This has led me to develop high standards. In order to thrive in our company, employees must both perform on an individual basis and comport themselves in a way that is consistent with our value of teamwork. Elements relating to teamwork are therefore central to our performance appraisal process for both managers and rank and file staff members.

**The Importance of Managers and the Four Es**
One of the many innovations championed by Jack Welch at General Electric was the use of the 4Es of Leadership to evaluate managers. With this system, managers were evaluated on the basis of the degree to which they performed on four parameters:

1. Has *Energy*
    a. Drive to succeed (fire in the belly)
    b. Embraces change
    c. In constant motion toward goals
    d. Makes thing happen rather than waiting for things to happen
2. *Energizes* others
    a. Ability to motivate others to perform
    b. Sharing credit and owning blame
3. Possesses *Edge*
    a. Competitive spirit
    b. Ability to make difficult decisions and take action when needed
4. *Executes*
    a. Performs consistently
    b. Delivers results

Note that having energy, a competitive spirit and achieving results is not enough. The top manager will also energize others. Managers who browbeat their staff into meeting short-term goals are not likely to be successful in the long-term. Their negative impact on morale is counterproductive and will erode employee engagement.

On the other hand, managers who avoid conflict and are more concerned with being well-liked than how well their teams perform will also not produce optimal results. I confess that I have often made this mistake. My instincts are to praise and encourage and I dislike criticizing. As a result I have sometimes put off tough decisions and failed to provide candid feedback, to the detriment of my company's performance. Recognizing this weakness, I have hired managers who are better at doing this than me, reducing the number of people I manage directly. I work hard to provide candid feedback and constructive criticism to this small group.

Each employee's direct supervisor typically has the greatest impact on his or her enthusiasm. I have seen first-hand how different teams in the same company, sometimes even on the same floor in an office building, will have markedly different levels of morale, driven by the degree to which the manager creates a culture that provides equity, achievement and camaraderie.

**Technical Skills Are Not Enough to be a Good Manager**
One unfortunate tendency in business is to require that people move into management to get ahead in the organization. Frequently, those who are excellent performers in a technical role will not perform well as managers. The skills required to be a good engineer, accountant, lawyer, consultant, statistician or other technical role are usually different from those required to manage people in a way that promotes enthusiasm. Some people obviously can be good at both roles, but this is far from universal.

When an excellent technical performer is promoted to management, the result may be that the company loses in several ways. If the individual lacks the skills to manage effectively, the productivity and morale of the team may suffer. In turn, the individual who may have previously been an energized, high-level performer may lose enthusiasm. He or she may become frustrated enough to leave the company, which many would rather do than face the humiliation of relinquishing the new position and going back to a non-management role. Furthermore, the firm loses the high technical output that was previously produced by the newly minted manager.

Being a manager requires a set of talents and skills, just as being an accountant requires a set of talents and skills. Sometimes these co-exist, but you should not assume this to be true. While I generally advocate promoting from within, it is better to hire a proven manager from outside of the organization than to promote a good technical performer who lacks management talent to a supervisory position. In order to make such a strategy work, it is necessary to ensure that good technical performers have opportunities to advance in title and compensation without moving into management. It is also useful to utilize a "trial run" period where an employee has a chance to try management for a limited period (say 3-6 months) with a prior agreement that if it doesn't work out, based on 360 degree feedback (i.e., from staff, colleagues and supervisors), that the individual can return to a non-managerial role without financial penalty or stigma.

**EQ is at Least as Important as IQ for Managers**
In his bestselling book *Emotional Intelligence*, psychologist Daniel Goleman asserts that four sets of skills drive leadership performance, which he terms EQ or Emotional (Intelligence) Quotient, as distinct from IQ or Intelligence Quotient. IQ tests are intended to measure a person's abilities to learn and understand new information, solve problems, and engage in abstract reasoning. In contrast, EQ refers to the skills of:

1. *Self-awareness* - the ability to read one's own emotions.
2. *Self-management* - involves controlling one's emotions and impulses.
3. *Social awareness* - the ability to sense, understand, and react to others' emotions.
4. *Relationship management* - the ability to inspire, influence, and develop others while managing conflict.

I am not a psychologist, but these descriptions make intuitive sense to me and the traits described are probably extremely important regarding the third of the 4Es, the ability to energize others. The most effective managers I have known have been able to inspire in others a strong sense of team spirit and a commitment to the company's goals and values. In part this arises from an ability to convince staff members that they are cared about as people, that their opinions count, and that they will be treated fairly, which includes being recognized for good performance and encouraged to increase their knowledge and skills. Goleman believes that these are not innate talents, but rather learned capabilities that can be developed to achieve high levels of performance.

**The Importance of Goals and Expectations, Driven by Clear Values**
The critical importance of creating clear goals and expectations cannot be overemphasized. In an earlier chapter about customer satisfaction, the importance of having clear and energizing mission and values statements was discussed. Mission and values must be known by employees at all levels and everyone needs to be held accountable for living up to the stated values. When an employee does not buy into the company values and acts in a way contrary to them, he or she must be held accountable. Failure to act in a way consistent with the company values should be reflected in performance appraisals and rewards should be withheld. Ultimately, those who do not buy into the culture will likely sense that your company is not a good fit and move on. Those who do not may need to be terminated.

Employees should receive regular, candid feedback on their performance – at least every six months. Performance reviews should not simply be the passing out of report cards, but, instead should be an exchange of ideas. This is an opportunity to discuss the employee's performance, but also a chance to obtain feedback about management's performance and ideas on how it might be improved and how systems or facilities might be improved to enhance efficiency and make the job easier and more enjoyable. In addition, the manager and employee can discuss the employee's aspirations and how he or she would like to see his or her role evolve over time and what training and guidance might be required to make this happen.

Finally, a performance appraisal is an opportunity to elicit feedback about how the employee feels about teamwork and camaraderie in the organization. Is he or she experiencing frustration with other team members or lack of cooperation from other business units? It is often easier to develop a sense of collaboration and teamwork within a business unit than it is to get business units to cooperate, particularly if they are required to "sell" services or merchandise to one another. Don't allow lack of cooperation between staff members or business units to go unaddressed.

**Maintain a Meritocracy**
As discussed earlier, General Electric's 20/70/10 system is a structured way to categorize performance. I favor giving a numerical rating between 0 and 100 (derived from scores on sub-categories within the 4E framework discussed earlier). Those who score 80 or higher (top 20%) should get the most rewards in the form of money, recognition and training. Those in the middle group (middle 70) should get proportionately less and receive clear guidance about what would need to improve in order for them to move up to a higher score. If only categories are provided rather than numerical ratings, this group can be split into upper middle and lower middle groups. I personally do not like letter grades because of all of the associations people have with letter grades from their school days. The key points are that evaluations should be as objective as possible and people should receive clear feedback on how they are performing both technically and with regard to the company's values.

Those in the bottom group are not making the grade. These individuals need to know that this is the case and be encouraged to move on. At larger companies like General Electric, it is feasible to actually remove the bottom 10% each year. With smaller companies, particularly after several years of candid feedback, it is not uncommon to end up with a group that is composed only of people who are making the grade. On the other hand, don't be lulled into complacency. Tolerating poor performers or those who do not display teamwork creates resentment among those who are pulling their weight and brings down morale. Set high standards and hold people accountable for meeting them. Reward performance and withhold rewards from those who do not perform, to the point of termination if necessary. The best and the brightest are attracted to companies that are run as meritocracies and developing such a reputation will help in your quest to get the best players on the field.

**Fill Buckets Frequently**
In the book *How Full is Your Bucket?* Tom Rath and the late Donald O. Clifton of the Gallup Organization use the metaphor of a bucket to reflect research findings about human motivation. Human beings are wired to get a psychological lift from praise and encouragement. Each time a manager provides praise or encouragement, this can be thought of as adding water to the employee's bucket. Criticism and other negative messages remove water from bucket. Research suggests that the optimal ratio of praise and encouragement to criticism is at least 5:1. Therefore, motivation and engagement are maintained at markedly higher levels when buckets are added to at least five times as often as they have water removed.

This does not mean that poor performance or areas that require improvements in skills and knowledge should be ignored. The importance of candid feedback has already been discussed. Instead, it means that most managers can do a much better job of catching people doing something right and offering praise and words of encouragement. This is true for individuals, as well as entire groups. Celebrate achievements. Acknowledge good behaviors and provide tokens of appreciation when someone goes the extra mile. A card, a $5 gift certificate, having lunch brought in for the team and other gestures go a long way toward filling buckets and sending the message that you care about your staff and appreciate their efforts.

In contrast, let me provide a real example that sent the opposite message. A manager that worked for me told me this story about her previous employer and said that this contributed to her decision to leave that company. A project they were working on required that study subjects spend a full 12 hours in the clinic. This meant that at least one member of her laboratory staff had to work a very long (13-14 hour) day. Because the subjects had to be fed lunch and dinner, she would order an extra meal for her staff member as a gesture of gratitude for the willingness to work longer than normal hours. This middle manager was called on the carpet by her boss for doing this. She was told that the employee was being paid for the hours and even getting overtime for any hours over 40 in a week. This short-sighted individual viewed a couple of sandwiches as an unnecessary expense. I view the sandwiches as a gesture of appreciation that would be likely to contribute to loyalty and engagement. The cost associated with replacing the employee or her manager is far greater than that of a few sandwiches. Trying to save money by reducing or eliminating gestures of gratitude is like cutting off a leg to lose weight. The number on the scale declines, but the long-term result is a handicap.

*Chapter 10*

# Leveraging Individual Strengths and Managing Around Weaknesses

*You cannot dream yourself into a character; you must hammer and forge yourself one.*

— James A. Froude

The book *Moneyball* by Michael Lewis describes how Billy Bean, the General Manager for the Oakland A's major league baseball team, was able to get high performance on a limited budget by using statistical models to assess the factors most associated with success and then building a team of players with complementary strengths to ensure that all of the necessary elements for success were represented on the team. Mr. Bean achieved impressive results (numerous trips to the playoffs), despite severe constraints on the funds available to pay players compared to other teams such as the New York Yankees.

Everyone - whether a professional baseball player, project manager, or carpenter - has strengths and weaknesses. In general, employees will get the most pleasure and satisfaction when they are allowed to do what they do best on a daily basis. A good deal of management time and effort is wasted focusing on areas in which an employee is weak and trying to get him or her to improve. While it is necessary to hold people accountable for following systems, it is usually fruitless to attempt to turn a weakness into a strength. Better results are obtained by helping employees develop their strengths in such a way that their productivity can be maximized.

Many managers believe that with proper training and encouragement any reasonably bright employee will be able to excel in any role. In theory this is true, but to quote Yogi Berra "In theory there is no difference between theory and practice, but in practice, there is." People tend to excel in roles that are good fits for their talents and to be unhappy in roles that are not. However, individuals often have a difficult time accurately assessing their own strengths, so it is usually helpful to implement structured systems for assessing strengths and working with staff members to further develop their talents.

**Knowledge, Skills, Strengths and Talents**
Knowledge and skills are attributes that can be acquired with study and practice. Knowledge represents information and an understanding of how that information can be applied to accomplish an objective. Skills are abilities that are necessary to execute the steps in a process effectively.

Talents and strengths are aspects of an individual's make-up that enhance his or her ability to learn or execute in a particular area. For the purposes of this discussion I will use the terms interchangeably, although many social scientists would take issue with this approach.

Research into top performers suggests that talents may develop somewhat haphazardly. For example, in the book *Outliers*, Malcolm Gladwell describes the curious observation that a very high percentage of Canadian all-star hockey players were born in the first quarter of the year. Their talents in hockey likely developed because of the way youngsters in Canada are sectioned into leagues based on year of birth. Those born early in the year are a few months older, which can be a big advantage in hockey during the early years among kids as young as 7 or 8 years of age. Because of this slight advantage, these kids perform a bit better and, consequently, they get more encouragement. In turn, they find hockey more enjoyable and are willing to put in the time and effort to improve their knowledge and skills. As a result, they become talented hockey players. Note that I am not using the term talent to indicate innate or genetic predispositions. This is a topic on which there is considerable scientific debate. From a practical standpoint, it is not important to know the degree to which nature vs. nurture contributed to the development of strengths; it is only important to know that they exist.

By the time someone reaches adulthood, he or she is likely to have developed a number of talents that have arisen out of the accumulation of his or her life experiences. While it may be true that with sufficient study and practice any two reasonably bright people could learn how to use an accounting software program to manage the books for a business, the effort required might be vastly different depending on prior experience. An engineering school graduate who has spent a great deal of time studying numbers and mathematical relationships would, in most cases, have an easier time than someone who graduated with a degree in English literature. In general, people have the greatest potential for exceptional performance in areas that are extensions of their pre-existing strengths and talents.

A few years ago I learned that I have a talent for driving golf balls. In contrast, I have little aptitude for chipping and putting. I don't golf often, but when I do, I find myself whacking drives 200 yards or more. Sadly, this is accompanied by a near inability to putt with any accuracy. Any advantage I have after a 250 yard drive evaporates during the 5 or 6 putts that I require to put the ball in the hole. With a lot of study and practice I could probably develop an average short game, but with study and practice I could likely develop a truly exceptional long game. Similarly, employees who build on their strengths and talents are the most likely to be able to produce exceptional results. The return on investment for time and resources spent building on existing strengths and talents, whether in yourself or an employee, is likely to be much greater than that spent trying to turn a weakness into a strength.

**Author's note:** I sent a near final draft of this book to several people for review, one of whom was David Sklansky, who is a business owner as well as author of the book *The Theory of Poker* and several other excellent books on gambling theory and other topics. He pointed out that I would improve my golf score more by working on my short game than I would by working on my already good long game, which is entirely correct.

For some business owners who run single-person, or very small operations, overall performance will be determined largely by performance in their weakest area, and investing time in improving weak areas will be unavoidable. This is true in golf, which is usually not played as a team sport. However, for many businesses, it is possible to engineer enough specialization into the operations to allow key people to spend most of their time working in areas where they are good with the potential to become great, and less where they are poor with the potential to become fair. Business owners in particular can often delegate tasks in which they are weak to people who will perform them better and more efficiently. This is discussed in more detail below.

As an exercise in effective delegation, I am considering bringing a staff member with putting and chipping skills along next time I golf. I will hit the drives and he or she will do the rest.

### How Talents Develop

The topic of talent development has been quite popular of late. In addition to the book *Outliers* mentioned above, the books *Talent is Overrated* by Geoff Colvin and *The Talent Code* by Daniel Coyle outline the process by which people evolve from novices to top performers. As described in *The Talent Code*, three elements are necessary:

1. Ignition
2. Deep practice
3. Coaching (feedback)

**Ignition**

Ignition is the process by which a person develops both the desire to attain a goal and the belief that doing so is possible. Often this occurs when someone the person is acquainted with, or feels some connection to, displays high achievement. In *The Talent Code*, an example is given of ignition occurring on the Caribbean island of Curacao when Andruw Jones, a major league baseball player from the island, hit two home runs in the opening game of the World Series during his rookie season. [Authors note: several people who read a draft of the book asked if I had misspelled "Andrew." I did not, his first name is Andruw.]

A few weeks later at little league sign-ups in his hometown of Willemstad, four hundred new kids showed up. A similar phenomenon occurred when golfer Se Ri Pak won the 1998 Ladies Professional Golf Association Championship. Before her, no South Korean golfer had reached the top levels in the sport. Ten years later South Korean golfers collectively won one-third of the professional events.

I experienced an ignition event at the 40th birthday party for my boss at the time, Dr. Michael Davidson. Michael is now the Vice Chair of Medicine and Director of Preventive Cardiology at the University of Chicago. Michael's father had died suddenly at age 47 from heart disease, which had shaped his world view a great deal, igniting in him a desire to become a preventive cardiologist and to do research on heart disease prevention. He started a research company at age 29 while still undergoing training in cardiology. Over the next several years he had grown the company successfully and ultimately sold it to a larger company, staying on as a manager while also retaining an academic appointment at a local university. He had been able to achieve the ideal espoused by founding father Ben Franklin of "doing well while doing good."

At his birthday party Michael gave a short speech in which he said that because of his father's death at an early age, he had always been in a hurry. He got married early, started a family early (he has four kids), started a business and sold it, all before the age of

40.  He had been both financially successful and made important contributions to medicine by conducting clinical trials to test new therapies for preventing heart disease.  Since that time he has been a leader in the education of physicians and other health care professionals through his work with the National Lipid Association, as well as through teaching and scholarship at two universities.

At the time of his birthday party I was newly separated from my first wife at age 31 and, after taking into account debt from my student loans, had a net worth of approximately zero dollars.  It occurred to me that I was in a very similar situation to Michael Davidson's when he started his company.  I knew him well enough to know that, while he was definitely an intelligent person, he did not possess any truly remarkable attributes other than persistence in working toward his goals.  This became a kind of "aha" moment for me.  In many ways he was similar to the owners of the hotel I had worked for years earlier.  Like them, he had been successful after mapping out a course and then working hard to turn this vision into reality.  If these people I knew personally could do it, why couldn't I?  That night I set some major life goals for myself.

I wanted to become financially successful so that I could work toward making contributions in preventive medicine and educating health care professionals without having to worry about money.  That night I decided that I wanted to be financially independent by age 40 so that I could devote a good portion of my middle-age and later years to teaching and publishing (which are generally not high-paying endeavors).  I achieved this goal, in part by starting two businesses.  I define financial independence as having enough net worth that, if invested conservatively, it would produce enough of an income stream that our family could have a reasonable standard of living indefinitely.

I am happy to report that today, at age 44, I have co-authored two textbooks and I am a member of the faculty of the National Lipid Association's Master's in Lipidology and Board Review Course that contributes to the training of physicians and other health care professionals in heart disease prevention. I give talks at least once each month at continuing medical education events or scientific conferences and plan to seek an appointment at a local university so that I can spend even more of my time on teaching and scholarship.

Don't underestimate your ability to provide ignition events for your employees. It is enormously satisfying to help others achieve their goals and providing a work environment that helps people to develop their talents is a winning strategy for you and them, which would make Ben Franklin proud. Find out what your employees want to accomplish and help them to develop the belief they can achieve whatever they are willing to do the work to attain.

A fascinating experiment is described in *The Talent Code* that illustrates how important cues from authority figures are in shaping performance. A group of children was given a series of tests, the first of which was easy. Each child was told his or her score and given a single sentence of praise. Half were praised for their intelligence ("You must be smart at this") and the others were praised for their effort ("You must have worked really hard"). After a series of additional tests the kids retook a test of the same difficulty as the initial test. Those praised for their effort improved their initial score by 30% while those praised for their intelligence showed a decline in their scores of 20%. The researchers were so surprised by these results that they repeated the experiment five times and got the same results. Carol Dweck, the psychologist who performed these experiments, was quoted as saying that all parenting advice can basically be distilled down to two items:

1. Pay attention to what your children are fascinated by, and
2. Praise them for their effort.

I would add that this same advice can be applied to employees.

## Deep Practice and Coaching

Ignition events are not enough. Talent development requires many hours of deep practice with feedback (coaching or self coaching) to allow development of the neural circuits necessary to attain high levels of performance. A neural pathway is optimized through the process of wrapping the nerve fibers with myelin (an insulating sheath) to enhance the speed and strength of the signals. This results from repeated firing with feedback to allow correction of mistakes, producing gradual improvement. In other words, through struggle and feedback the neural circuits are trained to perform the activity in the desired manner. In studies performed by psychologist Anders Ericsson with many types of skilled performers including gymnasts, dart throwers, musicians, nurses, Scrabble players and SWAT (Special Weapons and Tactics) team members, performance was directly related to the number of hours of deliberate (deep) practice with feedback to correct mistakes.

The feedback element can come from external coaching, but this is not always necessary. Examples of self-taught top performers in many fields abound. The key elements appear to be desire, passion and a willingness to put in the hours of deep practice with some mechanism in place to allow feedback and correction so that performance can be nudged toward the ideal. Desire and passion are necessary because, without them, an individual is unlikely to be willing to invest the time and energy to become a highly talented performer. Earlier I talked about the vital few (about 20%) individuals who are responsible for the great majority (about 80%) of the productivity in most companies. My guess is that these are the people who are willing to put in the hours of deep practice necessary to become top performers.

## Assessing Strengths and Talents as a Starting Point for Building Complimentary Teams

A discussion of tools for assessing strengths and talents in staff members is beyond the scope of this book. I recommend the books *First, Break all the Rules* and the follow-up *Now, Discover Your Strengths* by Marcus Buckingham and the late Donald O. Clifton of the Gallup Organization for readers interested in learning more about how to systematically evaluate strengths and talents.  However, I also believe that there is much to be learned by simply eliciting feedback from employees, managers and team members about the strengths and weaknesses of each employee. Just asking people what aspects of their jobs they enjoy and feel they are good at can be very helpful for identifying areas in which individuals excel and can be developed further.

Management consultant Peter Drucker emphasized that the best results derive from playing to people's strengths and managing around their weaknesses, so identifying areas of struggle and dislike are equally important.  It is not always possible to eliminate all aspects of a person's job that he or she dislikes, but performance will tend to be better when staff members are allowed to spend the bulk of their time (perhaps 80%) on those tasks they enjoy and at which they excel, and a minority (perhaps 20% or less) doing tasks they don't enjoy.  It requires some engineering and flexibility to systematically move staff members in the direction of their strengths while making their weaknesses irrelevant by managing around their weaknesses.  Doing so can take the form of building teams of people with complimentary strengths, outsourcing activities that are not well suited to the talents of the existing staff members, eliminating tasks that have a poor ratio of hassle to value, etc.

An example of just the opposite behavior by management occurred in a company I worked for several years ago.  The top performing sales executive was a woman who had a terrific ability to develop rapport with clients.  She also had an extreme sense of urgency and wanted to deliver information and high quality proposals to clients as soon as humanly possible.  She worked very hard and would hound people mercilessly when she needed information for a client.  Many staff members found this irritating, although her persistence often paid off because it was obvious to the client that our organization really cared about meeting their needs as quickly as possible, providing us with an important edge over our competition. Also, her sales and expense reports were chronically late and often required reworking to meet the requested specifications.  It was indisputable that she achieved exceptional results as her sales figures were often literally twice those of the next highest performer which, in my view, made her enormously valuable.

When that company was acquired by a competitor, several sales executives were offered positions, but she was not. The reasons given were that she was viewed as too demanding and unreliable in generating reports. When I heard this news I thought that the management of my new employer had taken leave of their senses. The intervening years have not softened my view, as the ensuing results suggest that my assessment was on target. Senior management apparently valued conformity above results and had no intention of playing to this person's strengths and managing around her weaknesses. When they pushed her out the door, several million dollars in sales left with her.

**Encourage Specialization Where Possible so Key People Can Focus Their Efforts Where They Can Make the Greatest Contribution**
In our company we have a Medical Writing group that is responsible for generating various types of documents such as study protocols, reports of study results, presentations for scientific meetings and papers for publication in scientific journals. Through experience we have learned that some people are very good at producing certain types of documents, but struggle with others.

This type of technical writing requires high levels of skill and knowledge (all of the members of the Medical Writing group have masters or doctoral degrees), and those with specific strengths seem to do best with one type of document or another. For example, writing study protocols requires an ability to keep track of many details to ensure that all sections are consistent and no language ends up in one section of the document that contradicts that in another section. It also requires an ability to think through the instructions that are being written to imagine how they will be carried out in the clinic. If you have ever tried to write out detailed, step-by-step instructions for even a simple procedure, you will know how difficult it is to convey such information clearly.

In contrast, writing manuscripts for publication in scientific journals requires a somewhat different set of skills. The writer must identify and counter as many potential criticisms as possible and build a case to support our interpretation of the study results over various alternatives. The process is much like that of an attorney building a case for (plaintiff) or against (defense) a legal claim.

Rather than attempting to have everyone work on all types of documents, we try to identify where each Medical Writer excels in order to engineer the position so that he/she devotes most of his/her time to the types of projects that align with these strengths. Of course, in order to meet deadlines we cannot guarantee complete specialization, but, consistent with our 80/20 approach, we try to match types of projects with employee strengths a majority of the time.

Since people are typically drawn to the types of projects that are good matches for their talents, employees and their managers can usually work together to match strengths with responsibilities. However, there are some situations where doing so is not easy. One example is the person whose views of his or her talents don't match reality. I once worked with a Medical Writer who had great enthusiasm for writing manuscripts, but whose papers were very difficult to read and unlikely to be reviewed favorably upon submission. No amount of feedback or encouragement seemed to improve the quality of the work. Eventually I was forced to the conclusion that this person's interests and talents were not well aligned. Since it was untenable to continue to rewrite these papers, the only option was reassignment to tasks that she enjoyed less but was more suited to completing with adequate quality.

**Manage Around Weaknesses**
Focusing on and further developing areas of strength is only half of the equation. Equally important is managing around weaknesses. This is necessary to ensure that all of the tasks that need to be completed get done in a timely way with good quality.

In the example used earlier of the high-performing sales executive who was demanding and couldn't get her reports in on time, a potential solution would have been to hire an assistant to help her accomplish these tasks. This would have added some additional cost, but given her performance, this could easily have been justified. In addition, being relieved of these duties would have:

1. Reduced her frustration,
2. Provided the people who bristled at her overdeveloped sense of urgency the opportunity to work with someone whose style was more suited to their liking, and
3. Allowed the sales executive to spend more of her time on what she did best – selling.

Thus, hiring a support person could have been a potential win-win-win solution with a high return on investment. Instead, we lost one of our vital few top performers. Rainmakers are hard to find and it is an unforgivable management blunder to let one slip away because of unwillingness to manage around weaknesses.

*Chapter 11*


# Preparing for and Managing Through
# Recessions and Other Crises


*There are no gains without pains.*

— Benjamin Franklin


Fittingly, this is Chapter 11, which is also the part of Bankruptcy Law that deals with protection of a business from creditors during reorganization. As I write this in early 2009, the US is in the midst of a major recession. Just a few months ago the financial system was teetering on the verge of a meltdown due to an enormous quantity of bad residential real estate loans made during the housing bubble from 2002-2006. For the first time since the Great Depression, prices of single family houses have been dropping nationwide because far too many units were built during the bubble, driven by ridiculous lending practices that artificially elevated demand and prices for houses, condominiums and townhouses. Millions of families are losing their homes to foreclosure. Distress in the financial system has created a credit crunch so that businesses and individuals are having a difficult time obtaining loans. The unemployment rate has risen dramatically as businesses and consumers have become very cautious about spending.

**Recessions Present Problems and Opportunities**
While this recession is particularly severe, recessions are not new and should be expected periodically in the future. As some wise

person once said, "Congress has not been able to repeal the business cycle." There are several steps that business owners can take to prepare themselves for economic downturns, even when they arrive without warning. In fact, if you manage conservatively during boom times you may find yourself in a position to capitalize on opportunities that would be unlikely to present themselves during the good years, leaving you with a stronger and more profitable business when the economy, or the segment of the economy in which you operate, improves.

## Be Fearful When Others Are Greedy, and Greedy When Others Are Fearful

Pathological optimism and pessimism are typical at peaks and troughs in the business cycle. Warren Buffett says that the statement above has been his guiding principle as an investor. In our rental property business, we have followed this logic and, as a result, have had no trouble navigating through the worst residential real estate bust in the U.S. since the Great Depression.

By sticking to strict rules for buying properties only when market rents were sufficient to provide a reasonable net operating income, with a reasonable down-payment and favorable loan terms (usually with 30-year fixed rate mortgages), we avoided overpaying and have been able to maintain positive cash flow. When those around us were starting to make what seemed like easy money buying properties and selling them a short time later for a profit, we chose not to participate. When a bubble formed, creating a situation in which the income generated from rents would not be sufficient to cover loan payments (with a 10-20% down payment), we stopped buying. We will not buy an alligator (negative cash flow property) because in a soft rental market an alligator can create such negative cash flow that you are unable to keep up, resulting in bankruptcy or being forced to sell the property at a loss.

## Use Leverage with Caution

The rental property business is one that depends very much on access to financing and the use of leverage, but the same logic applies to other types of businesses. Borrowing money to expand

and exploit an opportunity can be a smart move, but this should only be done with a careful analysis of the potential down-side risk. One prediction I can make with confidence is that there will be disappointments and unexpected crises in your business. Don't put yourself in a position where everything must work perfectly for your business to stay solvent. This is a mistake that was made by large financial institutions that went bankrupt or had to be saved from bankruptcy in 2008, including some that had been in business since before the great depression and were considered among the bluest of blue chip companies. A few years ago it would have been considered inconceivable that companies such as Lehman Brothers, Merrill Lynch, American Insurance Group, Fannie Mae and Freddie Mac would all become insolvent or essentially insolvent within the space of a few weeks, but that is exactly what happened. In each case the companies had used a high degree of leverage, which left them vulnerable to extreme circumstances. My advice for most entrepreneurs is to use leverage sparingly and to be willing to accept a slower, but safer rate of growth in revenues and profits.

In an economic downturn, what options would you have to reduce expenses? Loan payments are a fixed cost. Fixed costs increase risk more than variable costs that can be reduced during difficult times. What resources might you have access to if you were to experience a large decline in revenue? For example, my wife and I have enough liquid funds in retirement accounts to cover the debt service and property taxes on our properties for an extended period if we had several simultaneous vacancies. We might not feel good about dipping into funds that are earmarked for retirement, particularly with the taxes and penalties that would come along with doing so, but paying taxes and penalties on a few thousand dollars in a crunch time would be far preferable to losing all of the equity in one or more properties. Over the years we have passed up some good deals because we were unwilling to increase our leverage. On the other hand, we are still standing while many rental property investors are filing for bankruptcy or losing their properties to foreclosure. In addition, because of the down market, we have been able to buy lender-owned houses for prices that we would not have dreamed possible a few years earlier. With conservative financing, these houses will generate positive cash flow from the start and eventually appreciate in market value after the excess housing inventory has been disposed of (a process that could take a few years). By not being overleveraged, we were in a position to capitalize on some great deals, even though we also passed up some decent deals along the way.

**Invest in Ways That Will Make Your Business Stronger After the Recession**
Herbert H. Dow, the founder of the Dow Chemical Company, emphasized investing heavily during the down segment of the business cycle. This allows the business to be positioned to take advantage of opportunities when the cycle turns up again and possibly to acquire valuable assets at attractive prices, as my wife and I have done in our rental property business. In order to be in a position to do this, the business owner must manage conservatively during the up-portion of the cycle. This means developing cash reserves and avoiding excessive leverage. Weak or overleveraged competitors will go out of business during a downturn, which will allow you to build market share and emerge stronger when things turn around.

**Emphasize Training**
During downturns you will have employees who are not fully utilized. Even if you don't have employees, you may find that your time is not fully utilized. This is an ideal time to enhance skills and knowledge through formal and informal training. Ask key employees to read books and present key points for discussion at meetings or brown-bag lunches. Encourage staff members to obtain certifications that will enhance your company's performance and marketability.

**Control Expenses at All Times**
The time to start controlling expenses is not during a down-turn in the business cycle. If you have a culture that allows frivolous spending and has poor cost controls during the good times, you will never be able to successfully impose austerity during a downturn. Attempts to do so will be met with resentment. On the

other hand, if your culture emphasizes frugality at all times, there will be no culture shock during a recession.

I should caution, however, that frugality can backfire if taken to extremes. The trick is to cut fat without cutting muscle in the process. One place where we do not skimp is in the quality of the people we hire. We have nearly always been happy with decisions to pay more to hire highly accomplished individuals for key roles. Trying to save money by hiring or promoting a B-grade person when an A-grade individual is available, but at a higher cost, rarely saves money in the long-run. As Warren Buffett says, he is unlikely to be able to turn a 0.200 hitter into a 0.400 hitter, so he looks to partner with individuals who are already 0.400 hitters.

**Cut Staff as a Last Resort**
This has been covered previously in the chapter on managing for employee engagement, so will not be discussed in detail here. Employees understand that if the demand for your products or services decline you may have to cut staff. If you manage conservatively, the need to downsize will be rare. When layoffs are unavoidable, the attitude of the staff members who are cut (who have the potential to influence your reputation in a variety of ways), and of your remaining staff, toward you and your business will be strongly influenced by how you handle cuts when they have to happen. If you communicate regularly, exhaust other options before instituting layoffs, and try to help out those who need to be cut to the degree possible, you will at least be viewed as being fair. Don't delude yourself into thinking that people will not be angry, they will. But their anger will be less intense and long-lived than it would be otherwise and they are less likely to bad-mouth you and your company, particularly if they hope to be rehired during the recovery.

**Maintain Sufficient Disability and Life Insurance**
Sometimes other factors can cause a crisis in your business. If you or your spouse/significant other become disabled, this could severely impact both your business and household income. Disability insurance is expensive, but it is expensive for a reason,

namely that it is insurance for which you are reasonably likely to file a claim. Lifetime risk of experiencing disability of at least 90 days during a career is significant, ranging from 20-35% depending on age, sex and health status. For many people, particularly younger individuals, their most valuable asset is their earning power. I can't emphasize enough the importance of avoiding the risk of losing your business and your income due to disability. If you have a full-time job currently and are considering starting a business, I recommend buying a disability policy in advance of leaving your job.

Another way to avoid disaster is to obtain inexpensive term life insurance policies for yourself, your spouse and any key employees whose deaths would significantly impair your business. For example, at our clinics we have life insurance policies for some of our physicians because the death of any of them would require a significant investment of time and resources and our business would be less marketable for a time until we were able to find a qualified replacement.

*Chapter 12*

# Big Ideas from Warren Buffett, Charlie Munger and Berkshire Hathaway

*Both Warren and I insist on a lot of time being available almost every day to just sit and think. That is very uncommon in American business. We read and think. So Warren and I do more reading and thinking and less doing than most people in business.*

*— Charles T. Munger*

Warren Buffett is best known as an investor. He had been obsessed with investing since a very early age, but attributes much of his success to discovering the ideas of Benjamin Graham, who Buffett later studied with at Columbia University and worked for at Graham's investment firm (Graham-Newman Company) in New York. Buffett says that he had previously been focusing on technical analysis as a way to evaluate stocks, with average results. He experienced tremendous improvements in his results after discovering Benjamin Graham and his "big ideas" about investing. In Buffett's own words:

> Beginning in 1951 my performance improved. No, I hadn't changed my diet or taken up exercise. The only new ingredient was Ben's ideas.

Buffett has described his initial exposure to these ideas in Graham's book *The Intelligent Investor* as an epiphany, like "seeing the light" and "similar to that of "Paul on the Road to

Damascus." I confess to having a similar experience when first exposed to Warren Buffett's ideas about business management. His ideas have helped to create a framework for my thinking and have provided an example after which I could model my own behavior.

Like Buffett's discovery of Benjamin Graham, my discovery of Warren Buffett was a critical ingredient for my success as an entrepreneur. Many very good books and articles have been written about Warren Buffett, Charlie Munger (Berkshire's Vice Chair), and the managers of Berkshire Hathaway's wholly owned subsidiaries. Below are a few of the key success principles advocated by them. This chapter provides only a brief glimpse into what one can learn from studying the many excellent resources about these individuals. I can honestly say that the return on investment for the time and effort I have devoted to studying Berkshire Hathaway and its managers has been positive in the extreme. If you have read the prior chapters, most of the concepts below should sound familiar.

Many previous books have meticulously catalogued the sources for each of these principles by citing quotes from articles and from Warren Buffett's annual Chairman's letters. I have not done so here but, instead, tried to summarize and comment on central themes. Should you find any of my interpretations or attempts to paraphrase statements made by Buffett, Munger or Berkshire operating managers to be in error, the fault is entirely mine. Several excellent books are listed in the appendices for those interested in delving into these topics in more detail. Note that for convenience I generally refer to Warren and Charlie when discussing Mr. Buffett and Mr. Munger, respectively (I hope they will forgive my lack of formality).

**Do What You Love with People You Like**
One of the best aspects of owning a business is that you have a say in what you spend your time doing and with whom you spend your time (business partners, staff and customers). Warren suggests that taking a job that you dislike because it pays well is like marrying for money – a bad idea.

Charlie advises the attorneys in the law firm that still includes his name (Munger, Tolles and Olson, LLP) that they should choose clients as they would friends. The same goes for staff. Consistent with the 80/20 principle, a small percentage of people will be responsible for a large majority of your frustrations and headaches as a business owner. Don't be afraid to walk away from toxic relationships (or, better yet, avoid them from the start if you can). On the other hand, customers, business partners and staff members who share your vision and values deserve your loyalty. Doing what you love with people you like, trust and admire will have a tremendous positive impact on your quality of life.

At annual meetings Charlie often counsels people to associate with people better than you, as you will tend to move in their direction. The converse also applies and reminds me of an old saying – "If you dance with the devil, the devil doesn't change; the devil changes you."

**Have Heroes, but Don't Follow them Blindly**
It is immensely valuable to have heroes who display traits you can admire and emulate. Charlie advises that you not limit your heroes to the living. One of his heroes is US founding father Ben Franklin. Warren cites his father and Ben Graham as heroes. While I wholeheartedly endorse choosing heroes as success models to be studied and emulated, it is important to realize that, being human, they are not infallible and should not be imitated mindlessly.

Warren and Charlie are heroes of mine, but each has some views with which I disagree. Warren's father was a staunch Republican, but Warren has generally endorsed Democrats. Ben Graham used a purely statistical approach to assessing investment ideas, looking for companies that were statistically cheap, without much regard to quality. Warren initially modeled his investments after this approach, but showed independence of thought, even early in his career. In one case he was assigned by Ben Graham to execute an arbitrage deal that involved buying shares in a company controlled by Jay Pritzker (Rockwood) and selling futures to lock in a nearly risk-free profit. He did so for Graham, as instructed, but believed that there was greater profit potential in buying and holding the stock, thus betting on the same side as Jay Pritzker, which he did for his own account. He netted a much larger return on investment than his boss.

Ben Graham engaged in many extramarital affairs. Warren counsels that an important component of success is to be loved by people who you want to love you. Charlie suggests that the best way to have a wonderful spouse is to deserve one. Graham likely found that his philandering had a negative impact on his marital success (with all three of his wives). His experience reinforces the concept that it is useful to imitate the successful behaviors of one's heroes, and to avoid their mistakes.

**Set an Example**
As a business owner, it is incumbent on you to set an example. You will lack moral authority if you behave in ways other than those you preach. If you consistently treat people with respect and display integrity and thrift, you are likely to get those attributes in return from those around you. If not, you are deluding yourself if you expect your employees to do so regarding your business and your customers.

**Devote Significant Time to Self-Education**
Both Warren and Charlie are legendary for the amount of material they read. During dinner parties Warren was known to retire to a back room to read annual reports while his wife conversed with their friends. According to Charlie, "In my whole life I have known no wise people who didn't read all the time – none, zero." While working as an attorney, Charlie would sell his best hour of the day to himself by devoting that time to upgrading his knowledge and skills. At least once a week I remind my kids that "Readers are leaders, and learners are earners."

**Study Successes and Failures, Including Your Own**
There is a great deal to be learned by studying business successes. However, there is equal value in studying business failures. Learn from the mistakes of others. Charlie is fond of the Will Rogers

quote, which I will paraphrase as follows: "There are three kinds of men; the ones that learn by reading; the few who learn by observation, and the rest of them who have to pee on the electric fence for themselves." Knowing what to avoid can be as important as knowing what to do. Charlie points out that through an honest analysis of your own mistakes, and those of others, you can learn to make fewer errors and fix them more quickly when they occur; but there is no way you can live an adequate life without making many mistakes.

You should not agonize over mistakes, but you should engage in honest and critical self-analysis. Avoid after-the-fact rationalizations. If you made an error, admit it to yourself and others. Warren points out that it is important to recognize errors of omission as well as those of commission. Failing to act on opportunities quickly enough can be just as damaging to performance as acting impulsively. This also applies to unnecessary delays in confronting unpleasant situations. I have been guilty of this when giving problem employees third, fourth and fifth chances rather than undertake the unpleasant, but necessary, actions to terminate them. Warren cited his delay in acting to shut down the textile business when it was clear that no amount of effort could elevate it to sustainable profitability as such an error.

The examples above underline another tenet emphasized by Warren and Charlie - be willing to change your mind when the facts don't support your view. John Kenneth Galbraith said "When faced with the choice between changing one's mind and proving there is no need to do so, almost everyone gets busy on the proof." Ben Franklin said "One of the greatest tragedies in life is the murder of a beautiful theory by a gang of brutal facts." Several times in my career as a scientist I have come across study results that I could not reconcile with a long-held belief, forcing me to change my opinion, often with great reluctance. I have watched with discomfort as some scientists continued defending ideas with theological zeal long after it was clear that their views were no longer tenable. Hence the expression: "Science proceeds funeral by funeral." Some influential scientists have been known to attack new theories to the point that progress could only proceed unfettered once they were no longer living.

Charlie has spent a great deal of time studying and describing common human errors and biases, which he terms the psychology of misjudgment. He has given a number of talks in which they have been described in detail and these talks have been collected in the book *Poor Charlie's Almanack: The Wit and Wisdom of Charles T. Munger* (edited by Peter D. Kaufman), which I enthusiastically recommend.

**Understand and Stay Within Your Circle of Competence**
One of the most useful concepts espoused by Warren and Charlie is the importance of understanding and staying within your circle of competence. This applies to both your personal circle, as well as that of your company. They emphasize that, to be successful, your circle doesn't need to be large, as long as you understand where the perimeter lies. They recommend emulating Thomas Watson, Sr. of IBM, who said, "I am smart in spots – but I stay around those spots."

Warren has emphasized that many CEOs of large companies do not understand their limitations when it comes to capital allocation, which often leads to actions that destroy value, such as acquisitions intended to add "synergies" that never materialize. Many CEOs rose to that position by being exceptional performers in functions that did not involve capital allocation. They may be great operating managers or marketers, but not great capital allocators. Capital allocation is a skill that requires study and practice.

The good news is that most skills required to be successful in business can be developed with study and practice. However, one should not attempt to engage in activities that require such skills without first putting in the time and effort to become competent. As Charlie says, "If you play games where other people have the aptitudes and you don't, you're going to lose." However, critical self-examination and feedback from trusted advisors is required for most people to assess where they do and do not have an advantage. There is a famous study that has been repeated in many settings for various types of skills where people were asked to rate themselves as being above average, about average or below average in driving skill. Consistently, 80-90% rate themselves as being above average. Since, by definition, 50% must be average or below, this indicates that quite a few people are failing to accurately assess their driving abilities.

Successful entrepreneurs avoid operating outside their circle of competence. In part this is done by saying no to opportunities where they lack the background or understanding to fully evaluate. Warren and Charlie talk about having three piles, yes, no and too hard. Warren won't invest in companies like Microsoft or Intel because he doesn't feel that he has the depth of knowledge and understanding to predict with reasonable certainty what those companies will look like in 10 years. This is true even though he is good friends with Bill Gates, Microsoft's founder, who also sits on the Berkshire Hathaway board of directors. Warren often says that he and Charlie have not developed any special skill at solving difficult business problems. They are proficient at avoiding such problems. Instead of spending their time trying to clear 7-foot bars, they actively seek out 1-foot bars to step over.

Berkshire Hathaway is involved in a large number of businesses ranging from ice cream and candy to home furnishings to insurance and energy generation. These businesses are simple and stable enough for Warren and Charlie to understand their economics. On the other hand, neither is interested in running the day-to-day operations of Dairy Queen, GEICO or Nebraska Furniture Mart. Warren and Charlie have been successful by staying within their circles of competence while partnering with others who had complimentary circles, including the operating managers of the businesses they have acquired. They have chosen business managers to associate with based on long track records of exceptional results. They are not trying to turn 0.200 hitters into 0.400 hitters, but instead seeking out partners who have already demonstrated their abilities. You might say they are betting on horses with proven jockeys. Warren and Charlie have mastered Peter Drucker's concept of taking advantage of individual strengths and engineering their situations to make weaknesses irrelevant.

**Margin of Safety**

One of my favorite expressions is "In order to finish first, you must, first, finish." According to Warren, Berkshire Hathaway has always been managed according to policies that allow achievement of acceptable long-term results under extraordinarily adverse conditions, not optimal results under normal conditions. Warren says that a 99% chance of success and a 1% chance of total wipe-out (99:1 odds) are not odds that he and Charlie are willing to accept. This viewpoint is especially evident when it comes to debt. In 2008 a number of iconic financial institutions toppled because of excessive use of leverage which, to paraphrase Warren, left these companies swimming naked when the tide went out. There was never any danger of Berkshire Hathaway going under during the crisis.

Berkshire has always employed debt conservatively. Warren and Charlie refuse to put the entire company at risk for a few percentage points of extra growth. Their approach has been to borrow conservatively when conditions are favorable (or at least not oppressive) because when conditions deteriorate it will be much harder to borrow. In addition, tough economic times are when the best opportunities tend to occur. Warren says that he wants to have a loaded gun when a rare, fast-moving elephant happens by. This was the case in 2008 when Berkshire was able to buy $8 billion in preferred stock in Goldman Sachs ($5 billion) and General Electric ($3 billion). These instruments pay 10% dividends and also came with warrants that allow the purchase of equal amounts of common stock any time during the subsequent five years at fixed prices that are (presumably) below Warren's estimate of the companies' intrinsic values (present value of future cash flows based on a conservative discount rate).

This is not a book on investing or corporate acquisitions, so I will not spend a great deal of time on the concepts of intrinsic value and margin of safety in investing, but will review them briefly, as they are central to understanding the way Berkshire Hathaway is managed. Intrinsic value is a concept emphasized by Ben Graham. It is calculated by estimating future cash flows and assigning them a present value based on a discount rate. This discounted cash flow model can be used to value any type of instrument with cash flows, including bonds, common stock, whole businesses, real estate, etc. Early in his career Warren focused on buying businesses at cheap prices. Later, he focused on buying great businesses at fair prices. Great businesses were those with sustainable competitive advantages, which would allow them to generate above-average returns on invested capital over many years. If such a business also has significant potential for growth in revenue and earnings, all-the-better, although this has not been a prerequisite for Berkshire to acquire the company.

Warren believes that long-term competitive advantages nearly always result from a sustainably low-cost structure or from managerial excellence. Examples of the former (which does not preclude the presence of the latter) include Berkshire subsidiaries Nebraska Furniture Mart (profiled in the next chapter) and GEICO Insurance. GEICO uses a direct-to-consumer marketing model that avoids the expense of employing agents, thus can maintain lower costs than competitors that do employ agents.

Managerial excellence promotes a culture where employees think like owners. Top notch operating managers treat all stakeholders fairly and work hard to develop and nurture relationships with customers and employees, promoting long-term loyalty from both. This generates significant equity in the form of intangibles, such as brand and reputation, which are difficult for other businesses to reproduce. Warren refers to these barriers to successful competition as "moats" because they prevent competitors from breaching the castle walls and stealing the valuables inside (market share). As a business owner, your job is to run your business in such a way that continually widens the moat.

With regard to investments, margin of safety relates to the difference between a conservative estimate of intrinsic value and the price one pays. The greater the discount one can obtain, the lower the risk and the greater the potential return. Warren uses Ben Graham's allegory of the manic-depressive Mr. Market to describe how market psychology occasionally drives prices down to levels that allow one to buy partial ownership in a great business at a cheap price.

In 2009 during the credit crisis brought on by the bursting of the housing bubble, Warren Buffett told a group of students that the stock of Wells Fargo Bank (a long-time Berkshire holding) at a price below $9 is an opportunity that he would be comfortable sinking his entire net worth into (as I write this a few months later the stock is trading just below $27 per share). In other words, he believed that Wells Fargo was a great company selling far below his estimate of its intrinsic value. Berkshire added to its investment in Wells Fargo in the first half of 2009. Warren saw a similarly attractive opportunity in American Express during the early 1960s and sunk more than 40% of his investment partnership's funds into the stock. By developing the knowledge and skill required to consistently buy $1 of value for less than a dollar in price, one can achieve above-average investment gains with below average risk. However, these skills are by no means easy to attain, which partly explains the poor track record of value creation through acquisitions by large company CEOs.

**Independent Thinking**
Ben Graham counseled, "You are neither right nor wrong because the crowd disagrees with you. You are right because your data and reasoning are right." If forced to choose, I would say that the most important ingredient in the success of Warren and Charlie has been their willingness to think and act in unpopular ways, sticking to their convictions in the face of enormous criticism, the volume of which has increased in recent years due to their greater fame.

In 1969 Warren closed his investment partnership because the market had become overvalued and he did not feel that his investment approach was well suited for that type of environment. During the Internet craze in the late 1990s, the "new economy" was all the rage and investors were willing to pay enormous multiples of earnings, or worse, enormous multiples of sales for companies that had never turned a profit. Warren and Charlie did not change their investment approach. Recently, they have been criticized for selling put contracts on major market indices, essentially making bets that the world's stock markets would be above pre-specified levels on particular dates 10-20 years after entering the contracts. The criticism has been especially harsh because many incorrectly believe entering into these derivatives contracts was hypocritical, since Warren and Charlie have criticized the reckless use of high-leverage derivatives. (Incidentally, this makes about as much sense as denouncing someone who has criticized drunk drivers for operating an automobile.) What the critics fail to understand is that these contracts are essentially forms of insurance that fit entirely within the basic rules of running an insurance company that Warren and Charlie have articulated in the past. These are:

1.  Only accept risks that you can properly evaluate (including consideration of remote loss scenarios) and that carry the expectancy of a profit (i.e., you receive an adequate premium to compensate for the risk).
2.  Do not accept risks that have the potential to threaten solvency.
3.  Avoid moral risk. You cannot write good contracts with bad people. (While the counterparties for the derivatives contracts have not been revealed, it is reasonable to assume that this rule was followed.)

Berkshire could lose money on some or all of these derivatives and this would not necessarily indicate that it was a bad decision to enter into the contracts. Given what was known at the time, they were estimated to have positive expected values. In other words, for each contract the potential gain, weighted according to its probability, minus the potential loss, weighted according to its probability, produced a number sufficiently positive to make entering the contract worthwhile. Professional gamblers would call this a bet with an edge. A bet cannot be judged on the outcome, only on quality of the reasoning used when deciding to make the bet, given what was known at the time.

Despite the belief that these derivatives contracts have a long-term positive expectation, Warren and Charlie knew that entering into them had the potential to cause short-term pain in at least two ways. First, market fluctuations had the potential to create substantial fluctuations in Berkshire's earnings (in both directions) in the interim because these contracts would have to be marked to their market value on a quarterly basis. Paper losses generated by reductions in the market value would lower Berkshire's reported earnings, likely resulting in a reduced stock price. Second, in the event of a market downturn, the paper losses generated by these contracts were bound to generate considerable controversy and criticism, which they have in the aftermath of the market downturn of 2008 and early 2009. In going ahead with the contracts, Warren and Charlie were acting in a way consistent with their stated views that they don't mind looking foolish to others, as long as they don't, themselves, believe that they have acted foolishly. They focus on the long-term results and do not get overly concerned with short-term fluctuations. They have always said that they prefer a lumpy 15% return to a smooth 12%.

Warren and Charlie have regularly emphasized that, at Berkshire, they have the discipline to resist the "institutional imperative," the tendency to imitate the behavior of peer companies. This phenomenon shows up in many types of behavior, including the setting of executive compensation, acquisitions, growth, pricing and pursuing any number of fads and fashionable ideas.

The institutional imperative was in evidence in 2003-2006 when banks and other lending institutions engaged in massively nutty behavior by lending money to individuals to buy homes in spite of poor credit histories, little or no money down and insufficient income to provide a reasonable likelihood of repayment. The pull of watching others make large profits in the short-term by engaging in such lending during the housing bubble was enough to induce a stampede right off the edge of the cliff.

Similar behavior was apparent in the use of complicated, high-leverage derivatives contracts that Warren and Charlie were warning about in the early 2000s, calling them financial weapons of mass destruction. This was far from the prevailing view at the time. They were so convinced of the danger posed by these contracts that they sold off nearly all of the derivatives contracts acquired with General Reinsurance, incurring a loss of $400 million in the process. The losses would likely have been much larger had they not done so.

Warren says that he and Charlie keep internal scorecards and don't judge their behavior according to popular opinion. As long as they are acting in ways that they judge to be rational, they do not mind acting in ways that are unpopular.

## Grow Only When it Makes Sense

One area where Berkshire Hathaway has differed from most public companies is in its willingness to let its subsidiaries grow when doing so makes economic sense and not grow (or even shrink) when that makes economic sense. This is most aptly demonstrated in the super catastrophe insurance business. When the prices that can be obtained are sufficient to provide the expectation of a profit, Berkshire will write insurance policies. However, occasionally the super catastrophe insurance market goes through periods of unrealistic optimism, particularly if several years have gone by without major disasters, and therefore without large payouts. Companies will try to gain market share by underpricing their policies. When Warren and Ajit Jain (who runs this element of Berkshire's insurance business) feel that prices are such that it they cannot compete rationally, they will not lower their prices. Instead, they will be content to write fewer policies; in effect, to shrink. Warren has said that they will be perfectly willing to write one-fifth as much or five times as much insurance business from one year to the next. They will not follow their competitors off of a cliff.

There is nothing wrong with wanting your company to show growth in revenues and profitability over time. However, mistakes that I have seen made repeatedly include growing too rapidly, so that systems cannot keep up and service deteriorates, and using poorly analyzed acquisitions. Growing by acquisition is a reasonable strategy, but acquiring well means having the patience to wait for the right opportunity where the people and the economics make sense. As Warren puts it, "wait for the fat pitch" or, as market speculator Jesse Livermore said, "The big money is in the waiting."

**Do Not Attempt to Change People or Businesses**
Warren Buffett studied with Ben Graham, the father of value investing. The stereotypical value investment would be a business that is struggling and therefore the market is assigning it a low price. For this reason, many people assume that Berkshire Hathaway acquires struggling businesses and then manages them into high profitability. There may have been some truth to this idea during Warren's early years, but this is definitely not an accurate description of Berkshire Hathaway today. At one time Berkshire focused on buying fair businesses at low prices, but now favors buying great businesses at fair prices. In my view, there are some useful lessons here for the small business owner.

If you ever get the opportunity to buy a struggling business at what seems like a bargain price, remember Warren's admonition that managers who believe that they can take over and turn around a struggling business may have been overly influenced by the fairy tale in which the princess kisses a frog and it miraculously turns into a prince. Warren says that in his experience the miracle-to-kiss ratio is very low – in other words, turnarounds seldom turn. When it comes to taking on new businesses and partnering with their managers, Warren and Charlie stick to the tried and true.

For key management positions, it is generally a better bet to stick with those who have a proven track record. Great managers are few and far between and rarely do average managers turn into exceptional managers. Therefore, it is usually a better bet to pay up for a great manager than to undertake the effort of trying to upgrade an average manager. Through their acquisitions of businesses that came equipped with great managers, Warren and Charlie have been able to achieve their goals to "hire well and manage little."

When it comes to compensating key people, the overarching principle followed at Berkshire is alignment of interests. As Charlie often says, if you want to motivate in a certain direction, it is more effective to appeal to interest than to reason. Warren has echoed this sentiment by saying that appealing to interest works best because there are not enough saints to staff a good business.

Compensation systems should not create perverse incentives that reward short-term behavior at the expense of the long-term interests of the business. They should reward the manager for results that he or she has the ability to influence, not those that are due to outside forces. For example, a manager at an oil company should not be rewarded for an increase in profits driven by a rise in oil prices. On the other hand, it might be reasonable to reward that manager for keeping the cost of production low. Warren has said "The 0.350 hitter expects, and also deserves, a big payoff for his performance – even if he plays for a cellar-dwelling team. And a 0.150 hitter should get no reward – even if he plays for a pennant winner." In other words, they recommend running a meritocracy, with rewards tied to results.

### Integrity is the Most Important Trait for Those with Whom You Associate

Warren has been quoted as saying "In looking for someone to hire, you look for integrity, intelligence, and energy. But the most important is integrity, because if they don't have that, the other two qualities, intelligence and energy, are going to kill you." When evaluating someone for possible promotion in our company, I look first and foremost for signs of integrity or lack of integrity. When I hear people telling "white lies" for convenience or learn, for example, that a person lied to an insurance adjuster, saying that a pre-existing dent occurred during a fender bender for which a claim is being made, I know that I have an employee with an integrity problem. In an effort to promote a culture of high integrity, I regularly remind our staff of Warren and Charlie's aphorisms. They both say that it takes years to build a reputation, but that reputation can be destroyed in minutes by a single misdeed. Also, Warren reminds us that it is harder to get out of trouble than it is to stay out of trouble. Getting out of trouble is a 7-foot bar that I would prefer to avoid.

Integrity is not only an important consideration for you (as a role model) and your employees, it is also a good screening criterion to apply to potential clients. Warren and Charlie say that you can't make a good deal with a bad person. My own experience has been consistent with this principle. Every time that I have worked with a client whose integrity I questioned, I later regretted doing so. The stories range from not getting paid everything owed, to having my work misrepresented in advertising. All of these were painful, and sometimes costly, mistakes. One of the best parts about owning a business is the ability to choose to work only with clients who you like and trust. This may be tough for those just starting out, but in the end, more often than not in my experience, the integrity filter will save you time and aggravation, and possibly money as well.

**Understand the Time Value of Money and the Money Value of Time**

I once read that Warren Buffett never mowed the lawn at his house in Omaha. Whether or not this is true, choosing not to mow the lawn would be an economically rational decision for Warren. While Warren's financial success is a testament to the power of the time value of money due to compounding, a less appreciated lesson from Warren and Charlie is the money value of time. I am proud to say that I gave up mowing the lawn years ago, because mowing my own lawn was too expensive. We all get the same 168 hours in each week. Those who are most productive in our society will be the ones who figure out how to spend more of their time on high value activities and less on low value activities. Those activities that have a low value with regard to moving you toward your goals should be delegated, outsourced or eliminated. Elimination is a particularly important strategy. Most business owners would benefit from a careful, detailed review of how they spend their time over a period of a week or two. An honest evaluation is likely to reveal any number of activities that, if eliminated completely, would have no negative impact on the business whatsoever.  As Warren and Charlie like to say: "That which is not worth doing at all is not worth doing well."

Warren and Charlie have been brilliant at engineering their lives so that they can focus on what is most important and productive given their circles of competence.  They have learned to say "no" to many of the distractions that so often sidetrack business owners.  They have also acquired top-quality companies with good management that did not need a lot of day-to-day interaction and guidance, leaving them free from meetings, conference calls and other day-to-day operational activities.  It is useful for every business owner to regularly assess how he or she is "investing" time.

**Focus on What is Important and Knowable**
Warren has said that one of the reasons he didn't like living in New York was that he was constantly bombarded by stimuli.  He said that anyone with a normal amount of adrenalin is likely to start responding and might make poor decisions driven by emotion rather than reason.  In Omaha, with less stimulation, he feels he is better able to think.

Today, the information barrage has been amplified by new technologies such as 24-hour cable news shows, the Internet, cellular telephones and personal digital assistants.  Moreover, much of the information provided is of little value.  Turn on CNBC any day of the week and you will hear a constant stream of predictions about the stock market, the economy, the unemployment rate, Chinese GDP growth, etc.  Over extended periods many of these variables are somewhat predictable, but accuracy declines precipitously when predictions are made about the coming few weeks, months or quarters.

Warren and Charlie have made their views on short-term predictions clear.  Warren has said that the main value of economic forecasters seems to be to make fortune tellers look good.  Charlie has stated that listening to today's forecasters is just as crazy as when the king hired the guy to look at sheep guts to tell him the future.  For more information about the accuracy of short- and long-term predictions, I recommend the books *The Fortune Sellers* by William Sherden and *Irrational Exuberance* by Robert Shiller.

The best managers do not try to run their businesses based on short-term predictions about the economy, interest rates, prices, etc. Instead, they focus their attention on what is important and knowable. What is important and knowable? As described throughout this book the elements of SLEEC (sales and marketing effectiveness and engagement of employees and customers) can be evaluated objectively and they are unquestionably important. Expenses can be measured and managed. The business owner who keeps his or her eye on these balls will have the odds on his/her side.

**Invert, Always Invert**
When faced with problems to solve in your business, follow Charlie's advice to invert the problem. You should think through not only actions to move you toward your goal, but actions to avoid that move you away from your goal, or at least fail to move you closer. As an example, earlier in the book I emphasized 80/20 analysis, which can be used to identify subsets of your products and services, customers and employees who are responsible for a majority of your company's profits and productivity. Segmenting in this way is useful to identify the main contributors to your success, the top 20%. It is equally useful to identify the bottom 20%, which may provide important insight into what might be holding you back. Some of my most useful insights from talking to business owners have come from asking them not only about what they did to succeed, but also what mistakes they made along the way or observed in their competitors. This gives me insight into what to avoid. I have found Charlie's advice to develop the mental habit of inverting problems enormously helpful in many situations.

**Learn to Communicate Well**
In recent years Warren has been hosting groups of business school students in Omaha several times each year. One of the themes that he has emphasized at these question and answer sessions has

been the importance of developing good written and oral communication skills.  These are skills that can be improved through practice with feedback.  An important element of good communication is setting expectations.  Customer and employee dissatisfaction generally arise when mismatches occur between expectations and reality.  This also applies to much of the interaction between managers and those they manage.  If performance expectations are not clearly communicated so that they are understood by both parties, the manager is not likely to be satisfied with the resulting performance.  Furthermore, the employee may be frustrated because his or her efforts were not appreciated by the manager.  It is hard to hit the bull's eye when one has only a vague idea where the target is located.

**On Being Happy**
Warren and Charlie often cite the axiom that "a happy man is one who has what he wants and wants what he has."  Warren talks about having won the ovarian lottery by being born in the United States where high rewards for effort are achievable.  However, you should pick your goals carefully.  Major life goals always require large doses of effort and determination.  Since we all have only 168 hours in every week, time spent working toward these goals will not be available for other activities, including important relationships.  In the book *The Snowball:  Warren Buffett and the Business of Life*, Alice Schroeder paints a portrait of Warren as being obsessed with business and making money, often at the expense of time with his wife and family.

At one Berkshire Hathaway annual meeting Warren made a statement that I can't remember verbatim, but the gist of which was that money spent to take a family trip to Disney World is a rational alternative to investing those funds for retirement.  Warren does not use the word *rational* lightly and, I suspect, with the benefit of hindsight, he might spend a bit more time and money with his family at Disney World if he had a chance to go back and relive those days.

> **Authors note:** I sent Mr. Buffett a draft of the book and he replied with a hand written note thanking me for doing so. He said that he found no errors that needed correction, but also pointed out that he went to Disneyland with his family more than 20 times.

The admonition above notwithstanding, Warren and Charlie advise against obsessing over mistakes. Prior decisions should be critically analyzed as learning exercises, but you can only live your life forward. With apologies to Warren for mixing his metaphors, you can't live your life in the rearview mirror, so keep your eyes on the windshield.

A final bit of advice from Warren and Charlie is to avoid envy. Someone else's gain is not your loss. Findings from research on success and happiness show that the relationship tends to be relative rather than absolute. People do not judge what they have and have accomplished versus an absolute standard, but rather relative to those to whom they compare themselves. Getting on the treadmill of trying to keep up with the Joneses is a mistake. This is another area where Warren and Charlie's concept of an internal scorecard is useful. Decide what it is you really want out of your life, then work toward those goals. These might include goals related to business, family, health and recreation. Reward yourself for achieving these and try not to worry about what the folks down the street are doing. Remember what Warren and Charlie say: "Envy is the dumbest of the seven deadly sins because it is the only one you couldn't have any fun at." Lust, gluttony and sloth can be the makings for a great weekend, but envy just makes you miserable.

*Section 2*

# Profiles of Entrepreneurs

*Innovative ideas are like frogs' eggs: of a thousand hatched, only one or two survive to maturity.*

– Peter Drucker

The first section of *Tipping the Odds for the Entrepreneur* has focused on presenting a few of what are, in my view, the most important concepts and strategies that an entrepreneur needs to know to improve his or her odds for business success. The next several chapters will profile a few of the business owners I have admired. These include managers of family businesses acquired by Berkshire Hathaway, as well as entrepreneurs ranging from owners of start-up companies that are just getting off the ground to those that have been in business for decades. All in the latter category are people with whom I have had some personal connection as a customer, vendor or employee. The entrepreneurs selected for inclusion run their businesses in a manner consistent with the principles outlined in this book. I hope that you will find their stories both interesting and instructive.

*Chapter 13*

# Rose Blumkin, Bill Child and Doris Christopher

# Entrepreneurs Who Sold Their Family Businesses to Berkshire Hathaway

*Small opportunities are often the beginnings of great enterprises.*
— Demosthenes


One of Warren Buffett's central tenets is that his job is to identify great business managers to take on as partners and then stay out of their way. He encourages the managers of the businesses Berkshire acquires to keep operating just as they have in the past and often leaves a portion of the ownership with the family (10-20%) to ensure that his interests and theirs remain aligned. Over the years, Berkshire Hathaway has acquired a number of high-quality family businesses that had been built over a lifetime, or, in some cases, over several generations of family control. A few examples include See's Candies, Nebraska Furniture Mart, RC Willey and Co., Borsheim's Jewelers, Helzberg Diamonds, Iscar Metalworking Companies and The Marmon Group. These companies are certainly outliers that have grown far beyond the size of most family businesses. Nevertheless, studying the attitudes and habits of the managers of these family-owned enterprises provides a host of useful lessons for owners of businesses of all sizes, even those who have no intention of growing to a size anywhere near those of the companies profiled here. Fortunately, a number of books have been written that provide portals into the minds of these entrepreneurs from which I have created brief summaries. I strongly encourage obtaining the books referenced so that you can read about these fascinating individuals in greater detail.

### Rose Blumkin – Nebraska Furniture Mart

Rose Blumkin founded and made an enormous success of the Nebraska Furniture Mart, ultimately selling 90% of it to Berkshire Hathaway for $55 million in 1983 (nearly $120 million in 2009 dollars after adjustment for inflation). Rose was known as Mrs. B to everyone who knew her. Mrs. B's history is remarkable, but in some ways not unique. Many of the most successful family businesses in the United States were started by immigrants who showed amazing tenacity and drive to succeed. These success stories prove that an Ivy League business school education is not a prerequisite for entrepreneurial success.

As recounted by Alice Schroeder in the book *The Snowball: Warren Buffett and the Business of Life* (which was my primary source for this section on the Blumkins), Mrs. B came to the United States from Russia to escape political unrest and persecution of Jews. She and her husband Isadore ended up in Omaha in the 1920s, which had a large population of Russian immigrants. She didn't learn to speak English for years and never learned to read or write in English.

In Omaha, they rented and ran a pawn shop. When the business struggled during the depression Mrs. B devised a strategy to save the business. Her idea was to undersell the "big shots" by selling at 10% over cost. She handed out 10,000 flyers all over Omaha saying that they could outfit a man – underwear, suit, tie, shoes and straw hat – for $5. As a result they took in more than $800 in a single day, more revenue than they had made during the entire previous year.

Eventually Mrs. B opened a store called Blumkin's in a basement near her husband's pawn shop to sell furniture, carpet and other home furnishings.  Because Blumkin's undercut the prices of other retailers, they complained to local wholesalers who refused to sell to Mrs. B because of these complaints.  She responded by traveling all over the Midwest to buy overstock merchandise from stores.  Her motto was "Sell cheap, tell the truth, don't cheat nobody, and don't take no kickbacks."

During the Korean War in the 1950s sales slowed and Blumkin's was having a difficult time paying its suppliers.  A sympathetic banker gave them a $50,000 loan and they organized an enormous sale at the Omaha City Auditorium.  During a 3-day period they sold $250,000 worth of furniture.  This solved their cash flow problems and elevated their profile in Omaha dramatically.

Sadly, Isadore died from a heart attack that year.  Mrs. B kept running the business (now called Nebraska Furniture Mart) with her son Louie.  Nebraska Furniture Mart continued to sell at 10% above cost, keeping expenses to a bare minimum.  They continued to grow every year, drawing customers from a larger and larger area, including neighboring states.  By the early 1980s annual sales had grown to more than $100 million per year.

While in Omaha at a Berkshire Hathaway shareholders' meeting my wife and I stopped into the Nebraska Furniture Mart.  We needed a dining room set and purchased one at a price that we almost couldn't believe.  Even after the charge for delivery to Illinois we paid much less than the asking price for comparable sets we had looked at in our area.

Warren Buffett attributes the success of Mrs. B and the Blumkin family to hard work; a fanatical culture of cost containment, allowing the store to consistently offer the lowest prices (a sustainable competitive advantage); and staying within their circle of competence.  I would add persistence in the face of all obstacles.  Mrs. B never gave up.  When wholesalers refused to sell to her, she found another way to buy inventory.  When her husband's pawn shop was on the verge of bankruptcy she devised a plan and took action.  Evidence of her tenacity was present at an early age.  At age 13 she knocked on 26 doors in the city of

Gomel looking for work and a place to sleep. She offered to work for a shopkeeper if he would let her sleep on his floor. By age 16 she was a manager at the shop, supervising 6 married men.

One element of Mrs. B's managerial style that may be perplexing to some readers is the way she would insult her family and others. Apparently she would regularly call her grandsons bums and she was quoted in the newspaper as saying that Warren Buffett lacked loyalty because he didn't side with her during a dispute she had with her grandsons.

As an aside, at one point Mrs. B left the Nebraska Furniture Mart after a dispute with her grandsons and opened a competing store across the street. This occurred when she was in her late nineties. After two years she reconciled with her family and Warren Buffett. Berkshire Hathaway paid her $5 million to buy out the new store on the condition that she sign a non-compete agreement. The fact that Mr. Buffett insisted on a non-compete agreement with a 99 year old woman is indicative of his great respect for her abilities as a business manager.

I don't know how Mrs. B treated her employees who were not family members, but I suspect one of two scenarios or some combination thereof. One is that she was a hothead, but kind and generous at other times, so people would put up with her regular outbursts without developing resentment. Another is that her family members acted as a buffer, smoothing over the ruffled feathers generated by Mrs. B.

When I worked at the hotel, both of these scenarios played out to some degree with the patriarch of the family (his son is profiled in Chapter 14). Stanley would regularly blow up at me and others, including the occasional customer, often using profanity and saying wildly inappropriate things. I once heard him tell a customer who complained about a leaking pipe "Your head has leak!" At other times he could be encouraging and generous. However, his wife was uniformly easy going and treated all of the employees exceptionally well. Many times I recall her bringing me food or praising my efforts. She regularly let me know that my contributions were important and appreciated. She also encouraged me to take on more and more responsibility, even at a young age. At 19 I was weekend Housekeeping Supervisor. By age 20 I was a Guest Service Manager at the reception desk, supervising several clerks, some of whom were much older than me. Her example, encouragement and confidence in me were a tremendous boost to my self-esteem, which helped me to keep my sights set higher than they would have been without her influence.

**Bill Child – RC Willey Company**
In 2009 while attending the Berkshire Hathaway annual meeting I purchased a book that had just been published entitled *How to Build a Business Warren Buffett Would Buy: The RC Willey Story* by Jeff Benedict. I started reading it on the plane ride home on Sunday, and first thing Monday morning I asked my assistant to order a copy for every member of our management team. The book is mostly the story of Bill Child, who, at age 22, took over a 600 square foot retail appliance store in 1954 when his father-in-law (RC Willey) died after a short bout with pancreatic cancer. Bill had been helping out his father-in-law at the store while studying for a degree in education. He had recently graduated and been offered a job in education, but found himself at a fork in the road. His father-in-law's death forced him to take over the store because there was nobody else who could take over the business, which was supporting his mother-in-law and other members of the Willey family.

A number of unpleasant surprises awaited Bill, including an IRS audit, an unpaid construction loan, delinquencies in the accounts of a number of customers who had purchased appliances on credit, and payments to vendors and suppliers that were in arrears. Even though the store was on track for a record year in sales of $250,000 (a bit over $2 million in 2009 dollars), the store could not be sold for any significant sum because of its various obligations, some of which were threatening to put the store out of business.

Many 22 year olds would have been paralyzed, but Bill Child got busy solving problems. He approached a large bank for a loan and was turned down. He approached a community bank where the banker he met with was familiar with the RC Willey store and its good reputation and was extended a line of credit. This allowed the doors to stay open and thereafter he started chipping away at the problems one by one.

Amazingly, he obtained permission from the IRS to hire the agent that had been sent to audit the store and, with his new accountant's help, he negotiated a settlement for the payment of overdue back taxes. He took advantage of programs from Utah Power and Light intended to incentivize appliance dealers to convince customers to replace gas-powered appliances with electric versions. Bill needed to sell 150 water heaters and 150 ranges to pay back the loan. He located a company that was willing to refinance delinquent appliance loan contracts at a higher interest rate if Bill could convince the borrower to sign a new contract. He had to go to each delinquent customer's house with his pick-up truck and give the borrower a choice to sign the contract or give back the appliance. When the new contract was signed it became the finance company's responsibility to collect the payments. Otherwise, Bill had to repossess the merchandise.

RC Willey was a true family business. Bill hired his brother Sheldon to head the sales team and eventually the brothers even hired their father. After two and a half years, Bill was on the verge of his first year of profits unhampered by large debt repayments. However, he ran into a dispute with a manufacturer that had been selling washing machines with defective parts. The manufacturer refused to take responsibility, leaving Bill to decide whether to incur the expense of replacing the defective parts for hundreds of customers, which would wipe out nearly a full year of profits. As painful as doing so must have been, he went ahead and made it right for his customers, even though the defect was the manufacturer's fault. Though difficult in the short-term, this decision helped to cement his relationships with his customers and undoubtedly led to a great deal of repeat business.

The RC Willey store was located in an outlying rural area, but they turned this into an advantage with advertising slogans such as

"Drive out to the country and save" and "Lower overhead means lower prices because of our country location." Bill made a deal with a television station to buy unsold ad space at a discounted price. They used the slogan "Come save money with us, but never on Sunday." The store wasn't open on Sunday because Bill Child was a devoted Mormon and he saved Sunday for worship and family.

Bill didn't spend all of his time working in the business; he hired good people for key positions so that he could work on the business. After 14 years of successful growth and operation in Syracuse, a second RC Willey store was opened in Salt Lake City. In this larger market, RC Willey continued to grow and by 1995 their sales exceeded $250 million. This represents a compound annual revenue growth rate just shy of 19%.

Bill attributes the success of RC Willey to steady adherence to a few simple management principles that I have paraphrased below.

1. Be motivated by excellence, not money. The profits will follow if you are better than your competitors.
2. Offer true value on quality products.
3. Treat customers as you would like to be treated.
4. Enjoy your business and think about the future of the industry you are in.
5. Avoid unnecessary debt.
6. Be efficient. Waste drains profits.
7. Treat your employees well or they won't treat your customers well.
8. Pay attention to the details. The little things count when it comes to customer service and in creating the right appearance for your business.
9. Be honest! It takes years to build a reputation, but a single misdeed can destroy that overnight.
10. Hire good and capable people who you respect and will enjoy working with.
11. Make decisions with an eye toward the future – take the long view.

12. Differentiate your company with marketing. Good marketing maintains top-of-mind status.
13. Be willing and able to change. Don't be afraid to change when circumstances demand.

Bill Child was a longtime friend of Irv Blumkin, grandson of Rose Blumkin. Irv was CEO of the Nebraska Furniture Mart and Bill sought him out to discuss his situation now that he was over 60 years of age and thinking about succession planning. He had already turned down offers from suitors such as Heilig-Myer, Montgomery Ward and an investment bank, the largest being for approximately $200 million. Irv conveyed that they had been extremely happy since selling the Nebraska Furniture Mart to Berkshire Hathaway. Warren Buffett had kept every promise and the family was allowed to continue running the business.

Irv offered to talk with Warren about RC Willey and a few weeks later Bill Child got a call from Warren. After sending financial documents for his review, Buffett made an offer to purchase the company for $170 million, which was $20 to $30 million less than offers that Bill had already turned down. Nevertheless, selling to Berkshire Hathaway came with a promise that the family could continue running the business in much the same way they had when they were the sole owners. In May of 1995 they sold RC Willey to Berkshire for $175 million in Berkshire Stock (Buffett threw in an additional $5 million to solve some complex tax issues).

**Author's note:** After receiving a draft copy of this book Bill Child called me personally to congratulate me. Having interacted with him several times now via telephone and e-mail, I can report that he has proven to be every bit as gracious and impressive in these interactions as he was reported to be in *How to Build a Business Warren Buffett Would Buy: The RC Willey Story*.

### Doris Christopher – The Pampered Chef
I am not much of a cook and, truthfully, I paid little attention to The Pampered Chef until it was acquired by Berkshire Hathaway in 2002. One of our neighbors was a Pampered Chef "Kitchen

Consultant" and my wife purchased several items at Kitchen Shows. I remember once asking her about where she had purchased a particularly handy device for opening jars, which clearly indicated that this was a special product since I am unlikely to pay much attention to anything in the kitchen short of a live rattlesnake or a six-foot showgirl.

When Berkshire Hathaway acquired The Pampered Chef, I took notice and became interested in learning more. I was surprised to discover that the company's headquarters were in Addison, Illinois, which is close to where we live. In fact, one of our research clinics is now located in Addison. Doris Christopher, the founder, started the business with her husband Jay in 1980, using $3,000 from a life insurance policy as start-up capital. She ran the business out of their home in Elmhurst, Illinois for the first few years, proving that it is possible to launch a great company from a basement. Today The Pampered Chef has more than 60,000 field consultants and is estimated to have had $613 million in revenue in 2008 (source: http://biz.yahoo.com/ic/42/42750.html accessed October 2009).

In 2005 Doris published a book entitled *The Pampered Chef: The Story of One of America's Most Beloved Companies*. Warren Buffett wrote the foreword in which he says that the book has a lot to teach anyone reaching for the American dream. He advises the aspiring entrepreneur to read it, then read it again. I could not agree more. My wife Cathy and I listened to the audio book on a long car ride. When we got home I went straight to the bookstore and bought several copies, one for myself and others to give as gifts. Mine is full of yellow highlights and notes in the margin. I think Doris Christopher and her husband Jay are terrific success models. What follows is an abbreviated history of The Pampered Chef and some of the main principles outlined in Doris Christopher's book.

Doris and her husband Jay started dating in high school and married shortly after college graduation. Doris obtained a degree in home economics from the University of Illinois, briefly worked as a teacher, then took a job as a home economist for the DuPage

County (Illinois) Cooperative Extension Service, operated by the University of Illinois, teaching home economics to adults in suburban and rural areas. After six years Doris left her job to become a full time homemaker at the time her first daughter was born. Several years later Doris started to work part-time jobs to supplement the family income and save for their daughters' college educations.

In 1980, when both of her children were going to be in school, Doris wanted to return to full-time employment, but couldn't decide what she wanted to pursue because she didn't want to forgo being available full-time for her daughters. Using an approach straight out of Charlie Munger's playbook, her husband Jay suggested that she invert the problem and think about elements she didn't want in her new career. They soon discovered that her requirements (working only when the kids were in school, no weekend or holiday hours) would likely preclude most traditional jobs, so they decided that the best option was for her to start her own business.

Doris had always loved cooking and teaching, so they tried to figure out a way to combine those two things. Eventually Doris hit upon the idea of selling kitchen tools to women in their homes, using a model that had worked for such companies as Mary Kay Cosmetics and Tupperware (food storage containers). She correctly surmised that kitchen utensils would sell better if demonstrated because many women would not know from looking at an item how to use it, or how certain utensils could help to save time and effort. She recounts reading a case history of the Wham-O Company that had great success with the Hula Hoop and Frisbee by demonstrating how they could be used on television and with campus representatives who showed college students how to use Frisbees.

Doris envisioned in-home demonstrations for groups of friends in a relaxed atmosphere, with no sales pressure. She also believed that it would be ideal to have some low-priced items so that participants who wanted to buy something to be polite to the host would not have to spend too much. She wanted to offer quality products at fair prices and demonstrate them with simple, quick recipes. This approach allowed her to show attendees how they could use the products to quickly produce delicious meals for their families. The Kitchen Shows would be entertaining, fun and an opportunity for friends to socialize while learning useful skills.

The Pampered Chef was a one-person operation for some time, but Doris was approached in 1981 at the end of a show by someone who wanted to know if she could become a Kitchen Consultant. Doris and Jay worked out an initial compensation schedule that underwent several revisions over the first six months. By the end of the year there were 8 more Kitchen Consultants, bringing the sales force to 10. By the end of that year deliveries had become such a big job that it was no longer feasible for the company, so that was turned over to United Parcel Service. At the end of 1981 total sales were $67,000. By the end of 1982 there were 25 Kitchen Consultants and sales were $100,000. By the end of 1984 sales had grown to $499,000 and it was time to move out of the Christopher house.

By the end of 1986 revenues exceeded $1 million and Jay left his job in 1987 to join the The Pampered Chef on a full-time basis. The company continued to grow rapidly and by the time Jay left to start and run his own consulting firm in 1994 sales had grown to $135 million. Rapid growth is both a blessing and a challenge and I am certain that it was no small feat to do this in such a short period. Throughout there was an emphasis on the company's values of integrity, determination, hard work and respect for others that allowed The Pampered Chef to maintain the trust of its consultants and customers. The product line was continually expanded and upgraded. The approach to selling did not change. Kitchen Consultants sell by teaching, with no sales pressure. Also, management actively solicits feedback and suggestions from staff and consultants to improve the company's operations.

The Christophers set up a system in which the initial investment by a new Kitchen Consultant was limited to the purchase of a starter kit for less than $100 (at that time). Kitchen Consultants are Independent Contractors, not employees. In contrast to many multi-level marketing companies, no commissions were earned for signing up a new Kitchen Consultant. Commissions are only earned on sales. Overrides are paid by those who recruit, train and build their own sales force. The first rung on the ladder is Future Director, which is someone who has recruited two active Kitchen Consultants (a certain level of sales is required to maintain "active" status). The person becomes a Director when five active Kitchen Consultants have been recruited. Four additional levels exist beyond Director.

This structure allowed Kitchen Consultants to create a position that would fit their personal situations. Some wanted to work part-time and could do so without creating a sales force. Others wanted a full-time position with potential for significant earnings and upward mobility. This was also available and each consultant could put in as much or as little time as she wanted with almost no capital at risk (I say "she" because most Kitchen Consultants are women).

Performance is recognized at monthly sales meetings. Later, national sales conferences were put in place that include public recognition for performance. Various ribbons and pins are given to signify levels of achievement. Doris calls these gestures of recognition a process of "praising people to success." Travel incentives are provided for reaching milestones. Doris reports that these work particularly well with young couples who are often reluctant to spend money on vacation travel.

---

**Authors note**:  The information above is from Doris Christopher's book and may not accurately reflect the current terminology and organization of the company. The interested reader should visit the company web site (www.PamperedChef.com) for more information.

---

Doris outlines the following tips for start-up entrepreneurs.

1.  Follow your passion.

2. Stick to your knitting – have a clear idea what you want to do and avoid the temptation to diversify. Stick to your core business and do that well.
3. Find a niche – find a unique market, a unique method of selling or some other factor that will differentiate you from your competition and allow you to deliver your product or service faster, with higher quality, better service, at a lower price or to a group that with which your business will have special affinity.
4. Be the best you can be at what you do.
5. Make a difference in peoples' lives – find ways to enrich the lives of your employees and customers.
6. Keep it simple – develop systems to ensure consistent quality in your products and services. Root out and eliminate unnecessary complexity.
7. Watch your overhead – don't spend on lavish office space, furnishings, etc. Save some money during the good times so that you can withstand the inevitable downturns.
8. Go with your instincts – learn to trust your gut, but realize that your gut will sometimes lead you astray. You will make mistakes, but it is impossible to live an adequate life without making some errors.
9. Value your time and be a good time manager.
10. Brush up on your computer skills.
11. It's only a business – no matter how important your business is to you, remember that family and other relationships are what really matter. You should not let your business overtake all aspects of your life.

# Chapter 14

# Vlado Lenoch – Hotel Owner

## (www.WilliamTellBanquets.com)

*I know the price of success: dedication, hard work, and a devotion
to the things you want to see happen.*
– Frank Lloyd Wright

Throughout the book I have emphasized how important my years
as a hotel employee were in shaping my views about success and
entrepreneurship. I didn't know it at the time, but I gained
experience more valuable than an MBA while working for a
couple who immigrated to the Chicago area from Yugoslavia
(although they were of Czech ancestry) and went into the
motel/hotel business.

I had the good fortune to join Stanley and Zdenka's company in
1980 and I worked for them for just under 10 years. This included
part of my high school years, all of my undergraduate years, and a
significant portion of my time in graduate school. I alternated
between full and part-time status to accommodate my school
schedule and performed nearly every imaginable function on an as
needed basis. These experiences would prove invaluable to me
later as a business owner. In addition, these experiences helped
me understand that, to be financially successful, I would have to
own something. I started with investment real estate (like Stanley
and Zdenka did) and moved on to owning a service business. I

was fortunate to have the Lenoch family as role models and I owe them a debt of gratitude for the experiences and world view I acquired while in their employ.

Stanley and Zdenka's two sons, Vladamir (Vlado) and Josef (Joe), grew up working in the family business and now own a group of five hotels in Illinois and Colorado. Vlado was kind enough to talk with me to share his insights and advice for the small business owner in September of 2009.

KCM: I'm interested in hearing an encapsulated version of your parents' history, how they got here, and how they got into the hotel business.

VL:     Both my parents are Czech. Their great grandparents are from a small town near Prague. They were born and raised in a small town near Zagreb, Yugoslavia, which was a Czech farming village. The whole valley there were all Czechs who moved there prior to World War I because cheap farming land was available. Somehow, my parents got the notion they needed to go to America for more opportunity.

What transpired was my dad got a Visa by bribing the local government guy with extra bags of flour to go work on a construction project in Dresden, Germany on the dams they were rebuilding after World War II. So they went there and did that for a year or two. Then he had the opportunity from there to get an immigration permit. He already had an aunt living in America. She vouched for them. They got an immigration permit to go to the US.

They took a boat non-stop from Hamburg, Germany to New York Harbor, and getting off the boat, they were confronted with strikes and very limited job opportunities in New York. I think this was October 1956 when they landed. They hopped on the train and went to Chicago where my aunt was. When they settled, somebody got my dad a job in a cardboard factory. From then on, it's almost fate what he did. He realized that even though he was working in a cardboard factory, to gain wealth, he'd have to own something.

He somehow right away knew that real estate was the way to do it. Within a few years, he bought a small apartment building, fixed it up, sold it, made a little money, bought another apartment building, fixed it up, and sold it. Eventually, he found a job maintaining a synagogue in Hyde Park, Illinois. He started working there and gained a lot of experience in maintaining large buildings. All the while, still buying small apartments, fixing them up, and selling them. While he was working at the synagogue, one of the members of the synagogue noticed his expertise and hired him to manage two large high-rise apartment buildings in Hyde Park.

That further enhanced his experience and knowledge of operating a large facility. These were both 20 story, several hundred-unit apartment buildings. That helped his education on how to maintain a building like that. He was the head janitor, custodian, or building manager. I'm not sure what his title was at the time. From that he got the notion that he's got to own bigger properties, rather than these little apartments. He eventually found a small motel on Joliet Road in Countryside for sale.

Taking vacations driving around, we'd stay in little motels. He'd look here and there. I remember one vacation in California, we did hang out a couple days with a real estate guy looking at little motels, mainly in the Los Angeles area. When we came back, he found us this motel in Countryside, IL called Sunnyside Motel. That's what he bought. He put some money down and talked the bank into giving him a loan. The seller also took back a note. He paid it all off. Then he bought the adjacent land and another motel from another owner on a similar basis: part cash, part owner financing and a little money from bank loans.

He was acquiring land, which eventually enabled them to build the Holiday Inn facility that's there now. He ended up with about 25 acres. It was not developed at all, mostly just weeds.

KCM: Do you know about what year it was when he bought the Sunnyside Motel?

VL:     That was about in February 1967, which was the year of the record snow in Chicago.  We all remember how it took us about a week to move from the house in Chicago to Countryside because of the snow.

KCM: Bad timing.  What year was it when the hotel was built?

VL:     They built the first phase of the hotel and the restaurant building in – it was finished in 1974.  They subleased the restaurant operation to Louis [*last name omitted*], who managed the William Tell Restaurant on North Avenue in Chicago.  My parents knew that they had no experience in a restaurant, but they needed it to have a successful hotel.  They brought in another operator to run the restaurant with the operator just providing them with lease money.  The same bank that provided some of the financing on the Sunnyside Motel helped with the financing of the hotel.

KCM: I had part of that story not quite right.  I'm glad you gave me the proper history.  Do you remember how many rooms were in Section 1 of that hotel?  As I recall, it was right around 100.

VL:     Yeah.  It was actually 80 rooms.  It was amazingly small in a high rise setting like that.

KCM: For the Holiday Inn, there were two additions, plus then the atrium area was expanded.

VL:     In 1980, they added another 110 rooms to the end of the original 80 rooms.  They just extended the corridor and added another wing.  In 1986, they added the west wing, which was another 120 rooms.  Then also, two years later, they added the swimming pool.  Between all that, an atrium was added and a larger banquet area.  That was finished in, I think, 1983.  Also, what happened in 1983 was the restaurant was in distress.  Louis, the owner, he didn't pay some federal income taxes and he was defaulting on loans. I don't know why.

To me, the business always seemed viable, very busy, good volume. The assets went up for auction. Because my parents owned the underlying real estate, they were able to buy the assets for minimal money. Having watched Louis successfully operate the restaurant for ten years, my parents were willing to take on running the restaurant.

When they took it over, they had to learn really quickly. They never had a restaurant before. They made a lot of mistakes, but they learned pretty quickly. They learned how to run it through hard knocks.

KCM: I was there at the time. I remember doing everything from checking coats to banquet waitering and so forth as they were learning the ropes. There were some seminars in the school of hard knocks early in the process.

VL:    They knew they had to keep the restaurant running because it was a symbiotic relationship with the hotel. A large hotel like that has to have a restaurant. Several years later, they said restaurants aren't worth it, they're too much work for the return.

KCM: I assume you worked in the hotel motel business growing up. At some point, you left to go to school to become a pilot.

VL:    I just learned to fly in high school and continued taking lessons on the side. I went to a local high school airline township in LaGrange, IL. After that, I just went right on to college. My dad let me do the course work I was interested in, which was aviation. He didn't want me to learn to fly or be a mechanic. He wanted me to do something substantial, so I took aeronautical engineering. After going to school, I got a job at Boeing in Seattle. I worked there about five years. I was completely away from the property for five years.

When I was going to college in the summers or on vacation, I'd come home and work on the property. It was like coming back to the family farm, jumping right in and picking up; painting or working the switchboard. When I went to work at Boeing, I was completely removed from the property and wasn't involved in it. While at Boeing, I decided that I wanted to fly because I kept flying on my own. I was able to get a job in an airline. I stayed with the airlines for another five years. Being an airline pilot was probably the world's easiest job in those days.

You worked three or four days a week, and you'd have the balance of the week off. With an airline job, I could hop on a plane, come home to Chicago, and go to work on the "family farm." Once I got in the airlines, I was back at the hotel. I didn't have anything else I was interested in doing. Were you there at the time when I was back and forth with the airline?

KCM: For the first couple years I worked there, I don't recall meeting you. But after that, you were around more. Later in my tenure, you moved back to Chicago and were there all the time.

VL:    Halfway through all my airline flying, the airline in Denver, Frontier Airlines, shut down. I got a job with another airline in Chicago, and that's when I was in Chicago much more often. That's why I could be there.

KCM: I remember arguing with the car company about the time for your pickup to go to the airport. I'd say, "They're not going to leave without him. I promise."

VL:    Then when my mom died, I quit the airline all together to come back to the hotel and worked full time.

KCM: What year was it when your mom died?

VL:    I think it was January of '87 when she passed away.

KCM: That was toward the end of my time at the hotel.

VL:     Then you went onto full time college or grad school.

KCM: I think I went to graduate school for a year while I was still working on weekends over at the Hampton Inn. [The Hampton was a property built next to the main Holiday Inn in 1987, a few years before I left the company.]

VL:     You got some internship or something and needed to be with that full time.

KCM: My schedule didn't allow me to have the part time job for a while, and I moved on to working in a hospital. I was working the overnight shift there, which was not so bad, since I had done it for years at the hotel.

VL:     After that, it was just my brother and me running all the properties. Back in '67 after my dad first bought the Sunnyside Motel, he bought the Plaza Inn down the road. We managed that place. We had a couple of live-in managers. It was an independent hotel. In the franchise hotel, as we took out older furniture that was still good, we'd send it over the Plaza Inn, which was an unfranchised motel. It was good to have that furniture over there. Carpeting, sinks, lights, bedspreads, towels. Everything that was still usable, we sent to Plaza.

Plaza had about 120 rooms. It was a very low overhead property, partly because we provided it with our own used furniture and equipment. Its profits were pretty good. We ended up selling it in 2003. The area was a big trucking, industrial and manufacturing area. As you know, manufacturing has left the United States. It started to leave the South Side of Chicago. Our corporate guests were starting to go away. We decided to sell that at the time. We got a pretty good dollar for it compared to what it cost to operate over the years with our low overhead.

KCM: How many properties do you have currently?

VL:     Right now, we have the Best Western next door, which was a Hampton Inn. That was built in 1987, and its license expired in 2007.  Hampton doesn't like to renew licenses.  Their standard policy is when a hotel license expires, they want to not renew it and have the owner build a brand new building somewhere.  With that building, we converted it to a Best Western, which is the least expensive franchise.  We still own that one.  In about 1989, we bought the Crestwood, IL Hampton Inn.

We owned that until about 2000.  We sold it, then we built a Hampton Inn in Carol Stream in 2001.  We still own that one.  In 2003, we bought the Hampton Inn at the airport in Denver.  We still own that.  Right now, we're finishing construction on a Baymont Inn at the airport in Denver.  It's not open yet.  It'll be open in about two months [late 2009].

KCM:  Probably decent timing, as it looks like the economy is picking up again.

VL:     The business at the airport has always been good.  The Chicago hotels were down from 20 to 30 percent in business and revenue, but the worst the business was ever down at the Denver airport was 10 percent.  Right now, they're down 5 percent compared to last year's September levels.  Being an airport property, it has all together different trade characteristics.  It bounced back pretty quickly and still has good business coming through the doors.

KCM:  It's always interesting to look at different niches and markets and how they fare.  In our business, the recession has not been too bad because we do a lot of business with food companies.  While everyone else was hurting, food companies were doing reasonably well because people were eating at home more.  I wouldn't have predicted that a year ago, but that's the way it turned out.

VL:     We're really busy here.  We've reduced hours on regular line employees just as a reflection of business.  Labor costs have to match the volume.  On the restaurant side, we have about the same amount of business – we have a little more in weddings this year than we did in '08. It's interesting what sectors out there are still really active and which are down.

KCM: You run this business with your brother Joe. What are some of the challenges of running a business with a family member?

VL:    It has to really be communication. If there's something that needs to be purchased, he has to know. He's a co-signer on all of the loans. We have a system that anything over $1,000 we have to both sign. That's a requirement we've placed on ourselves so we force ourselves to communicate about major purchases.

The other problem in dealing with a partner who is a family member is he may have a different idea on what direction a certain aspect of the business should go versus myself. For example, if we've got two projects that need to be done, which project should go first? I might think we need new mattresses, the guests need them. He has a very strong idea about redoing the exterior with major landscaping work. How do we come to an agreement?

Those issues come up maybe once a quarter. Some we can talk about and resolve quickly. On others we dance around for days or months, or we just shelve it and come back and talk about it later. That's probably the biggest problem. If I didn't have a co-owner who is a family member, it might not be so stressful because it wouldn't be a family member. The way I internally resolve it is to think of Joe as a shareholder.

If it was just a private business with just me and I didn't have to answer to anybody, it'd be very easy. But it's not, these are the cards dealt. I have a partner who is my brother that I have to remind myself, "I have to tell him," or, "I can't let this contract go out without him seeing it," and either initialing or at least agreeing with the direction we're going. It's work, but that's why I get paid, to perform my ownership duties.

KCM: Have you ever had any non-family investors in your business?

VL:　No. The last time was this Louis who ran the restaurant. He was a tenant of the building. That was the closest we ever had. After the nightclub shut down – I think you were there until that shut down.

KCM: It shut down shortly after I left.

VL:　It was vacant for two years. Then we converted it to an area for breakfast, only for hotel guests. Then we shut that down and moved breakfast back to the dining room. Later we converted it to a banquet facility. My brother wanted to get back into the nightclub business. Four years ago, we slowly started moving into redecorating, redesigning the interior using to make it a nightclub. With the bad economy, we just stopped the project altogether for the last year. Before the economy went bad, we talked to a few other people about being investors in this. Being that it was my brother's primary focus, it was his baby to do that.

We were talking to a couple possible investors. After a while, he decided he didn't want to have investors. He wasn't sure how they'd perform, what they'd demand. When you say you are looking for investors for a nightclub, all kinds of people of various levels of social quality come out. After seeing a few resumes and meeting a few folks, he said it's better to be on his own. It's safer. He could make decisions completely on his own and not have to worry what a partner is doing.

We grew up in the neighborhood and my brother went to school with a lot of guys in the police department. He knows everybody around here. Everybody knows him. He's got a good, clean reputation. Nobody ever doubts the way we operate. Nobody wonders if we are dealing drugs, money laundering, or any of those types of things. It's safer not to put that reputation at risk by bringing in a partner.

KCM: Just a few weeks ago, Planet Hollywood in Las Vegas had their nightclub closed down, apparently because of issues going on with the way the tenants were operating it. Reputation is like fine china. Easily broken; never fully repaired.

VL: We've got enough challenges on our own. We don't need sidebar drama going on with an investor.

KCM: Seems like a good strategy. Are there any business people who have been influential for you? Obviously, your parents were. Outside of your family, is there anyone you've admired and who has influenced your approach to management?

VL: It's an interesting thing. Growing up, there were all these heroes I wanted to emulate, like the astronauts. We come from that era. Now that I've gotten in the business of working every day and the company is on the line, the bank loans are on the line, and we've got to make payroll and make all the business operation decisions, the people I look up to are people who have similar challenges.

I like to look and see how they've operated and gotten through problems. A lot of these people were written up in the industry trade journals and hotel magazines. They'd pick a guy every quarter and write about where he's from and what he's done.

KCM: One of the things that has been a driving force in our business has been the importance of repeat customers. The person who first drilled that into my head was your mother. She once told me something along the lines of, "It costs five times more to get a new customer than to get a happy customer back." I have this acronym I use. We want our business to be SLEEC, which stands for top notch in sales/marketing and with loyal, engaged employees and customers. What are the central themes you think about in terms of how you manage your business?

VL: The basic thing is we want to be in every [marketing] venue that is appropriate for the business we have. We try to spend in the venues where our target customers are going to see us. The regular customers who provide us the bulk of business, we want to maintain them and keep them happy.

We always say in our sales meeting to grab the top 20 and go visit them. Make sure they're happy. We have a sales person who will go on a sales blitz or a campaign in the neighborhood and the first thing we want him to do is <u>not</u> to go look for new business. It's more expensive and harder to find a new customer than it is to get that old, familiar customer and enhance their business at our property. Make their visit and view of our property as somewhere they want to go to and send referrals.

KCM: How about the best and worst aspects of running a business? What do you like best and least?

VL:    The best is doing a certain project and having it happen, be it remodeling, a sales campaign, or a certain advertising contract. Entering into these projects and having them turn out successfully, and even exceeding expectations. The worst is dealing with people problems, maybe from an unhappy guest, one that might have been handled wrongly, and we are trying to right that wrong, or the basic thief and crook. That can sometimes be an employee. It can be wrenching to have to deal with employee issues when there's a big tussle going on. He said, she said.

They claim one thing, and we claim another. That's no fun when dealing with stressful personnel issues.

KCM: I can relate.

VL:    That's probably the hardest thing. Everything else is more of a project or defined goal you can modify or work at or tweak and come to agreements. Personnel issues are tough.

KCM: How about business books? Are there any ones you've read that you've found particularly useful?

VL:    Yours, of course [*Beating the Dow with Rental Houses*]. Over the years, there have been a lot of books. I tend toward books that have similar material to yours. They're the ones I tend to read to reaffirm what I'm doing and reaffirm the business model we are using. We haven't become such a large grandiose corporation where we're doing Class A, Class B stocks, bonds, etc. We're still operating as a privately held operation, albeit with corporations or LLCs.

From reading over the years I can see that real estate holdings and wealth development have basically been the same, but have been tweaked, modified, and improved upon by various authors. It's fun to read those books. I gravitate to those areas.

KCM: I have to say that working for your parents was hugely influential in my life, and it makes me really think about how my life would be different if I had not had those experiences. It'd be enormously different in many ways. I was always interested in science, and I pursued education in science. Because of working in the hotel I got interested in real estate and business, in many ways those experiences set me on a new path.

VL:    Yeah. Pretty lucky to have been exposed to that.

KCM: I often wonder, "What if I had just worked at the McDonalds?" I'd probably have a different view of the world.

VL:    What if you went to college and just studied the stuff. Would it have had the same effect? Probably not. And this job is so much real world that you can't replace experiencing it with an internship. They just don't quite equate.

KCM: Absolutely. I owe your family a big debt of gratitude. How about bits of advice you'd give to someone considering starting a business? If you could give them a few pieces of information on what to do, what not do, what would they be?

VL:    Probably one of the things to do is show up every day. Be on-site absolutely every day, even if only electronically. Cell phone, fax, computer. You've got to be there every day. Even if it's a real estate job that doesn't require your presence, make it so people feel your presence and know that you are aware of what is going on. Staff will then have a certain respect for you as a manager, operator, owner, etc. Another thing is to be in very easy speaking terms with the business-banking department at your bank.

You can stay in touch with them on what's happening. As you learn, you can teach the bankers about the current trends. Then they look at you as the expert, and they're more comfortable in a lending situation. Be a member of appropriate associations. Either an owner's association or a civic association. There are a lot of civic associations, and unfortunately, a person doesn't have time to be involved in every one.

You might end up joining 20 at first. Then you've got to whittle it down to those that are valuable for the business. You really have to make every membership count and participate in those that align with your business motives.

It's good to have hobbies. A hobby is a good stress reliever, and it gets your mind completely off job stress and gets your batteries recharged to go back at it again. I think those are a few bits of advice.

KCM: How about mistakes? Any particular mistakes you tell people to watch out for?

VL:    Don't sell yourself short. Don't think you can't qualify for something. You've got to think you can qualify for everything. Let the other party say no rather telling yourself no. Go ask the bank for a loan rather telling yourself, "No, I'll never get the money. I shouldn't bother." Also, just like I talked about before, don't get involved with unethical partners or contractors.

Don't buy any make money quick stories. That just doesn't exist. That kind of money doesn't exist. You can gamble for entertainment, but get rich quick schemes really don't exist. People make money the old-fashioned way, and I think that'll happen forever.

KCM:  I like to say your typical overnight success had ten or 15 years of hard work preceding the overnight success.

VL:  Yep.

KCM:  How about promoting a positive culture?  How do you promote that within your employees and on your properties?

VL:  One way is to communicate very openly and continually with the staff so everybody knows what personality and goals you have.  It's sort of constant communication.  People know what level of quality you are, what kind of standards you want, what kind of goals you want for the business, where you want it to go, and what expectations you have.  You don't have to be demanding, but constant communications will transmit that information to the staff.

That way, they'll be able to sign on to the goals of the company.  That way, they all have a clear idea.  That really helps their motivation.  They're much happier when they know where the ship is going.

KCM:  I was surprised a couple years ago when I called the front desk at the Holiday Inn.  The guy who answered the phone is someone I trained 18 years earlier.  I noticed you have a fair number of people working there who I knew 20 years ago.  You've been very successful at keeping some key individuals.  What do you attribute that to?

VL:  Communication.  If you talk to everybody continually and keep everybody involved, they're much happier.  As an owner, you're much happier that they understand where we're going.  It is a unique thing when you look at our hotels.  We have a very low turnover.  Much lower than the industry on average.  For example, a typical restaurant has a – I heard a number like a nine or 12 month average turnover.  Our average employee stays several years.  I guess eight, nine, ten for all staff positions.

It's an interesting thing. We don't get involved in the staff socially to where we go to family's parties. We still visit with everybody on the job, talk to everybody, make sure they're doing okay, and continually stay in communication with them. It helps all the way around.

KCM: One of the things I cover in the book is research done by Bain and Company in which they identified the two strongest predictors of profitability, which has held up in industry after industry. Lower employee turnover and lower customer defection were the factors associated with higher profits. It doesn't surprise me that you have continued to do well, given my experiences in your company, and I was there for ten years. I think you've got both of those profit predictors.

VL:     Yeah, like I talked about the employee status that people tend to stay a long time here. If a customer is on the verge of leaving, it's like a 20 alarm fire. We go all out to get a hold of them, rectify what was going on, and make them happy with the appropriate services or prices. It's a major thing. If a customer is ready to leave, we don't take that lightly at all. I think everybody on property knows that. In the early days of the Holiday Inn franchise, back in the '80s when we first signed on, they had one of those catch words in their training – it was empowerment. We tried to identify what we could do to empower line employees and line managers to keep a customer happy. Part of that is we give them power to give discounts or comp things. We tell different employees and managers that if you've got to do it, do it and we'll stand behind you. As long as it's keeping the customer happy. To make sure everybody is honest, we just say, "Document it." Give me as much information on who that person was, or what company they were with, and what the problem was and what you gave away. As long as they're documenting everything, it keeps employees on an honest level.

KCM: One of the stories I recount in the book is a film I saw of Steve Wynn from Las Vegas who was just about to open the Wynn Resort. He was giving a talk to his entire staff. He was saying, "I can't be everywhere. You have to be there for me. I want you to make it right for the customer. If the customer has been wronged in some way, if an order got screwed up, the room service order wasn't right, or something took longer than it should, do what you need to do to make it right. Keep them happy." I'd recommend visiting the Wynn property if you get a chance to. They're exemplary in customer service.

VL:    We were there a couple years ago. We saw Steve Wynn walking around in a lounge jacket or something. One of those old Hugh Heffner smoking jackets. He looked like he just came from dinner at his house. He personalizes the whole business.

KCM: He sure does.

VL:    That's important.

KCM: Are there any questions I should have asked but didn't?

VL:    Not everything is for everybody. My brother, on his own, he tried to get into apartment buildings. That wasn't his cup of tea. Everybody has a different personality and temperament. The most basic way a person in America can achieve wealth is through real estate or business ownership. It's up to that person to find out what they can tolerate as far as risk, stress, and the type of business they want to deal with. That takes real honest introspection. It may take a couple false starts like my brother with the apartment building, but you've got to go out there and do it. You've got to try it and see what flavor it is.

KCM: I knew from working with your parents that I wanted to get into real estate. I thought about apartment buildings and other approaches. I eventually ended up with single-family houses, which worked well for me. That's been a good fit with my goals and what I like to do.

VL:    Everybody has a different personality. They need to be able to work that into their goals for the same reasons you said.

KCM:  Any other thoughts or comments or burning ideas you want to communicate to the world?

VL:   Have a good lawyer and a good accountant you can trust to do your taxes and watch out for you.  As a business operator, you're probably not a real expert in all the ever changing tax laws. So it's good to have somebody that's easy to talk to and is a real expert in those areas.  The money you pay sometimes seems expensive, but it's worth it in the long run.

KCM:  Very good advice.

*Chapter 15*

# Rose Hanbury – Night Light Designs

## (www.NightLightDesigns.com)

*A goal is a dream with a deadline.*

– Napoleon Hill

Rose Hanbury is a former employee of our clinical research company. She left our company for the best possible reason – because her side-business had become so successful that it made more sense for her to do that full-time than to work for us as an employee. Now in its fourth year, her company has done so well that her husband recently quit his job to join her on a full-time basis. Rose has taken an unconventional path to entrepreneurship and I hope you find her story as interesting and inspiring as I have.

KCM: Thank you for agreeing to an interview.

RH:   Thank you very much, Kevin. It's a pleasure to be here. Thank you for inviting me.

KCM: Tell me about your history. You started out in art school, and then you ended up in neuroscience, and somehow, you evolved from art school to neuroscience to night lights. How did that happen?

RH:     I went to art school back in Detroit, but didn't finish.  I went for three years, then decided I could do it on my own.  I didn't need a degree to do photography.  I moved to Chicago and worked for a couple photo houses.  They closed.  Then I went back to UIC (University of Illinois at Chicago) for biology.  So I got my undergrad degree there.  I just happened to have taken this one course in which they took us around to all these different places.  It was kind of like a fieldtrip.  We were at Rush [University] in one of the labs.  The person who was giving us this tour was a PhD.

Just before we were leaving, another doctor says, "Hey, anybody know photography?"  I said "I do."  Back then, in scientific publishing, figures had to be black and white photos.  So I got in there doing volunteer work, and they sucked me in.  I got my PhD from there.  I got a post-doc [post-doctoral fellowship] here at University of Illinois at Chicago.

There was nothing else going on.  When the grant money ran out there, this really cool company hired me.  Very cool company. [Note:  that would be when the author hired Rose.]

KCM: They've got a great reputation, I've heard.

RH:     Yes, they do.  It was a pleasure to work with them.

During that time when I was toward the end of being here, my husband, Bob, who worked in information technology, kept getting laid off.  Companies weren't hiring.  They were hiring for only three months at a time.  He was really kind of disgusted with that.  He said, "We need to start our own company."  When we got married in Vegas, we went to a Monet exhibit.  We found a really cute light.  We bought it.  I think it was a Van Gogh.

KCM: Was it a night light?

RH:     Yeah.  It was a light we bought, and we loved it.  It was the coolest thing I'd ever seen.  About a year after that, Bob says,

"Why don't we do something like that, but only do custom." So that's how the business started, custom night lights. Since he was laid off for three months, he could do all the early work. That's how we got that cool web site. We started doing custom photos. Little by little, it started growing. Not a lot in custom, but because we had that website, which gave us great credibility. Our website was very small at the time, but it was nice and professionally done.

We had gone to the French Market in Wheaton [Illinois] and thought, "I'd love to sell night lights at the French Market," but we were only doing custom. You can't really sell a custom product there. Our nightlights are more of an impulse buy. People want to take something with them. So we found 24 images and displayed them on the original boxes Bob built.

They're green. They're shadow boxes. We got that idea from IKEA in the frame department. How do you display night lights? It looks tacky on a light strip. We wanted to look professional. So 'Bob the builder' built two light cases; each with 12 lights. We had to come up with 24 images. We bought images. I had one. We made a couple. We were trying to go for that French market feel. Everything had to do with flowers and vegetables. That was our imagery. We obtained a Vegas image.

KCM: Vegas is universal.

RH: We got the idea from Vegas, so that's why. We had the 24 images. This is going into our fourth year, so three summers ago. This is our third summer doing it. We had our 24 images. We didn't know what we were doing. We invested so much money into it. There are big minimums [for orders from wholesalers].

KCM: The night light frames, how many were in your first purchases of those?

RH: Fifteen thousand. Originally, we were going to do ten thousand. That was the minimum, but it was only one direction, portrait, not landscape. We had only bought portraits, but a lot of the photos we were finding had a landscape orientation to it. We had to have another 5,000 landscape. It turns out, landscapes were bigger sellers. Hey, live and learn. You've got to know who the audience is. You just go with it. So we had our 24 images. It was the beginning of April. We actually sold $200.00 worth of lights, and we were only selling them for $10.00. So we sold 20 lights on our first time out there [at the French Market].

We sold enough to pay for our booth for the rest of the month. After that, we thought, "This is all gravy." We started looking for holiday images – people started asking us, and we started listening to what people were requesting. "Do you have this?" Then we write down the ideas, go home, search the internet. Bob was really good with this. He found a few Christmas images, so he contacted the artist. She says, "This is my licensing agency. You need to talk with them." So we did, and that's how I got started with the licensing. So that snowball effect is huge.

KCM: The licensing agency probably has lots of artists, and that would give you more opportunities.

RH:    Right. I think the first – she was kind of country – Theresa Kogut. Her images are on a lot of paper products. You've probably seen her stuff around on cards, paper. Great artist. It was not her, but her licensing agent that gave us our first break. Who are we? But we had that website that made us look very professional. So we showcased her. I think she's still showcased on the website. Once you get one licensing agency, others started contacting us and it was easier to get more. We pay on time. We are very professional about it.

It's a small little community with those licensing agents. So the word gets around. They started coming to us. We started with 24 images. Those we own outright, those first 24. Now we have over 1,400. I think about 70 percent are all licensed.

KCM: So you pay a royalty to the artists through the agency for each sale you make.

RH:     Exactly.  We have to track those sales.  Today is my deadline for sending in royalties for the last quarter.  We have to make our deadline.  The payment is going to be in the mail today.

KCM:  What were some of the biggest challenges, the difficulties, or what things created the biggest roadblocks for you when you were getting started?

RH:     Everybody knows that stuff is made in China, so the communication was big.  Especially when dealing with large production like that and minimums.  It seemed to go okay.  I don't consider that a huge roadblock.  That was a challenge.  The next challenge was money.  Where do we get the money?  They don't give you a business loan if you haven't been in business.  They still don't give you a business loan even if you are in business.  So we used a $25,000 home equity line of credit.  During the year prior to starting the business, we were afraid Bob was going to be out of a job so we had established this credit line.

So we had our equity line of credit.  I guess we were lucky in that we had a friend that developed the website.  That was key for credibility with people who have never met us and want to do business with us.  Time is always an issue.  We were both working full time.

To find the time takes a lot of work.  Because Bob was laid off, that could have been the biggest roadblock.  It should have been, but he couldn't find a job for three months.  Him being laid off helped us enormously.  What he did in three months probably would have taken close to a year just to do if we were both working.  I guess we were lucky in that sense.  We didn't have any huge roadblocks.  Roadblocks came later on when we wanted to expand the business a bit and trying to get a loan or line of credit.  That was a nightmare.

KCM:  That was some bad timing.  [That was about the time of the financial crisis and credit crunch.]

RH:     Yeah, again, a friend who was a bank manager got me a line of credit and we were able to do everything we needed to do: buy more computers, buy more printers, buy more paper. All those things cost money. That took six months for me to finally say, "Can you help me? I'm having a hard time getting a loan. I can't even get $20,000 on my equity, and I have a lot of equity in my house." That was frustration beyond frustration. That was a huge roadblock, but that worked itself out, too.

KCM: It sounds like having relationships with people who could help you out was very important.

RH:     Absolutely. That goes for a lot of things because you can't do everything when you have a business.

KCM: Absolutely, it not's possible.

RH:     It is impossible, and people who think it is possible probably fail. That's my best guess. You need help. Our next is getting a really good accountant because we're going to have payroll in the fourth quarter. Uncle Sam is going to want his cut every quarter. That's okay because I'm going to rely on employees to help me with this business. That's another one of those things.

KCM: So you're moving to that next level where it's more than just you and Bob. Scary times.

RH:     Little bit. But we've got to take the chance.

KCM: You have to do it if you want to get to the next level. You can't do it all yourself.

RH:     You have to take the risk.

KCM: Knowing what you know now, is there anything you'd do differently?

RH: Yeah. We did a trade show that was run by the Craft and Hobby Association, the CHA. We have art kits. We thought, "Let's showcase the art kits. We'll have all these buyers." It was the Chicago area, so we didn't have to pay a lot for transportation. We just pay the cost of labor and the booth. We get there, and we're in the general crafts area. We come to find out that 80 percent of this very large trade show was scrapbooking. All the buyers that came were buying for scrapbooking. We're talking big buyers. Michaels and all the stores like that.

You hear screams and yells, and they're having a party ten aisles down. You hear crickets in general crafts. Nobody was there to buy general crafts. I think we need to do a little more research into the type of tradeshow that it is now compared to what it used to be. That was a lesson learned. We lost money on that. That was a hard lesson learned.

KCM: What percentage of your sales are from the website versus various in person booths and shows and so forth?

RH: I'd say 80 percent of our income is face-to-face retail. The other 10 percent is internet sales and 10 percent wholesale.

KCM: Soon you can send out an announcement to everyone about the kiosk that you're going to be having at Woodfield Mall.

RH: Yeah, that's another one, too. We have that on the website already. That's a done deal.

KCM: What about night-lights versus your Glowtastic!® U Draw Night Light Art Kits, which I think are super cool?

RH: They are cool. Kids really like them, and any markers work, so it's not something that you need special equipment for. Everyone has markers around the house if they have kids. Bob said to my daughter, "Here, draw something." She did. She drew a turkey. We put it in the night light, and we thought, "Wow, we've got ourselves a new product line."

They've started gaining more popularity, but they're taking a slower ride than the pre-design. I think maybe just because the pre-designs are a broader thing. The people who purchase the night lights are women from 35 to 80. I would say 35 to 65 definitely. That's our buying population. People do buy them for their grandkids, but they don't buy them as much as we hoped they would. They are maybe 15 percent of our sales. We got an actual registered trademark.

KCM: I saw that. Did you do that through an attorney?

RH: Yeah. The process is quite interesting.

KCM: They have to do the searches.

RH: Yeah. It took about a year. I was expecting it to take longer to get that little R [®] on the end of it.

KCM: What about marketing? What do you do when you're going to shows and having your website, how do you let people know you're out there?

RH: We don't advertise on the internet, but we're connected to enough – what are those little things you click on other peoples' sites – we come up when you search for night lights, we're on the first page of Google.

KCM: Yeah, I found you on the first page of Google.

RH: That took a couple of years.

KCM: So it took a couple years to move from Page 11 to page 1?

RH: Yeah and we were trying to think of ways to get up higher in accent lighting. For accent lighting we're on the third page, and the pre-designs are definitely accent lighting, too. They're not just night lights. We started putting that in the first page of the webpage. We did a lot of that with trying to be more creative and trying to get on more peoples' websites and that kind of thing. I think that helped us a lot that we're on so many websites.

KCM: Getting to that first page is the Holy Grail. What percentage of your sales do you think are repeat customers versus people buying for the first time?

RH:     Repeat customers are huge. I would say at least 60 to 70 percent are repeat customers. It probably goes even higher if they refer somebody. You see these little pockets of areas like in South Carolina. We have a little following. In New Jersey, we have a following. It's definitely – if it's not a repeat, they have told somebody about us.

KCM: Word of mouth and repeat business. Have you tried using any lists to send out information to people who might have similar interests? Hobby craft kind of lists.

RH:     No. As far as the marketing goes, toy directories, TD Monthly is a website, and it's associated with the toy industry. I've been with them about a year. I did a lot of advertising with them. Unfortunately, the people who actually contact me about the Glowtastic!® product are people who are closeout buyers. Lots of closeout buyers. So I dropped that advertising, but I'm still on their magazine website. It wasn't that expensive, but that got the name out there a little bit.

KCM: Do you have retail outlets? I know in the past, we've talked about hotel gift shops and that sort of thing. How many of those do you have?

RH:     That's climbing. As far as how many – it's usually in the Midwest. Minnesota, Wisconsin, Michigan, Ohio, Indiana and Iowa. Just because that's where it's close enough for them to drive in. We've got to be close to 30 now.

KCM: What kinds of retailers are there? Are they mostly in downtown shopping areas?

RH:    Yeah. I think so. I'm starting to get a lot of historical museums with their own image of some kind of landmark specific to their hometown.

KCM: Can they provide you with the picture of some sort, and then you can create the night light for them?

RH:    I tried to sell that. "Well, if you don't see anything you like," because they have their badge, and it says, "New Zealand." I would say, "Let me tell you what we can do." So we're getting out there with the retail.

KCM: A lot of success in business comes from building a reputation and building trust with your customers.

RH:    I 100 percent guarantee everything.

KCM: How do you build trust? I put that question in because I saw your guarantee on your website, which I thought was great. Tell me how you build trust, and maybe have you had any disputes with customers, and how did you handle those?

RH:    First of all, we pride ourselves on our customer service. We bend over backward to keep a customer happy if possible. They'll pass on a bad word, and bad words travel. I tell people, "Bring it home, plug it in. If you don't like it, bring it back and I'll give you your money back or you can exchange it. No problem." A lot of people love that. I tell that to everybody when they're hemming and hawing about something.

Or if they bought it as a gift for somebody and the person doesn't like the image, I say to just bring it back. I'll refund you. Because we're dealing with tens of thousands, there's going to be that small percentage that don't work or break. We replace it with no problem. We try to help people out. If they're really dissatisfied, we'll say "pick out an insert for your troubles." We try to really push the customer service and make sure they're buying something without buyer remorse.

They can return it if they want to, but they usually don't. We've only had one complaint, and it had to do with the mail. The address was correct, but their post office returned it to us. The customer was really irate, so we sent them out a brand new one by overnight courier, which cost us about $50.00. So she got it on time for whatever she needed it for. She still blamed us. That's out of my control. We really haven't had to deal with anybody else who was irate. We try not to even have that scenario occur.

KCM: Prevent it, but some are unpreventable.

RH:   Exactly.

KCM: If you can at least have the person leave feeling that they were treated fairly, even if they weren't completely happy with the outcome.

RH:   I had a woman from Iowa write me a long letter with how displeased she was saying, "I just bought this light and it broke." There was no phone number and nowhere to contact her. I mailed back a brand new base, and then I put an extra LED that should last for eight years. I mailed that with a thank you for your troubles. Stuff like that. Keep the peace. Build trust. They'll tell somebody that these people are great to deal with. Even all the licensing agencies love to deal with us, too.

We're always on time. Even though we're a small company – and their artists love our products. Our artists that we license from buy nightlights from us with their images inside.

KCM: They buy their own picture.

RH:   They do, but because they don't get the 6 percent or 10 percent royalty from those sales, we give them a discount.

KCM: So, if you were talking to someone who is thinking about starting a business –

RH:   Don't do night lights.

KCM:  What advice would you give someone if the person said, "What are the most important things I'm going to need to know about starting a business?  What would be those one or two things?"

RH:  It's not going to happen overnight.  You can't think that what you see as far as my business comes overnight – that wasn't built in a day.  It was one brick at a time, and it took us a full year to get us up and running until I was in that French market. You've got to do the steps, be patient, don't rush it.  Do it right.  Ask people.  Definitely hire a lawyer.

KCM:  There's all sorts of things.  Product liability, trademarks, you have to incorporate.

RH:  Yeah, in order to get any of that, you have to incorporate. That takes a couple of months, and it costs a couple thousand dollars.

KCM:  How is your business structured?  Is it an S corporation?

RH:  Yes, 500 shares.

KCM:  I only have 50.  I love your answer about being patient and doing it right from the start.

RH:  Thank you.  We really had everything in place before we went live.  You can't run a business if you don't have a bank account.  And you can't get a business bank account without being incorporated.  You can't get a resale license without being incorporated.  There are all these little steps.  It costs money. Yeah, but think of it as an investment, but you'll get a return on that investment.  It's just a temporary loan.

KCM:  It's a temporary loan, and the business is going to pay you back with a lot of interest if you do it right.  What about mistakes? What mistakes would you tell someone to avoid who is just getting started?

RH:    Make sure you do your research.  If you're talking a few hundred bucks, you don't know if it's going to be a mistake or not, try it.  If it is, it's not going to be heart wrenching.

KCM:  Try a bunch of things and keep what works.

RH:    You have to try stuff – you can have a business plan, but sometimes that doesn't always go in the direction you want it to.  You try to force it to, but it doesn't want to go that way.  Don't make the mistake of forcing it to go that way.  If your customers want you to do something, you do that.

KCM:  As it turns out, one of the things I say in the book is you can't sell people what you think they need.  You can only sell people what they want.

RH:    That's so true.  You have to listen to the customers.  I think that's why we have so many images now.  Bob is working with a woman he met at one of the shows.  She says, "You have no Indian stuff."  We got on Flickr, Shutter Point and bought some more commercial artwork in that genre.  Now we're going to have Indian and Kwanza images.  Just listen to what people want.

KCM:  Yeah, I really picked up on that when you said you go to the French market or go other places, and people would ask you if you have this.  You'd write it down.  That's great to get that feedback from customers.  Are there any individuals that have had a large influence on you?

RH:    Good or bad?

KCM:  Is there someone else who had a business, and you said, "Wow, I'd like to be able to do something like that?"

RH:    Yes.  One of my best friends, Shari in Detroit, ran a one hour photo lab for many years.  She had it for about ten years.  I always admired the fact that it was her business, she ran it, and she owned it. I thought that was the coolest thing.

KCM: You mentioned a business plan. Did you have a formal business plan?

RH:   No. Very loosely in our heads kind of business plan.

KCM: What about goals? Do you set goals on a regular basis for the business and write them down?

RH:   We don't write them down, but we do set goals. We want to be doing this by X date. It's funny because Bob has his little area he's good at, and I have my little area I'm good at. So I'm the one who is pushing the trade shows, pushing the retail. He has to build the cases. The goals change all the time, constantly. Our goal right now is – depending on how this Woodfield [shopping mall] kiosk thing goes, if it goes well, that's a new direction where we can manage several kiosks.

KCM: Can you see yourself having many kiosks that are run by other people?

RH:   Absolutely. We've already discussed and talked about that. He's building the prototype. He won't be building these anymore if it goes well. This is the prototype. This is what we want.

KCM: That's the way you guarantee it'll look the way you want it to look, and then you can say to someone who is going to build it, "We want it to look like this."

RH:   Exactly. The funny part is that I don't think anyone else could have built it how we wanted it because we both know exactly what we want. We both have the same vision because we've been doing it for three years. Where the lights should be, how it should look, how many should be in there. You don't want to overcrowd it, but you don't want it to look too sparse because then it looks ridiculous.

KCM: There's definitely a balance.  Studies in psychology show that if you give people too many choices, they don't buy anything because they're overwhelmed.

RH:     I think we have 96 lights.  We could have fit 108.  I said, "No, it's going to be too much for them to be looking at a wall of lights.  If we break it up a bit and stagger it, at least it's not a line.  Your eye doesn't just go straight across and it becomes one big light."

KCM: It's like an ad in the newspaper.  If there's white space around it, people are more apt to notice it.

RH:     Right, the negative space.

Yeah, our goals are always changing.  When we first started, our goal was to just do online.  Then like, "I want to do retail."

KCM: I love your story because it started as something small and became bigger and bigger.  Now I'm looking at this and saying, "Wow, if this shopping mall kiosk works, I could see your company having many kiosks."  I was just recently reading a story about a guy who had a restaurant.  He ended up getting involved in the movie business.  He didn't have any idea what he was doing, but he bought a mobile kitchen.  He had nothing to compare it to since he had never seen this done before.

He provided much better quality food than the folks on movie sets were accustomed to getting.  His business took off from there.  He started with this one mobile kitchen.  When he bought it, he produced a high quality product.  He painted on the side of it, "Mobile Kitchen No. 3."  So he'd look like a bigger business.  Now a lot of top level actors are having it written into their contract that his service must provide the food.

RH:     See.  Gain trust.

KCM: But now he has 50 of these mobile kitchens. That made me think that you could have 50, 100, 200, 400 kiosks all over the country. That's kind of exciting.

RH: Yeah. About a year ago, somebody asked me – you know the pickle guy? A little franchise. I think that's what they're called. Really good pickles. All different kinds. They do kiosks in smaller malls. A couple years ago, he said, "You should do a kiosk in a mall like we do." I said, "Yeah, I bought pickles from you guys in a kiosk." He kind of planted the seed for me. I looked into it. I've got to go for the top, the best. It's going to cost you a little extra money, but the traffic and people that come through there.

KCM: So that'd be another person who was kind of a model for you. So the pickle guy had a model that you could maybe adapt for your business. Are there any business books you've read that you've found useful?

RH: I like those tapes you lent me that one time. Piranha Marketing. We must have been doing something right because a lot of what they said in there, we've already done or were going to be doing. Those are good, helpful tapes. I read a lot online, the Entrepreneur.com. I read the articles there if I need to know something.

KCM: What are the best and worst aspects of running your own business?

RH: The best, of course, is you're your own boss. You can run things the way you want. No one is telling you what to do, how to do it, or blah, blah, blah. The worst is you're never not working. You're constantly working. Always working. But you love it. I wouldn't have it any other way. It's quite nice.

KCM: Most people I know who have run businesses and had some success with them say, "I can't even imagine going back to a job."

RH:     No, I don't think I could.

KCM: It's hard.  Being able to do things the way you want.  It's hard to think about it any other way.

RH:     It is.  It's true.  You don't know until you try it.  It's like, "Oh, that feels good."  You're right.  The downside is you're a slave to your job, to your baby.

KCM: There are always things waiting to be done.

RH:     Yeah.  We have – speaking of back to goals, I'd like to expand the product, but right now, everything is so tight time wise and money wise.  Woodfield is going to suck us dry on rent.

KCM: The flip side is if it does really well –

RH:     Oh yeah, I'm sure we're going to do very well.  I already started doing other products, but I had to put those on hold and will have to wait until next year.  That's one of my goals.

KCM: I totally understand.  We're trying to get our website up and everything with our publishing business, which is a new venture.  I've got this other business to run.  It's hard to find the time for what needs to be done over here.

RH:     Now you've got to get laid off of your current job so you can work on your new job.

KCM: I don't think that will happen.  Are there any questions I should have asked you but didn't?

RH:     No, I think I've been a motor mouth.

KCM: Are there any ideas, thoughts, or words of wisdom that you'd like to convey to people who read this book?

RH:     If you are going to try to do your own business, it takes time.  It's not going to happen overnight.  Don't give up on it.  If you believe in it, don't give up.  Definitely listen to your customer base.

KCM:  I heard a great quote the other day.  It was, "Largely, success is a matter of hanging on when everyone else has let go." Listen to your customers.  Be patient.  It doesn't happen overnight.  Be persistent, and listen to your customers.  Right?

RH:    Right.  And always look for new avenues.  How can I sell my product?  Where can I sell my product?  Who is selling my product?  Who is my competition?  That kind of thing.  It's trial and error, too.  You're probably going to fail at half of it, and the other half will do really well at it.

KCM:  That's the famous line about, "I know that half my marketing budget is wasted.  I just don't know which half."

RH:    That's about it.  That's all I can think of it.  Unless you have more questions.

KCM:  Thank you.

RH:    You're welcome.

*Chapter 16*

# Anthony Curtis – Huntington Press and *Las Vegas Advisor*

## (www.HuntingtonPress.com and www.LasVegasAdvisor.com)

*Your ability to learn faster than your competition is your only sustainable competitive advantage.*

– Arie de Gues

I have been a long-time subscriber to the *Las Vegas Advisor* and a big fan of Huntington Press. Years ago, when I was a graduate student, I earned a portion of my income playing blackjack (counting cards) in Las Vegas (putting my training in statistics to good use). I still love going to Las Vegas and stop in for a few days whenever I am traveling to the west coast. I also go to Las Vegas regularly when working on a book. I can only write effectively for about four hours a day, so it is great to be in an interesting place where I can have as much solitude as I need to get my writing done, but also have interesting things to do after I am finished writing for the day.

Anthony Curtis's *Las Vegas Advisor* is, hands down, the best source I know of for up-to-date information on what is happening in Las Vegas. A subscription is a great deal at only $50 for 12 issues a year. In addition, the newsletter comes with a coupon book containing roughly 150 valuable coupons for hotels, dining, entertainment, gambling and rental cars. Using just one or two of the coupons often generates enough savings to more than pay for the subscription. People who live in or near Las Vegas can literally obtain hundreds of dollars in savings. Anthony's publishing company (Huntington Press) produces *The Las Vegas Advisor* as well as software, strategy cards and books, including mathematically rigorous gambling titles such as *The Theory of Blackjack, The Frugal Gambler; Frugal Video Poker; Knock-Out Blackjack*; and the poker tournament books *Kill Phil* and *Kill Everyone*. The Huntington Press title list also includes such items as *Kidding Around Las Vegas*, *Gay Vegas*, *Golf Las Vegas* and *Hiking Las Vegas*. In addition, it contains books on topics ranging from casino management (*Casino-ology*) to getting the most from casino player program (*Comp City*). When it comes to all aspects of Las Vegas, there is no more authoritative source than Huntington Press. Anthony is a sought after expert on Las Vegas and games of chance and he regularly makes appearances on network and cable television. You have probably seen him if you have watched a few of the many shows about Las Vegas on the Travel Channel.

I met Anthony in his office in February of 2009 during the midst of a terrible recession. Unemployment in Las Vegas had climbed to more than 10% and large casino companies such as MGM and Harrah's were scrambling to stay solvent. While most business owners were hunkering down to ride out the storm, Anthony was planning significant expansions. In the several months since the interview, two new *Las Vegas Advisor* companion web sites have been launched and several new titles have been added to the Huntington Press library. Below are the questions I asked and his responses, with some editing due to space constraints.

KCM: Tell me about your history. How did you come to start the Las Vegas Advisor?

AC: Essentially, what happened was I was just a kid growing up in Detroit and I was game player. And by that, I mean, that's what we did in my household. I was playing Pinochle with the grown-ups, when I was 4 and 5 years old, and by no means, any math prodigy in that regard, but I did pick up gambling, card games and games of skill.

I also had pretty much an innate ability to understand probability before I was taught it, so we would play games like Monopoly, so I was understanding probability, and I was applying that to game playing. When I was – I believe I was probably a junior in high school, somebody gave me a book on card counting. I read it and I got it, and I saw what card counting could do, so from that point forward, from about 11$^{th}$ grade in high school through college, I was spending more time reading books on gambling than I was other subjects.

[Note: card counting is a method used to obtain an advantage over the casino in the game of blackjack. It involves keeping track of the ratio of low and high value cards that have been dealt. Since the deck or shoe of cards is not shuffled after every hand, the remaining cards in the deck will be advantageous to the player when there are a lot of high value cards left and more advantageous to the house when there is a high concentration of low value cards left in the deck or shoe. This is one of the legal methods that advantage players can use to play with an edge against the casino.]

So I was a high school wrestler and I was pretty good. I was a runner-up in Michigan State, Class A, so I got some good offers from college, and I went originally to Georgia Tech, and then subsequently, to Duke on wrestling scholarships. So as I was nearing 21 and I transferred from Duke to UCLA, so you can see what I was doing. I was getting closer and closer to Vegas. And when I did turn 21, I just dropped out. I didn't even get my college degree. I left and came to Vegas, as soon as I turned 21.

That's when I began to try it. I think I came here with about 2,800 bucks and that lasted about three days. So I got a reality check real fast. I kind of gutted it out for the next year, living off coupons and things like that and figuring it out. And then, I came under some pressure from my folks, who were saying, you know,

"We didn't get crazy when you dropped out of college and all of that, but you've gotta show us you can do something." So that's when I became a stockbroker. I went and applied at Merrill Lynch and did that for about a year. I passed the Securities exam, went to New York, did that for about a year.

KCM: How'd you like that?

AC:    Oh, I hated it. I envisioned, well, this is a job I can do because it's all about quantitative analysis and so forth. Well, it wasn't. It was about picking up the phone and cold calling, which I couldn't do, so that lasted about a year. I was that dismal. I couldn't sell anything. And I got out of that, and just got back onto the playing side, and got into running the streets again, this is in the early '80s.

And one of my last jobs was as a bouncer in one of the big clubs here, so I was the smallest bouncer in Vegas. But at that point, is when I sort of hooked up with Stanford Wong and some of those guys. I started to get a little bit of a reputation of being someone who had some staying power, had been around and knew what he was doing. And so that's pretty much the chronology of it, and that's when I got into the full-time playing.

Skip ahead, maybe a decade after that, a little over a decade, the shelf life for me ran out because we were – we became such a high-profile group, and we won a lot of big tournaments. And I played with some other guys, and we did a lot of counting on teams and things like that. So that was the whole, sort of, the gambling part of the career. And I just got too well known, you know, I just got well known, it was getting too tough, and I'd always told my dad that I thought that there would be things to do. Because my father was a university professor, by the way. My father had taught at SUNY Albany, Wayne State, Michigan, Fresno State in California.

KCM: What field was he in?

AC:    He was in Communicative Disorders. I don't even know if that's what they call it anymore, but essentially, it was brain interpretation of sounds. So there's a lot of statistical analysis involved in this and quantifying test scores and things like that. He really understood the math of probability and stats. So when I showed it to him he understood why it would work and he thought it was reasonable.

But he never really bought into it until I told him that I would consider publishing someday down the line. Because actually, the way it went is I said, "You know, there's gonna be more opportunities that will spring from this," and he said, "Like what?" And I said, "Publishing," and I'll never forget, he turned around, he smiled at me, and he went, "Now, that's a good idea." So it was always in the back of my mind, and I just decided, probably around the '90s, early '90s, that this would be what I would use my knowledge of Vegas and gambling for because I wasn't really allowed to play at the level I wanted to play any longer.

The goal is to make money, not to be the world's greatest gambler. I knew there was a ceiling on how much I could make. So I think I'll make the decision basically get out of gambling as a vocation and get into publishing. So that's pretty much the story.

[Note: At this point I told Anthony that I had published a mathematical analysis of an approach to card counting in a publication called *Blackjack Forum* in 1996 and that Anthony Curtis' Las Vegas Advisor Top 10 List was on the next page after the end of my article.]

AC:    I'll be darn, that's cool. As you can see, I was writing. I had articles that were beginning to get published. I was looking for the bridge between gambling and publishing, so I was writing for trade periodicals around that time, but it was on the side.

KCM: What was the first Huntington book?

AC:    We did Peter Griffin's *Extra Stuff*; that was Griffin's follow up to *The Theory of Blackjack*, and then we got the rights to *The Theory of Blackjack*. I was a Griffin disciple. I read his books over and over and over again and I read all of his papers. He and I ended being almost best friends. He was my mentor. So when I got a chance to publish his book, it was great, but I didn't know where I was going with that [publishing].

I was already doing some weird version of Las Vegas Advisor (LVA). LVA's come and gone in three or four different incarnations. Again, I was just kind of dabbling.

KCM: When did that become serious?

AC: I didn't really get serious with it until probably about '89 or '90. And by serious, I mean, I came back and said, "Okay, I'm not going to do the one-pager any more. I'm gonna actually do a monthly." That would be some time in the early '90s.

KCM: How many subscribers do you have currently?

AC: Well, it's kind of amazing. Real legitimate LVA subscribers, meaning those that pay the full membership, we've probably got about 15,000. We've got some joint venture package deals that include LVA such as with Club WPT. So, because of that, we've actually got over 28,000 subscribers. We get remuneration from WPT, but it's not the full subscription rate. We send out 28,000 electronically or in the mail each month.

KCM: That's a pretty good thing to grow from something you put together as a couple of pages.

AC: Yeah, plus there's synergies of all sorts because every one of those guys and girls become one of our customers, and we market our books to them.

KCM: I'm curious, the prostate cancer book sort of stood out as something that didn't quite fit with the rest of your titles – I was wondering if that was related to Peter Griffin [who died from prostate cancer]?

AC:    Actually, not.  You would think so, but it wasn't.  It was just that this particular author, Lee Nelson, became a phenomenon – he's one of our hottest authors right now because of his *Kill Phil* and *Kill Everyone* books.

He had written this book prior to the poker books, and I knew him because of the gambling world.  He's a very, very famous player out of Australia and New Zealand.  He wasn't well known here at all.  Now he is because of his books, and because he's just been tearing it up all over the world.  But he actually had written that book originally, and was gonna do something with the Milken Institute.

At the Milken Institute they were all for it, they just thought it was the greatest thing in the world.  And they had a change at the top, and they got a new policy about what they would and wouldn't endorse, and so he got caught in the middle.  And he said, "Do you wanna publish this book?  It's done."  And we sent it out to a couple of people, and he showed me the testimonials he had from some of the biggest names in the business, the biggest PhDs in the field.

So we published it and got in trouble immediately with the Milken Institute because we left on a quote that we weren't supposed to, so we had to scrap a printing.  The whole thing turned out to be miserable, but I'm still proud we did it because I've gotten lots of response on that one; people say it's a very good book.

KCM: On your web site there was mention of your having gone through some lean years, which I think were when you first arrived here in Vegas.  Have you had lean years with the publishing business?

AC:    In terms of the business, the leanest years that I've ever had are now.  The business has grown strictly on cash flow – cash flow dictating growth.

I own 100 percent of it.  It's private, obviously.  I never sold off, not a penny of it.  It can only grow out of profits.  You're starting to make me feel successful here.  The growth literally went from me starting in the early days, with the early advisors, out of a two-bedroom apartment.  I moved to a house and got a little more serious about it, and hired an employee, who's head of my marketing right now - still here after 20 years.  And building and building and building up to 17, 18 employees that we were at, our zenith.  Now, we're down to about 16, so I've almost kept full staff.

None of those people were fired, we just lost them from attrition, and at this time, we haven't rehired those spots.  In the early years I was playing and I had good income coming from gambling, which helped to feed the business.  But we very much just grew in a kind of a linear fashion.

KCM:  So good example of boot strapping, and not taking on investors or equity partners –

AC:     I wouldn't do that for a couple of reasons.  One is that then you've gotta share control, and I didn't want to have to fight about it.  I wanted to be in control, and often accused of that [needing to be in control].

KCM:  Not the worst thing in the world for an entrepreneur.

AC:     Yeah, I think delegating is a problem, and you know, when you're a control freak, you sometimes don't delegate properly, and it's something I've had to remedy, and I'm still trying, but I didn't want to share control at all.  Second, is I honestly was never sophisticated enough or didn't have a clear enough vision to know what I would do with outside money.  You know what I mean?  I look back at all the times where I was offered X amount of money for X percentage of the business, and I think to myself that would've been the worst thing in the world.

I was able to do those things by waiting a little longer, whether it was a year or two years or whatever, out of my own cash flow, and I had a more defined understanding of what direction we needed to go.  I mean, even now – I've got a fairly aggressive growth idea now, which would eventually result in selling off pieces of the business for proper valuations, but now is not the time to do that, although publishing has been really a pretty hot multiple. I have a better idea now of what I would do toward the end of making the most money possible out of the business, but doing it early [selling] is a deadly mistake, in my opinion.

KCM: I started Provident with a partner and we ended up buying her out.

AC: Boy, that gets rough, because you're usually gonna have to buy all of it at a premium. I just didn't want the hassle. I wanted to be in control, I wanted to pay money to people that were working for me for an agreed upon contractual wage, with no promises down the line.

KCM: Good thinking. One thing that I was really interested in is *Bargain City*, which is the book you wrote that is out of print. Any thoughts about ever bringing that back?

AC: I mean, I've had thoughts about it, but *Bargain City* was a fun thing. *Bargain City* is the most error-fraught book I've ever published. It was just filled with typos and things like that, and the reason for that was I wrote it in 20 days. I wrote that book in 20 days because my son was about to be born. And my Senior Editor here, Deke Castleman, who's been my editor for 15 years or more, said, "Once your son's born, you're not going to get it done."

So waiting for his mother to give birth, I worked my brains out and wrote it. But we didn't have time to do good fact-checks on it and everything else. I was very proud of that book. I go back and look at it a lot, there's some strong stuff here.

KCM: I've got an old copy. I used to come to Las Vegas every month and I carried it with me because it had so many phone numbers and addresses and other things that were useful. I pulled it out in preparation to come here and talk to you, and I thought to myself, wow, I can't believe this is out of print. I thought, with the economic downturn, this is a good time to bring it back. Maybe *Return of Bargain City*.

AC:    I thought about it, but I won't because a) I don't really have any desire to be an author. It's so weird, I have people come to me and they just can't wait to be an author and see their name on a book. Of course, I've done it with *Bargain City* and *The Art of Gambling*, as well. I was co-author on that one. To be an author doesn't really jazz me, and it would take a lot of work for me to do it. And with my name on it, I'm not gonna wanna hire somebody to do it. I'd wanna do it myself. We've got something coming out that's similar. It's called, *Frugal Vegas* by Deke Castleman and Jean Scott.

Honestly, I thought *Bargain City* was a great guidebook and a lot of people did. It's one of a very few of the books that I've published that I've actually seen people walking reading. There was just something about that book that resonated with people. I probably should've kept that going. It's the only one I ever let go out of print when it was hot. I kept everyone else's in print.

KCM: I am an audio book fan. Whenever I'm in the car, or even walking around, I'm always listening to audio books or podcasts or other things. Have you ever thought about having audio versions of your books?

AC:    Yeah, we're looking into it right now. We've got audio books on our mock titles, I believe. I think we've got audio, *Battle for Vegas*. I think we might have audio of *Cullotta*. The whole rights thing that's part of my bigger growth plan. We've been selling rights now, especially foreign rights and audio rights, all of that kind of stuff, is a very lucrative side part of publishing. And the problem is it's harder to do than it would seem. It seems like you would just contact somebody. Well, that's easier said than done. Contact who? Who are you gonna contact in Germany, who are you gonna contact in Italy?

Our plans going forward from this point on are to open up foreign rights in a big way. And we've recently sold books to Germany,

France, Italy, and I'm starting to see how easy it is. We've probably got about 20 deals for different books. We've got them in China, we've got them in Japan, but these are all things that just came to us. And we are actively pursuing now, going out and getting these things and that includes audio. I mean, a lot of these books could work very well on audio.

KCM: An idea that's been rattling around in my head is that there are all of these classic gambling [advantage play] books that were never made into audio books, and some of them are out of print now. I've often thought that could be a business to create audio books from those.

AC:  It probably could be. My only feeling on that is that audio books are still very, very niche. They really are, and another example is e-book. That's where it's at. The future is in e-book. I look at audio and I see a market this big. I look at e-books and I see a market already this big, but will soon be this big. It's gonna be huge.

KCM: And what about the Kindle, do you think that's gonna drive the market?

AC:  I think that Amazon's dedication to the Kindle is definitely gonna drive it. I think that Bezos is a real driver of perception and policy. He's one of the most influential, I think, of the whole computer-age, and he's committed to this, to Kindle. Now, Kindle's got a lot of flaws, and the biggest flaw of Kindle is not the price, even though it's very pricey right now, and everyone talks about that. The flaw of Kindle is the interface to get your books to Kindle is very, very poor.

You have to do a lot of work to make your books Kindle-ready that they don't do for you. The first book we put into Kindle took us three weeks to converge, using like two or three of my staffers in IT. It was really painful, and I said, "I don't care. I sure hope that this curve gets less steep and we can do these things faster." And we are now, we're now turning Kindle books out in about a tenth of the time or maybe an eighth or a seventh of the time, about three days maybe, to convert a book to Kindle.

And I think the Kindle is gonna drive the whole e-technology, but there's lots of e-technology. We sell almost every book we do now in electronic format, which is a downloadable PDF. And I mean, I think it's brilliant, you know, because why do you need to hold it, all you wanna do is read it. Now, you can print it out, if you want on regular paper, or sit at night in front of your computer or your reading devices. Phones are gonna start happening, and you can sell these things at 60 percent discounts. So take the recent Bob Dancer book, which was $25.00. This is a very important book on video poker and we can sell it in e-book format for $10.00.

KCM: Well, you'll be happy to know that I both bought the book and downloaded it, and I think you'll have a lot of people doing that.

AC:  We're seeing it begin to ramp up, and I mean, this is one area where we've been very proactive. I believe that e-format reading is gonna be the future, and they'll always be a place for this kind of book. The hard book people will always wanna have it hard book, but the market will open up where people can get the information in a $25.00 book for $10.00, and instantly.

People don't realize how good "e" can be. I mean, it's perfectly searchable. It's like you've got the built-in master index. You can bookmark it yourself, as you read it. You can index concepts that you like and put it in there, always go to them. It's the future for people who are voracious about getting their knowledge.

KCM: Yeah, I was really pleased to see that you're getting into that. In Japan I understand that it's huge, people that are reading books on their telephones. In the U.S., it really hasn't started moving quickly up in the S-shape curve, it's still in the sort of flat portion of the curve, but I think, you're right, it's gonna ramp up.

AC:  It's moving right now. I mean, the amount of time that we spend on it, it sucks. The return – the short-term return on this, it doesn't equate, but I've run my business like a gambler my whole life, you know, the expected value equation. We're not doing it, based on what we can get today or tomorrow, but we expect it to pay off in time.

KCM: Actually, that leads into one of my questions, which is about marketing. So marketing is in many ways expected value, you know, you're making a bet, you're spending time, money, resources to try and sell something, and you hope that your return on investment is gonna be positive. So do you approach marketing issues that way, and how do you track return on investment on things you do in marketing?

AC:    We are probably a very poor marketing company. We're a very good PR company; we're very good at getting our name out, and making things happen like that. So we're very good at leveraging.

KCM: I thought I'd like to interview you is because you're a bit of a celebrity. I see you on cable television all the time. When somebody reads about someone that they know is an actual individual it brings more credibility to the message.

AC:    A lot of people in casinos will come up to me, and they'll ask for autographs, they'll take photos, they'll ask me questions. The way we take advantage of that is that I tirelessly do it. I do it all the time, like some time media whore. And it's not because I desire so much to be on another TV show. I'm really kind of fizzled out with it. I was just on the *Today Show*. I knew it was valuable though, so I traveled to New York and I did the show.

Now, did we leverage that very well? Not really. I am quite unsophisticated, even after all these years of marketing. I simply cannot quite get my head around paying for something, and trying to get a return that's greater, and being able to track it and quantify it. I'm just not very good at it. That's been one of my weaknesses. Now, you look at certain pitchmen-types, and I've seen tremendous growth in certain areas from other groups, which we don't get because we're not that good in marketing.

So it's something we have to work on or eventually, get to the point where we hire the experts to do that sort of thing for us. However, that said, our marketing is natural marketing, in a way with the publicity and the media, and we do have one of the biggest Web sites, and we do have one of the biggest publishing companies in this area, so obviously, we're doing something right.

KCM: PR is often the most cost-effective kind of marketing.

AC:  For a guy like me, who's literally afraid to spend hard dollars in marketing, PR's the only way, and you can't undersell the value of that because our marketing efforts have been good enough for free, and for what we've done through publicity, which, by my definition is free. So it's a weird one, you know what I mean? People say, "Man, you're great at marketing." I say, "No, not really. I'm just good at getting on TV."

KCM: Well, that's definitely a skill that I think a lot of people wish they had.

AC:  Well, when you're talking about – I'll tell you what, when you're talking about doing – when you're talking about a how-to book, if you really do, you know, my advice on that is if you really know your stuff, what you wanna do is tell as many people in the media as you can. We did that early on with lots of press releases, offering me up for interviews, and then when you get your chance, you're gonna nail it. Once they get one, they don't wanna take any other chances. They want to go to the go-to guy, and the go-to guy will remain the go-to guy until he just absolutely crashes and can't do it anymore, or won't.

So once you get in that pipeline, it can be very, very good. So, early on you wanna know your subject inside and out, and hopefully, you can talk about it with some kind of pizzazz, but then you wanna tell the media what you know, and when you get your chance, you wanna nail it.

KCM: So you mentioned Peter Griffin, as a big influence on you, were there any other individuals that have had a big influence on you, particularly, businesswise?

AC:     Yeah, Wong, Stanford Wong, no question. I mean, Stanford Wong is a Finance Ph.D., and Wong really, really knows business. He gave me lots of early pointers. Those two guys, Griffin and Wong. Wong also on the gambling side. Wong spent a lot of time teaching me, and clarifying things for me because I played on his tournament team. And both Griffin and Wong, the two of them, were the reason that I got so solid.

But on the business end, I would say Wong probably more than anybody, and I would throw my own father into this mix too. Because my father's always been – he's very intelligent and he's always been extremely supportive. My mother too for that matter, but when we're talking about father figures, you know, it's kind of been those guys, my real father and Wong and Griffin.

[Note: Stanford Wong is a pseudonym used by a very well respected advantage play expert and author with a long history of playing and organizing teams of advantage players.]

KCM: How about books, any business books you've read that you especially liked or were influential?

AC:     I really don't. I used to read biographies. I used to read biographies about wealthy people, and I read a lot about, you know, of course, Howard Hughes and Jimmy Ling. So I'm trying to think of some of the old-timers that are a little off the beaten track. Corcoran, although he's still big, and then I read a lot of magazine articles, just tons and tons of magazine articles.

I read business articles like crazy. I read two or three papers a day, including the *Wall Street Journal* and *USA Today*. I read *Time, Newsweek, Business Week*, religiously. I mean, that's where I get my stuff, and I get ideas about it there, but never formally business trained at all, and never read a lot of how-to biographies in business. There's only so much time. I'm editing, I'm checking, you know, I don't have time in a day.

KCM: I've made sort of a life's work of studying successful people, and what I always hear from them is that they read biographies about other successful people. I'll make one recommendation to you, if there's one business book that you ever read, I recommend *Winning* by Jack Welch. Boy, that book is fantastic.

AC: Really, *Winning*? Maybe I'll try it.

KCM: In your experience, what are the best and the worst aspects of running a business? What do you like the most and least?

AC: The most is obvious, you know, that's just success for me. Some people would say it's freedom, but I don't see it as freedom. It's very confining really, if you're gonna do it right. So success is it. It's really an amazing thing to look at where I was [compared to where I am now].

KCM: How do you measure success, other than financially?

AC: Well, I totally have a problem with that. I've been told by all my exes that I'll never stop, but sometimes I do reflect. And I told you I started some of these ideas in a two-bedroom apartment, just working out of a one room. And now, I drive to work sometimes, and I go "Wow, I own this whole corner here and it's a pretty powerful corner." This is a fairly high-rent district, believe it or not. I mean, you look around you and go, it don't look so good out there, but it has proximity to the strip and casinos. This is valuable land and I own the buildings on it and everything.

When you look at that, and you go wow, man, I grew that out of my own cash flow. It feels pretty good. I mean, you actually look at that, and you kind of can pat yourself on the back a little bit.

I'm a gambler. In gambling you make big hits. And even professionals usually lose more often than they win. They lose on more occasions, but they have bigger wins [that more than make up for the losses]. Business is very much like that too. There are many, many defeats, and when you get those – when the defeats start to pile up, it begins to manifest, in my mind, as unfulfilled potential. And unfulfilled potential also relates to inefficiency. And if you're like a real nit about it, like I am, you hate that, you hate unfulfilled potential, you hate inefficiency, and it begins to really work on you. And it's not the hours I hate, and it's not the lack of flexibility, those things kind of go with it. But recognizing inefficiency and wasted potential is really hard for me to deal with, and that's what bothers me the most.

KCM: We have a business that's grown from two people to about forty-eight at its peak. We shrunk down a little bit this past year, but what I found is I could be extremely busy, and I wouldn't be stressed or discouraged, as long as I was making forward progress. As soon as the forward progress stopped, I would start to get stressed.

AC:    You get into a situation where you kind of run around in circles and nothing's really happening, and that's very – that's hard for me to deal with. I don't like that. That's the worst part. That's when I think, all right, I've had enough of this and stop. I think that for about half a day and I then I go, nah [and keep going].

KCM: If you were talking to someone, who was about to start a business, and had never done this before, if you had one or two pieces of advice, what would they be?

AC:    Reconsider would be number 1. You'll probably get that from everybody you interview. You gotta have one or two things. You gotta have a lot of money behind you when you start, or you gotta have a lot of time. You gotta have one or the other. I had the other, I had time. And I was doing other things for money and I didn't mind slow growth.

But you either gotta have a lot of money in backing, or you gotta have a whole lot of time and patience; and with this generation, it seems like that's not in abundance with people. They want instant results and gratification. So you've got to be willing to just stick it out and that's gotta be in you. If it's not, you're not gonna make it.

KCM: I agree completely. What mistakes would you tell them to avoid?

AC:    Mistakes, trying to get too flashy off the top. I mean, you know, with the best storefront, the best letterhead, the best business cards, over-spending. It's almost more dangerous, going back to what I just said, if you are capitalized to some degree, because you are more likely to over-spend. That's the biggest problem that I've seen is really over-extending by spending too much or leveraging too far. We've always been very moderate. We've never been super flashy. We've tried to make it through a good, strong, solid information, a good, strong, solid vibes, good customer service that sort of thing, and we're really kept flash out of it.

I've tried real hard to keep costs under control. Hiring too fast – that's a problem. That's been my biggest problem in business because once you hire them, you – unless you're the hardest core, tough ass, you're gonna have to be in red at times because you're not gonna wanna throw them out.

KCM: Hire in haste, regret in leisure.

AC:    I'm taking some of the people that I have that I probably, in all reality, should downsize. And I'm taking them out of what their main job is, and putting them into revenue producing jobs like what I said before, how do we get to the point where we get those foreign rights that I'm discussing? Well, you take an editor and you take a customer service person. I'm trying to transition everybody who has spare time on their hands into revenue-producing activity.

KCM: We went through kind of a slump. There were a lot of projects we were supposed to start last year. Everyone got scared, the market crashed and so forth, and so a lot of things got delayed.

And so I've been trying to take people, who are specialized in this area, and get them to do other things, but I've had limited success.

AC:    Well, it's kind of hard because you're asking people to go out of what they expect that they're gonna do. And I mean, this kind of goes back to your other question like what are biggest disappointments. Overall, without fudging, I would say I've got a good staff and I've got good workers and all. But when they let you down, it's really – it's hard because you feel like you're working for them, and you're doing everything you can, and part of my biggest problems with running a business or being on top is being let down by employees sometimes. You know, not trying, when it doesn't mean as much to them. Then you think about it and say "Well, of course, it doesn't."

KCM:  So one of my beliefs is sort of the way you treat your employees is likely to be the way your employees treat your customers. And having had a good number of interactions with your office staff here, as a customer, I can say they've been uniformly good. And there were a couple of issues where there were minor problems, someone always got back to me right away. They were pleasant, courteous, so congratulations on that.

AC:    Thank you. I like our customer service. We get a lot of people telling us it's good. We've always stressed it, and anyone who's surley or nasty, doesn't last long here, that's for sure. That's the only reason I will fire people, by the way. I've fired lots of people for things like not being good to the customer. These are the good employees, the ones I have here right now that maybe I can't quite fill their days. I ain't gonna let them go.

Yeah, we stress it, and they get a lot of feedback. I make sure they see it. I make sure they see when people tell me how good they are. We've always been generous with bonuses at the end of the year. Now, that's a tough one too because if you're good with bonuses when things are good, and you can't bonus when things are bad, that's a tough hurdle. So you've got to be careful of not jumping out of your skin on bonusing because they come to start planning off of this bonus that they think they're gonna get at the end of year.

We've always done that, we've never given a turkey, even in the worst of times, we've given a couple hundred dollars, even to the lowest employees and they appreciate that check. But there's been times, you know, some of the top people have been getting four and five-figure bonuses, and you know, all of a sudden that's cut to three figures, and that's tough on morale.

KCM: How do you promote a positive culture with your staff?

AC:    Well, that's the hardest part. I mean, that's probably the hardest part of all, especially now, when things are so tough. It's really palpable sometimes when there's a bad feeling around, when people feel that things aren't going well, when there's no action. We try to do events. By events, I mean like I say, "Everybody, all right close it up 45 minutes early, let's meet downstairs, everybody's required to have one beer and then you can leave or stay." Half of them go and they take advantage of the early out, and half of them stay and party a little bit and that sort of stuff.

So it's a really fine line you gotta walk, but nothing succeeds like success. I mean, you can party them, you can get them early outs, you can give them nice bonuses at the end of the year, which I think is very important, but nothing is as powerful as there being a buzz around the office when things are really happening. I mean, we got a new book coming out and everyone's working on all cylinders or we're launching a new Web site and everybody's excited and the phones are ringing because maybe it's holiday time. There's nothing better than that because everybody comes to work, and they feel that they're part of something vibrant.

The problem is you can't always manufacture that, and all you can really do is try to get from good project to good project, when you've got a group like this, and try to keep people engaged.

KCM: I think one of the things that I've struggled with, and maybe you can comment on this, is that I have to spend a lot of time working in the business. And sometimes, I don't provide enough of the feedback and other things that you need to do to keep your employees motivated because I'm dealing with problems and putting out fires and so forth. So how do you avoid doing that?

AC:　I should've brought it up because that is part of the culture here and I stay on top of it. I have very much tried to give credit where credit is due, always give credit for an idea. If somebody comes up with an idea for the company, make sure that they know you know they came up with it. Make sure that their co-workers know that they came up with a good idea, that's very, very important. E-mail makes that easy. I mean, you can copy a bunch of people and go, "Look at this great idea from Gail, this great idea from Laurie. We're gonna go with this." I think it's huge, as a boss, not to take someone else's idea and run with it without credit. That's a killer.

KCM: That's death, yeah.

AC:　You cannot break a person's spirit more than by not acknowledging that it was their idea, you know, and that you liked it. Because after all, you're a boss, you're like the captain of a team, whether it's a debate team or the football team, you know.

And everybody wants the person they work for, or the person who's in this authority position to recognize that they've got something good going on in their heads. So I mean, yeah, for me not to have brought that up on my own is remiss because that's a very big part of the culture here. Anybody who comes up with a good idea, I make sure the whole company knows whose idea it was.

KCM: Jack Welch talks about money recognition and training. Their culture is very much one of growing managers, so training is all about helping people to learn new things, new skills, new knowledge and so forth. Recognition is key and that recognition often means a lot when it's in dollars.

AC:     Well, I think so too. And I always get yelled at about that by people who know well. You put too much on this financial remuneration. I think you can tell people they're doing a great job, give them great working conditions. I make sure that they got benefits, and everyone under salary has got health benefits. So we take care of all those things, and that's financial, to a degree. But nothing is as financial as the amount of money you're making, and right now, there literally have not been raises here for a couple of years. But they also understand that we're at 10 percent unemployment and they're very happy. It's a form of a bonus just to be able to keep a job, and they all understand that. So I know that money is extremely important, it's number 1.

One other thing, I drive a crapped out 1999 Dodge Caravan. I don't do anything extravagant for myself, nothing. There is no way these people are not getting raises, and I'm gonna show up here with a new BMW, no way. You asked about mistakes, there's a big mistake. For bosses who flaunt it while the others are not making gains that materially affect their life – that is a big mistake.

KCM: Well, you'll be happy to know that my wife finally made me trade in my 1991 Honda Accord, so I traded that in for another used Honda Accord –

AC:     You know, I'm not saying that you don't deserve it and you shouldn't have it. I mean, there are certain things you ought to have, when you worked your brains out. But when things are really tough, when you're not sharing the wealth a little bit, then you shouldn't be taking it all. I know other business guys, you know, who have done that and they're hated. They are hated by their people.

KCM: Share the wealth and share in the pain.

AC:     Yeah, exactly.

KCM: So you've answered this in part, but any thoughts on, you know, we're in tough economic times now, what are you doing in terms of strategies to navigate through what is looking like it's gonna be an extended recession?

AC:    Working more hours.  I mean, really working, trying to figure it out, a lot of thinking about it.  Honestly, my feeling is that in terms of my business, if this business is gonna get any bigger, it's gonna happen right now.  I'm a game player, and where other people are sticking their heads in holes, I'm aggressively trying to expand, and that's been made tough because the banks are running scared.

So my banks have indicated to me they don't wanna support me with some of these ideas.  So I'll seek new banks.  So we're actually embarking on our most aggressive expansion in the history of our company right now.

KCM:  The founder of the Dow Chemical Company had as one of his guiding principles that downturns are when you really invest because you'll be in a position then to capitalize on opportunities when things turn back up.

AC:    You just said it; it's getting to be a time where you should be getting into real estate and things like that.  You know, when there's blood on the streets, even if it's yours.

KCM:  Just as an aside, I published that book in 2003 [*Beating the Dow with Rental Houses*].  I stopped selling it at the end of 2004 because prices had gotten crazy, and I didn't wanna be encouraging anyone to be buying when the return in the future was not likely to be good.  Now, I'm dusting it off, and going to start selling it again because there are bargains to be had, if you can get the financing.

AC:    Yeah, it makes sense.  We're gonna open a sister Web site to LasVegasAdvisor.com, which is SinCityAdvisor.com.  Sin City Advisor will be kicked off by our next book called, *Topless Vegas*.  We're publishing poker player Annie Dukes' next book called *Decide to Play Great Poker*, and Annie is on *Celebrity Apprentice* [Donald Trump's hit show].  Our stuff is all lined up, so we'll attempt to grow powerfully right through this thing.

KCM: So are there any questions that I should've asked that I didn't?

AC:    No, I mean, you kind of covered the whole thing. Like I say, I don't think I've given you anything brilliant that you're not gonna get from everybody else you talk to.

KCM: Well, I don't know, the interesting thing is you've validated many of my main messages. I hope that I don't interview people, who say things completely contrary to the themes of the book. And almost every answer that you gave, I can point to a place in the book, where I say something very similar. Like most small business owners who have been around for a while, you have to develop certain beliefs and attitudes or you don't make it.

You're showing the beliefs and attitudes that I see in most successful business owners. The second thing I like is that you, view the world through the eyes of a gambler. I'm always calculating expected value. That's one of the themes and the title of the book is *Tipping the Odds for the Entrepreneur*.

AC:    It's nice.

Well, I'll just add to that where people really don't understand about gambling [advantage play] is that you're going to win. I mean, done at a professional level, or on an expert level, it's not gambling, I guess. It's advanced game playing in applied mathematics. They call it gambling, but there's no gambling about it. It's about being in a market and always having the best of it [a mathematical advantage] – you will win money. So those are obviously very strong concepts.

Just to give you an example, this weekend, I was busy, but a friend of mine called and he said, "On the UNLV, the Rebel game, for the first half is minus ten at Pinnacle," which is a very, very efficient online betting community. You can pretty much take it to the bank that minus ten is pretty close to the efficient number that it should be. Yet the leader at sport books all around town have it at 6 ½.

We went around and I bet a bunch of money, and it was a strong play. You make that play every time and you're gonna lose a few of them, but your gonna win in the long-run. So you look at that and think it's too big to pass up. We figured we had an edge between 20 and 25 percentage. Too much to pass up, so we ran around and did it, and that's what you gotta do in business. Overall, you're not a gambler doing business, you're an expert game player doing business [with an edge].

KCM: So that brings up a concept. I talk about customers making purchase decisions, if they're gonna purchase a product or service, they consider time, price, quality, convenience and risk and then quality has a couple of sub-components, you know, the quality of the service or product itself and the quality of the experience. So what would you say is your main competitive advantage?

AC:    The utility for the user of our product. I mean, what the user wants very much is to succeed. What are we talking about? We're talking about some people had all the money at gambling, and how to optimize vacation, two important things. So our value is in debt utility, so I guess, I don't know what category of quality. First of all, obviously, we're very quality-driven.

So I would say that, and the utility they bring to the user. That gets into price because we're often telling people how to save money [good value for the price paid].

KCM: And one other question I forgot to ask, which is you have had to set up a number of partnerships, in a sense, with casinos, from whom you get coupons, as well as with other people whose interests may not be fully aligned with yours such as retailers selling your books. I'm especially fascinated by the fact that casinos are willing to give you coupons and you're selling books telling people how to exploit their systems.

AC:     Yeah, the reality of that is that people and – I don't think this is disingenuous on our part because I freely admit to everyone and anyone – but that people just aren't going to do the things we tell them.  And again, utility is an extremely important underrated concept in math and economics.  The customer is getting utility, the customer is getting information he or she wants to help them do the things they wanna do, even if it's sometimes not in their best financial interest to play these games.

They chalk it up to entertainment value.  I know I'm gonna lose, I don't mind paying for this product, which is my fun on my Vegas vacation.  The casinos know that.  The casinos know that people come – this goes all the way back to Ed Thorp publishing *Beat the Dealer*, and blackjack players came in droves, who couldn't beat the game because they took the book and they passed it under their nose.  [They didn't do the work necessary to become an expert player.]

Casinos know that's human nature, and we know that too, but we do encourage people to learn and some people do.  Some people become expert players that beat the house.  There's got to be somebody, who comes out ahead in this, and I think that in the end, it's us and the casinos.  And I think the end-user is probably the one leaving utility out of it, who loses money.  But when you add utility in, they come out okay together.

KCM: The casinos, you know, they're doing their expected value calculations and saying, we're gonna get more people through the door.

AC:     Exactly, so I mean, really it's a very interesting triangle that I've thought a lot about, and I know that some casinos do – they take little umbrage at what we teach, but the smart ones say "go teach whatever you want."  Don't teach them how to break into a slot machine, but other than that…

KCM: Any other thoughts or ideas you wanna share, anything that you think my readers would be interested in that I didn't cover?

AC:   I will add one thing.  For anybody's who's got a business, if they're making money, they've got money coming in, then they're viable.  We do make a lot of money.  We have a lot of cash flow because you can then sew up leaks, you can patch them, you can change certain direction and you can downsize.  I am the most downsizable business in the world because once a book gets published, it's published.  I don't need staff; all I need is an order taker.

So I can downsize to two, you know what I mean?  I can write the LVA myself.  We would truncate our upside by doing that, but I can downsize at the snap of a finger, at the expense of employees and at the expense of growth.  It's nice to know, as the guy in charge, that you got an out.  You don't wanna take it, but if you're making money, you've got options.  That's the thing.  As long as you're making money.  Now, if your revenue started drying up, and people aren't buying your product, now you better start worrying.

KCM: Cash is king.  Gotta have cash flow.  Thank you.  I really appreciate your taking the time to talk to me.  I know you're busy and probably these days, you're busier than usual.

## Chapter 17

# Annette Norwood – Posh Salon and Color Bar

## (www.PoshSalonAndColorBar.com)

*The secret of joy in work is contained in one word – excellence.*
*To know how to do something well is to enjoy it.*

– Pearl S. Buck

KCM: I appreciate your coming in for an interview. Thank you very much. Maybe we can start with a brief history of what led up to you opening your own hair salon.

AN: Basically, I've been a hair dresser for 20 years, and I've been behind the chair for that whole time. What led me to where I am today was not being able to treat my customers in a way I felt was best. It was hard to work for somebody and have to follow rules when I disagreed with many of those rules.

KCM: Fair enough. That is what stimulates many people to start their own businesses – wanting to do things their way, so that's a perfectly legitimate reason. Tell me a bit about how you got started. You left one salon and opened your own business a very short time later (one week later). How did you get your first customers through the door?

AN:    I had worked for one salon owner for ten years and unfortunately was actually fired from that position.  I moved on to another salon for ten years.  I think about that first salon owner all the time.  She ran a great business, and I want to do the same.

I always remember what she said; "Treat the customers well.  Have great customer service.  Never stop marketing.  Have a referral program.  Give back to your loyal customers."  So I'm trying to get back into doing what my first mentor taught me to do.

I've been doing a ton of marketing in order to make this happen so quickly.  We did a direct mailing and offered our clients from the other salon discounted service to try our new salon.  We thought that if we got them through the door we would keep them with our great customer service.

KCM: Great.  So it's customer service.  Keep your customers happy.

AN:    Keep your customers happy.

KCM: How about some of the biggest challenges?  You've only been open a few weeks.  What were some of the biggest challenges that you ran into – maybe things that you weren't expecting?

AN:    Mostly things that came from the city, especially signage, which turned out to be a huge problem.  Because I was working at the other salon while preparing to open, I had a big communication barrier.  It was not easy to communicate with the vendors who were preparing our marketing materials and signage.

It was hard to delegate to people, to tell them what needed to be done while I was continuing to work at the other salon.  You can't be in two places at once, and you can't do everything all at once.

Now my staff enjoys helping, and enjoys having tasks to do. They feel a part of, and they feel like they've helped get this off the ground and have a vested interest in the business.

KCM: When you refer to your staff, is everyone an employee, or are some of them independent contractors? How are the relationships organized?

AN: Our staff is commission-based, and they are employees of Posh Salon. I get a percentage of their sales for services and products.

KCM: Do they have goals for the number of new customers they bring in, or at least the number of appointments they need to fill each week?

AN: Not yet, but this is something that we want to implement. We want to have incentives. We want to have goals. We want to have rewards. We want them to feel appreciated. And we're working on putting together guidelines for these things.

Because it's just a new company, and six weeks old, I'm still getting my feet wet as far as figuring out exactly what those incentives are. I feel myself sometimes making the mistake of promising too much. But I definitely want to make them happy.

KCM: Everyone that you have working as a stylist has been doing this for a while?

AN: We range from seven years to 25 years of experience.

KCM: If you were restarting – and you're only a few weeks into it, so this may not be a completely fair question – but if you were restarting, what might you do differently?

AN: What would I do differently? I would learn how to have an outline and stick to it. It's very easy to get pulled in different directions, and get off your daily agenda. So my advice would be to have your outline, stick to it, and also take time out for yourself to enjoy and breath a little bit. In many ways it has been overwhelming.

KCM: A, B, C, D planning – the A activities are things that you absolutely must get done, the B activities would be nice to get done, and ideally if you can delegate those to someone, you do. The C activities can be put off and the D activities can be deleted.

AN:　Correct.

KCM: As a business owner, I can guarantee you'll find yourself doing a lot of things that have low value and you have to think about identifying low value things and then decide, "I will not do those because I need to work on high value activities."

AN:　Exactly. That is my biggest challenge right now.

KCM: Eighty percent of your results come from 20 percent of your activities. The more you focus on the 20 percent, the more you will get the right things done. We all have the same 168 hours in a week. Marketing is a high value activity. How do you market the salon?

AN:　Actually, marketing has been really interesting. This is a whole new world for me. I have always been a big fan of Welcome Wagon. I've been doing hair for 20 years, and I would say 80 percent came from Welcome Wagon. We give a free haircut to anyone who moves into the neighborhood. We also provide incentives for referrals. If you refer a client I will give you $20 off your next visit, and our new client will also receive $20 off.

Now we're in a whole different world with the Internet, I still mostly rely on the old way of doing things. I think it's effective, but now I have to have new eyes. I hired someone that actually does web design and web-based marketing, so I have now been able to delegate that to that person, which has been awesome.

We are also working within the local business community. We're trying to cross-promote Posh with other small businesses in the area. We have linked up with Grant's Chocolate, and the Bank Restaurant, the Pilates across the street, and the wine shop.

KCM: When you say, "hooked up with," do you mean you have flyers, or coupons, or other things in their businesses?

AN: We have flyers and coupons within their businesses.

KCM: Have you thought about doing any joint venture mailings where a local business may be doing a mailing to their client base? If you can include some of your materials in that, then you can say, "Anyone who comes in as a new customer because of this mailing, we'll give you a commission because it's coming in through your database."

AN: Right. It's funny you'd mention that. I did this with two people today. We linked also with Wheaton Towers newsletter that goes out once a month. We buy ad space at a discount and 2,000 residents at the Wheaton Tower get the discount at Posh. We also have a feature in the First Trust Bank corporate office building newsletter. We've already had four new clients, and it just went out yesterday.

KCM: Are you getting a lot of walk-in customers?

AN: Unbelievable amounts of walk-ins. I feel that because of where we are, the location that we have, plus being together in the same building with a yogurt store, really gives us a lot of exposure. We are seeing one to two walk-ins a day, and about four to five referrals a day.

KCM: Fantastic. You're right near the train station. Have you done anything relating to handing out flyers, or in some way leveraging the large number of commuters that are walking very close to your business every day?

AN: You know, I haven't got to that point yet. The only thing that we've done as far as walking around and introducing ourselves would be the Friday-night car show.

KCM: There's that personal connection from being the business owner and so forth, but in terms of volume, just having somebody hand out flyers to people who are getting on or getting off of the train, assuming that's okay with the city, would be worth considering because there's such a large number of people who live in the area and are walking right by your business on a daily basis.

Trust is an important part of the selling process. How do you promote trust in your interactions with your customers?

AN: We believe in what we sell, and we believe in what we do as far as service. We stand by everything, and that's the biggest idea that I want to get across to everybody. We want to be trustworthy in all of our interactions with clients.

KCM: What do you do if a customer buys a product, takes it home, uses it, and is unhappy with it?

AN: One hundred percent guarantee. There are no questions asked. As a matter of fact, I had this situation happen to me today. My client came in and said, "I was very unhappy with this styling product." Absolutely, no problem, "I will be more than happy to refund your money, or let me show you something else that might work and you can trade for that." We stand by our products and services.

KCM: Great.

AN: I can't sell anything that I don't believe in. And I could never let somebody walk out the door with something just to make money for me. I won't do it. I would go broke before I would sell them something that I don't believe in.

KCM: Good policy. What about maintaining relationships. Let's say a customer has been coming to you for some time, and then stops coming in. What things might you do to try and get that customer back?

AN:  Well, there are a couple things that we do. We do emails, but that is a bit impersonal. Let's face it, the hair dressing business is a little bit like the doctor business. You're touching that person. You have to have mutual trust, so it's almost easier to actually call the person.

Sometimes people may feel uncomfortable about it, but I think that if they hear your voice, and know that you're concerned about them, they usually respond. If they don't answer the phone – we have caller ID nowadays – if they don't want to talk to you, you can leave a message and at least they heard your voice."

We send, "Miss you," cards. We may also send birthday cards – anything that's gonna be a spark to restart the relationship and let them know, "I'm still thinking about you."

KCM: What advice would you give to someone else who is just about to start a business?

AN:  I'll never say again to anybody, as long as I live, that I could do it better. You try to do it better, but don't promise anything. Don't promise anything, and stay focused. Stay on your roadmap. That, to me, is the biggest challenge, being pulled in too many directions. Set up a business plan. You're going to veer off here and there, but the plan will keep you on track.

KCM: How about mistakes. What mistakes might you advise the person to watch out for and avoid?

AN:  Trusting too much. If you haven't done it, you don't know what to expect; people come into your life and you trust them too much. Also, make sure your finances are exactly in order before you do it.

KCM: Are there any individuals who have been a big influence on you in terms of being a model for how to run your business?

AN:   Actually two people in particular – one was my old boss. She molded me into the person that I am, and like I said before, I want to run my business the way she ran hers.

I thought that she ran her business extremely well. I think that she managed her time well. She managed her employees well. She was able to have a family life, and be married, and have kids, and have a business, and manage all that on her own without having a manager for her salon.

Another girl that was my role model was somebody else that I worked with at the same salon and she taught me everything that I know as far as actually cutting hair, and how to treat the clients. I would sit and watch her and say, "I want to be her when I grow up."

And the funniest part about the whole story is that the second woman now owns her own salon across the street from mine in downtown Wheaton. I was worried about how she would react when she saw that it was me moving in across the street. And guess what? She walked into the shop and gave me this big hug and said, "I'm so happy it's you."

KCM: I ran a business unit in a company for ten years. The guy who hired me has been very supportive, and we've worked together on a number of projects, and we remain good friends. He's not concerned at all that I've gone into competition with him. We're friendly competitors and we help each other out when we can.

AN:   And I think that that's how it should be.

KCM: Are there any books that you've read, or seminars that you've gone to where you learned useful ideas for how to run your business?

AN:    There is one person in particular – his name is Michael Cole.  His focus is salon owners and hair stylists – teaching them how to market, how to save money, how to invest for retirement.  Unfortunately, in this type of business, we don't have a retirement plan.  We don't have 401(k) plans.

KCM:  Does he have a book, or seminars that he gives?

AN:    He has books and seminars.  He gives you guidelines on how to use your time wisely in the hair dressing business.  He gives you guidelines on how to add on services, how to reduce your hours to have a better quality of life.  He gives you the tools to give you referral programs, and the incentives that make them work.  He also shows you how to sell hair products and get a commission from the retail.

KCM:  Great.  What do you think are the best and worst aspects of running a business in your experience thus far?

AN:    The best experience is happiness.  We have a whole different feeling there.  That, to me, says it all.  To see my staff come in and want to work more hours, and be busy, and enjoy it.

As far as the worst, the worst would be managing my time, delegating and managing staff.  I've never been on this end of being the boss.  Having to manage a staff is a whole different world.  They look at you differently.  I don't really like that part of it because I'm just the same old Annette that they knew when I worked with them as a colleague, but with a lot more stress.

KCM:  More responsibility and more demands on your time so that you have to figure out how to balance your own clients, marketing, and other things for the business like the bookkeeping.  And now you have to devote some time and energy to making sure that other people are happy, and their issues are getting resolved, and conflicts between people which are inevitable, are getting resolved.  Those things all take time and energy.

AN:   Starting a business wasn't the hard part.  That was the easy part.  The hard part is keeping it going.

KCM:  Yeah, the hard part is keeping people happy – your customers happy and your staff happy, but doing it in such a way that you can keep yourself happy because  you're not going to be happy if you're working 14, 15 hours a day and focusing on everyone else's needs and letting your own needs go by the wayside.

AN:   That's exactly where I'm at right now.  My other challenge is, I'm behind the chair.  It's very hard for me to be behind the chair and hear what's going on around me, and not want to step in.  But I can't walk away and fix the problem because I'm cutting hair.  I'm wearing two hats right now, and I stress to my staff that if there's somebody in my chair, I cannot be pulled away.

KCM:  You're taking care of your customer.  Everything else has to wait while you deal with that – except a fire or some real emergency.

AN:   Yeah.  And that's what's been hard is to say, "You handle it," or "That can wait 'til later," or "I have a half-hour until I'm finished, then we'll address the problem."  Time management – it all comes down to time management.

KCM:  And also setting ground rules and showing people that you're going to stick to those rules.  In a sense it's staff training.  You have to let them know what to expect and what you expect of them.  They need to know that they will be held accountable for following the ground rules that you've laid out.  That's sometimes difficult, especially when you've been a colleague, and now you're the boss.

AN:   Right.  That's been one of my biggest challenges, definitely.

KCM:  What do you do when you have a customer who is just difficult to the point where you can never make him or her happy?

AN:  I have a few of those, but I feel that you can't take things personally either, and you almost feel like there have to be other things going on that are driving the unhappiness.  So you put that aside and just keep servicing them to the fullest.  And you know what?  When the client comes back, you know you're doing something right.

KCM: If you were to describe your philosophy about running a business in just a couple of sentences, what would you say were the bullet points?

AN:  It's definitely honesty and trust.  I think that you need to show that you're a loyal person, and you believe in what you do.  I wouldn't be here right now if it wasn't for people who believed in those same goals.

KCM: I predict you're going to be very successful.

AN:  Thank you.

*Chapter 18*

# Seattle Sutton – Seattle Sutton's Healthy Eating

**(www.SeattleSutton.com)**

*There are no shortcuts to any place worth going.*

– Beverly Sills

Seattle Sutton is a nurse who worked for many years with her husband, Kelly, a family practice physician, in his office in Marseilles, IL (about 70 miles southwest of Chicago). Many of her husband's patients had medical problems related to obesity and unhealthy eating habits such as diabetes, high blood pressure and heart disease. Seattle provided basic nutrition education to these patients, often with frustrating results. One day a patient said to her "I know I should do what you suggest, but I am certain I won't. But I will follow your plan if you cook the meals for me." This comment provided the inspiration for a business that provided 21 healthy meals per week to people who wanted to lose weight, eat more healthfully, or for those who had a difficult time buying and preparing healthy food, such as the elderly.

In 1985, at the age of 53, Seattle started her company, which was originally called Diet Carry-Out, but was later renamed Seattle Sutton's Healthy Eating. She started with three employees and sent out 231 meals the first week, mostly to friends in the local community. I recall seeing commercials for her company in the 1980s and '90s on late night cable television. I later learned that Seattle would set her alarm for 1 or 2 o'clock in the morning, just before a commercial was going to run, so that she could answer the telephone, take orders and answer questions herself.

Today, the number of meals that go out each week number in the hundreds of thousands and annual revenues are in the tens of millions of dollars. In addition to the main facility in Ottawa, Illinois, Seattle Sutton's Healthy Eating franchises have been sold on a state-by-state basis. Each facility provides meals to hundreds of local distributors from which customers can pick up meals twice weekly. For people who live in a state that does not have a facility, meals can be ordered for shipment by courier through the company web site.

In June of 2009 I visited Seattle at her company headquarters in Ottawa, Illinois where a large staff works to prepare, package and label meals for delivery to distributors in Illinois, Indiana, Iowa and Wisconsin. After meeting with Seattle, several family members who are involved in the business, and a number of staff members, I can attest to the fact that they run the business according to what Seattle describes as "small town values", including patience, compassion, nurturing and trust.

KCM: I read your book, which gives me a good picture of where your business was in 2004. How do your 2004 stats compare with your current numbers?

SS:    Right now we have seen a bit of a decline because of the economy, but we've only had about three lay-offs, which I think is good. I'm an optimist, if I weren't, this business wouldn't be here. I feel like we're on a bubble with about five or six different things happening with the company, and it's almost like we're going to be exploding [with growth], and I'm very excited. Because of the kind of company we are, and the results we have, I really think that our future is just excellent.

KCM: Well, certainly you're results to date have been very impressive. You've recently expanded, so you're in more states now and you ship nationwide.

SS: Yes, we developed a Wellness Incentive Program, and so many of the larger companies wanted to make our meals available nationwide to all their employees. It doesn't even matter how many employees a company has, it can participate in our Wellness Incentive Program if it has 6 people or 50,000.

KCM: That's great. How many employees do you have here at your headquarters? I saw quite a few people.

SS: I think it's approximately 140 employees. That includes our drivers. We have 11 refrigerated trucks that deliver the meals to our distributors for our Illinois distribution, and they go all the way up into Wisconsin, like Madison and Milwaukee, Menomonee Falls, up in there. Then they go east to Indiana and also into parts of Iowa. Then we have a franchise kitchen that's in Minnesota, and they're our longest running franchise. And a couple years ago, they purchased their own facility and enlarged the operation.

Then we also have a kitchen in Michigan, and they do only one day ground shipping, and do not do distributor retail. They have just recently purchased Ohio as another franchise and that's also one-day ground shipping. Then we have a franchise that covers Kansas and Missouri and we prepare their meals because we're close enough. They have their own refrigerated trucking that comes here and picks them up. The new franchise kitchen facility in Arizona is now up and running.

KCM: Fantastic. I thought your book was very inspiring. When you started it in 1985, what were some of the biggest challenges you faced?

SS: Not that I didn't know so much about business, because I had really managed my husband's family practice and got it incorporated and all of that. So that was not really a problem.

The biggest problem I think was that I knew that my program was not just a weight loss program, and yet, I knew that I wanted weight loss results for the diabetics, and it was also healthy eating across the board. I didn't want to follow any bad diets that were just for weight loss, and so I had no model to follow.

All the ideas I incorporated were really what I felt was necessary. So having not been in the food business, one day I just picked up the phone, and I called Dr. Kahn at University of Illinois, and he said, "Well, come on down." And I'm actually now embarrassed at what I brought down there to show him as far as our meals, because I didn't know how to analyze the calories or anything. So he was very cooperative and thought it was a great idea. He had his students do an analysis of our meals.

And honestly, I can't remember exactly how it turned out; I just know that we made a lot of changes. So he was very helpful. I also had the local community college that had a small business association. In fact, a good friend of ours, Boyd Palmer, ran that until he became the director of the local Chamber of Commerce in Ottawa, Illinois. So a lot of times we were advised by the small business association of the local community college. That was helpful, but I think the fact was that here, I was not just starting a business, I was starting a whole new idea, that was the biggest challenge.

KCM: It was a new concept.

SS: A whole new concept that had never, as far as I know, been tried before. Honestly, I can tell you that since I started it and people have heard about us all over the country, I think I probably have read or heard about 300 people trying to do the same thing, and they have failed. So I think that one of the biggest challenges is you have to surround yourself with honest people, with people that are ambitious, and people that have the same philosophies that you have. I think that's really important in starting a business, and that also means you have to have a corporate lawyer, ours is Stuart Hershman, you have to have a good CPA, ours is Kevin Alsvig, and all those things have to be in place.

I actually started out with only three employees, and of course at that time I was still helping my husband in his family practice, and I promised him I wouldn't quit because he was kind of dependent on me, and he was cooperative with me in attempting to do this. Our five children were already gone then, and so I had more time. I knew that the statistics on starting a business and also the statistics on trying to develop a whole new business idea; they weren't very good.

KCM: You were not betting with the odds.

SS: And I can tell you that things didn't always go smoothly. I didn't want to complain to my husband, who has always been very supportive, because I didn't want him to say "Why don't you just quit?" I'm an optimist so I just kept moving forward and we got through a lot of things that I thought were real obstacles, but many of which really turned out for the best. Like sometimes, they do if you're switching jobs or something, it can turn out for the best. So I just plodded along and everything always seemed to come out okay at the end, even though I lost some sleep and all that, but I educated our children and grandchildren, they all know grandma says, "Nobody ever died of lack of sleep, just get up and go." So it worked and I found that a lot of my best thinking and planning before starting this company, was during the night, and I would get up and make notes.

KCM: I always recommend to people, keep a notepad next to the bed because you never know when that good idea's going to hit.

SS: Exactly. Things are quiet, you can really think. So that's true, that's very true.

KCM: The weakest ink is stronger than the strongest mind, in terms of remembering.

SS:    Oh yes, I definitely believe in making notes and getting things organized. I guess that my real challenges, my favorite challenges have always been planning because, even to this day, I love to plan – we have a group that we travel with, a group of eight people, two of the husbands died, so it's down to eight, but I always like planning vacations for the group. I think we like the planning more than the actual vacations. I'm a planner.

This Sunday, we're having a birthday party for my husband. We don't know whether we're going to have 50 or 200 people, and I wanted to leave it that way so that I could say, "Well, I think just a few people will be coming" because he never really wants to be honored with things like a party. But it's his 80th birthday, so I decided it would be such great fun to have our friends and former patients come by and wish him a happy birthday.

KCM: Running a business is all about problem solving and figuring out ways to overcome challenges.

SS:    Yes. We had three birds get into a transformer and cut out our electricity –

KCM: Three different days?

SS:    Yes, in the last two weeks. There's something in that transformer that brings them in.

KCM: Do you have a generator?

SS:    Yes, we've got to get a bigger one, this one is old.

KCM: That could be a real problem on a day when you've got to get food out.

SS:    That's right. The first time, we lost a lot of food, but it could've been worse. And I always have to add—I told you how important it is to surround yourself with good employees. Brian Emerson is one of our managers and he is doing very well, and I'm very proud of him. The way we got him is he simply sent in a resume that we couldn't resist. He was in charge of the meals for former Presidents Clinton and Bush at Camp David. But he came back here to retire in Illinois, just a few miles south because he had always told his wife that that's what he's going to do, come back home for her. So we get this resume and we thought, "Oh, we can't lose him." So we hired him. So he's got pictures of his family with the Bush kids and it's been really great.

KCM: So you've never had outside investors. I know at one point you sold the company.

SS:     The reason I sold it was because – well first of all, we were contacted by Campbell's Soup Company, and they said they were interested. So they had their head of new development come out to visit us here, we were at the old place downtown, and he had brought different groups out like the financial group, the nutrition group, about seven groups from the company. Then he and his wife became personally interested, and I don't know for sure why, I think one reason was that Campbell's Company themselves were no longer interested or maybe because that was right at the time the president of Campbell's Soup Company suddenly died.

Anyway, he and his wife became very interested, and they had investors. He had his Masters degree in business from Harvard, and back then, I think this was in April of 1991, and I was also thinking that eventually I hope this goes nationwide. So I sold the business to them in April 1991, they failed in 1992, and in 1993, I decided to reopen the business. So that's basically the story.

KCM: So that was when you changed the name?

SS:     Well, actually I started a new corporation because I didn't want to be liable for any debts from the old company. And Ed Sutkowski, our franchise attorney, suggested that we change to a less generic name. He said, "Well, why don't you use your name?" And I said, "Well, I want people to know what it is too." So we came up with the name of Seattle Sutton's Healthy Eating, and it's been that ever since.

KCM: So you've got lots of family members working here, which is really great.

SS: Yes, and they're all over, Washington, California, Texas, Indiana, and Illinois. They live all over. Two of our granddaughters recently joined the company after completing college, Erin Borgstrom and Anna Egofske. Needless to say, we get along very well, and they do very well.

KCM: You have a lot of distributors, and in many ways, they're the base of the company.

SS: Exactly. They're sort of all of our clients, really, and I think it was a very unique way that my accountant suggested I set this up rather than them being employees. So we're the manufacturer and they are the retail, they sell the meals retail. My daughter Ruth is in charge of all the distributors and deciding where to locate them, and so forth.

KCM: She was a distributor.

SS: Yes, she had experience being a distributor actually during the time I had sold the business and she saw all of the mistakes the new owners made. So it all worked out for the better, really. Yes, after having had that experience she came to me and she said, "You know what, mom, let's do it. I won't even charge you, but I'll help you." And I thought she would be an excellent person to be involved.

And she had three little children that she would drag with her and was working full time nights in the hospital, and was a distributor. [All three of Seattle's daughters became nurses.] She thought, "Well, I can still help you plan it and all of that." So we did, and we knew the changes to make, we knew the changes that needed to be implemented in our distributor manuals and all of that. So I thought, "Okay, let's do it."

KCM: One of the things I really like is that with your plan, people can choose it one week at a time. Less than one week, I think, doesn't make business sense. But with one week at a time, it gives people flexibility, they can take a trip and stop for a week or two.

SS: Yeah, I think that part of the reason I am successful is because I knew what the people needed. As a nurse, talking to people at my husband's office, I really knew what they needed. So I knew that it would have to be the healthiest eating possible, freshly prepared meals including fresh fruit and salad, fresh vegetables, and dairy. So I knew that in order to make sure that I was going to have results, I knew that I would serve every meal for the week, and some people of course would say, "Well, you know, I can do my own breakfast, and I just want lunches and dinners." I said, "Well, no, because I also know that you could undo what I do for you." And I said, "The price is the same." That's what stopped it all. [The food has to be purchased in one week groups of 21 meals.]

Every time a new distributor started and they were asked, "I just want dinners." We'd say, "I don't know why I can't just sell them dinners." And I said, "No, because No. 1, it doesn't keep it simple, we've got to keep it simple." And I've never veered into doing any catering; it's a whole different business. So I knew that it would have to be the healthiest possible, fresh meals, no gimmicks, no contracts to sign, and it would have to be at least a week.

Sometimes people call me and ask if we guarantee weight loss. And I say, "Yes." But if you call me and you tell me you didn't lose weight, I would tell you, "You either cheat or you're laying there in a coma." But basically they know the point I'm trying to make, and they really like it because then they know that, hey, I can go on this and I'm going to have results – it is 100 percent really.

KCM: If they don't cheat.

SS:     Even getting out of bed, they're going to wear off more than 1200 calories.

KCM: The laws of physics say that if they're alive and they're moving around at all, they should lose some weight at the 1200 calorie level.

SS:     They should, yes that's right.

KCM: So if you were talking to a group of young people who wanted to be entrepreneurs, what one or two pieces of advice would you give them?

SS:     This is America; go for it, that's No. 1.  No. 2, don't expect it to be a 9:00 to 5:00 job.  You're going to have to give it a lot of thought, and you're going to have to work very hard in order to be successful.  So you've got to expect that.  For example, like in the business I started, I knew that how we answered the phones was essential.  The person answering had to understand what we had to offer.  And so I answered the phone myself at first, my 800 line, until 1999..  We went to an interactive voice system and have the distributor call the customer back because we couldn't keep up with our advertising.  We would get like 70 calls with one 30-second television commercial.

And I think in particular, I knew that our meals were just really great for the elderly because a lot of times we've kept them from going to assisted living.  They might be able to live at home, but can't do their own planning, shopping, cooking, and cleaning up.  Our meals are a great option for them.

Then also we get a lot of people when they're discharged from the hospital, in fact, we're working right now with hospitals to be involved in their discharge procedures where they provide our information.  We had a company that helps hospitals with their major problems, and the subject came up at board meeting, and our name was brought up, so we're getting involved in that.  That can be a major problem because in little communities like here, everybody has 20 neighbors that step in and help, but sometimes in the bigger cities, or when they're new to the area, they have nobody right there that can help them.

So it's very handy and convenient to have the meals delivered right to their door and twice a week, nine meals on a Monday, 12 on a Thursday, and it is healthy eating. And most of these people, if they've been hospitalized because they have heart problems or they're diabetic, well they know that their eating has to change. Many families too, they call us, maybe a wife from a husband's bedside –I want to take care of my husband, but the cooking's really a problem. So they call and order the meals.

KCM: In fact, that brings to mind one of our employees, whose mother had surgery. She was off her feet for quite some time, but her husband who hasn't cooked a meal in the last 60 years, is having real difficulties with the shopping and the cooking and so forth. So Seattle Sutton's would've been just the ticket for that.

SS:     And we find that a lot of people buy gifts, and even pregnant women or somebody that's delivered a baby, and they wonder what to do for that person. Well, they're going to come home with this baby, they're going to nurse the baby of course, if they're health conscious at all, and yet, they know what they eat is really important, and they feel frustrated because they don't have all that time. So we've had that happen a lot, that pregnant women or nursing mothers will be on our meals to eat healthy. We do all the work for them.

KCM: When you first started, you didn't really have competition, but you do have some today.

SS:     And you know what, I just like to think that as long as we concentrate on making this the very best possible and follow the nutritional scientists' suggestions, it doesn't really matter if we have competition. I don't think there's ever anybody that's really set out to do what I do, including the fact that every meal has a nutritional fact sheet, and every meal has the ingredients. I just think that we can't be beat, that's not just because I own the company, its true.

KCM: I look at the elements that people use to make decisions about purchases: time, price, quality, convenience, and risk, and I see advantages in a number of those. Good convenience, good quality food so people will keep buying it, it saves them time. There are a lot of elements of the main criteria that you're fulfilling, so it's not a surprise that you have been successful.

SS:  It's also cost. I'm very proud of the fact that we actually went ten years without a price increase, and that was because we were growing so rapidly, and when you're growing a business, many things stay stable. Cost stays stable because you can get better prices with larger orders, and so the more you can produce, the longer you can go without price increases. But, of course, the last couple of years with the huge increase in food costs, and our trucking, they're all diesel trucks, we did have to increase prices the last couple of years.

Another thing, we are always interested in helping as many people as possible. I think that right now, our pricing provides very good value. We have five-week rotation with repeating the same meal ten times a year; they only get that meal ten times a year. And I think that there isn't anybody that could actually do what we do for them for the same price, and we are better than hiring your own chef because we don't even mess up your kitchen doing it. I know that we've had many celebrities on our meals, and of course, some go under another name when they order.

KCM: We were talking earlier about how I ordered something in a restaurant that was loaded with sodium, but I really had no way of knowing. I thought it was the healthiest thing on the menu.

SS:  And what you ordered, I figured out for you, you could've eaten three days of our meals and not had that much sodium.

KCM: So thinking back to that group of young entrepreneurs, what are some of the mistakes that you would counsel people to avoid?

SS: Well, in a way, I wish that I would've been one of the franchisees and had everything handed to me on a platter, the whole plan. If I had known everything that I know now, which is what we teach our franchisees when we train them on how to do what we do, that would've been a lot easier. So I think buying a franchise is a good business. Then you really have to have a good idea, and maybe even a good story, like how I got started with my husband's patient in the office. I could tell he wasn't listening to me and suddenly he said, "Look, Seattle, I'm going to be honest with you, I'm not going to do all that work" because I was trying to help him plan his diabetic meal plan.

Then I think also the experience that I talk about with my own father, who weighed 385 pounds when I went off to Jamestown College School of Nursing in North Dakota in 1950. And I thought then that, my gosh, if they just had somebody to do the work for them, they would see results, and he would be okay. And of course, back then, I wasn't ready to start this, and until I started this, there was nobody even attempting it.

There are bad diets out there, and I think that's probably true in any business, there is false advertising, and I made up my mind right away that I would not get involved in false advertising. I would not, for example, show a before and after weight loss person that wasn't our own client.

KCM: One of the things that I always advise people is maintain high integrity. It takes years and years to build a reputation and five minutes to ruin it.

SS: That's right.

KCM: Like fine China, easily broken, not easily repaired.

SS: That's right, and I also knew that I wasn't really interested in selling a franchise to just anybody.

KCM: It's more than just a business, you believe in what you're selling.

SS:     Yeah, because I, myself, could never sell something that I thought was wrong or didn't believe in. So I would never want a distributer or franchisee that didn't believe in it too. And we've never really advertised for distributors. I think that almost 100 percent were on our meals and were impressed and wanted to get involved in this company.

KCM: You started out, and it's very interesting to read in your book about how you would place ads to run at 2:00 in the morning and set your alarm, then go answer the phone when people would call after watching the spot. What advice do you have for people just starting out in business about sales and marketing?

SS:     I think No. 1 would be you have to give good service and that means answer your phones. People don't want to be put on hold for ten minutes, they don't want to have to go through a big rigmarole get to somebody to tell them what it's all about. And it has to be people that are working for you, that are going to make the sales, you have to be sure that they know what you're all about and can answer questions, and not just somebody that's reading a script. It just doesn't work, especially when you're starting a new business.

You have to be sure that the person answering the phone is doing it properly and is friendly and knows everything about the company, and will spend time answering questions. Like our distributors, they have to be willing to spend time and we always tell our distributors, we don't care if you forward your phones to a cell phone. But answer your phones because it might be an elderly person that needs the time changed on their home delivery, or something. And they get really frustrated and worried if they can't get in touch with someone. We also say that if you don't want to be interrupted during dinner, for example, then don't be a distributor.

That was never a problem with me because my husband was in family practice; that was really before cell phones, he finally had pagers at the end, before his retirement. But we never turned our phone off because my husband said at that time, it was his duty as a family practice doctor, and he felt he had his patients really educated very well not to bother him if it wasn't necessary. So we answered our phones. In fact, really, before they had emergency room coverage, doctors took turns covering the emergency room, and it would be for two-week periods, and it was really tough. So we were really used to never turning off the phone.

KCM: Those are elements of good service.

SS: Exactly, and also when you're dealing with all ages, it's important to have really good phone coverage and have good employees that explain your product.

KCM: Are there any books that you've read that you found useful that might be helpful to somebody starting out a business?

SS: You know what? One of the best was by Ray Kroc from McDonald's. One of his main ideas was "keep it simple." He talked about how you must keep everything simple. For example, when I sold the business, started giving people a lot of choices, and when deliveries went to distributor sites, they often had to make another trip back because some part of the order was wrong. It was no longer simple. They had to go back track to almost every location, every week, twice a week, and that was very costly.

I've often wondered when I look at some restaurants who have these pages of menu, what their waste is.

KCM: I wonder the same thing, and I've also wondered how old the food is. Again, if I order something that is only ordered once every two weeks.

SS: We also had to teach our vendors that we're going to call them and we're going to send it back, if it isn't just right. So they don't unload things on us, believe me. They know better. And I think that the people that you deal with have to know your expectations.

KCM: So you've really built in a lot of efficiencies by keeping it simple, and there's a cost to complexity.

SS: Absolutely, and that's another reason why I haven't ever been interested in catering. I also knew that by keeping it simple, it was good for the clients. I wanted them to have results.

KCM: What advice do you have about selecting staff members?

SS: In most cases, there is a 90 day probation period where you can tell if that employee, not always, but you can tell if that employee is really good or not. I also think this goes way back to parents. I think parents should tell their children to do better, that if you go to work, do better than as expected. Some people, they seem to have the attitude that, well, they're going to get this job, but this company better be good to me.

However, I think that it is important to be good to the employees, and it's also good to reward them, and it's good to give incentives, and to promote those that really do well, that's so important.

KCM: So you run a meritocracy.

SS: Yes, and I think that all business owners should keep that in mind, and that's the best way to run the business, really. But I think parents need to teach their children that they must do a good job if they expect to move along with the company.

KCM: Do you write out a business plan every year or specific goals every year?

SS: No, I don't, but you know what? We have meetings and we do set goals. I don't know if you could call it an actual business plan as such, but we set goals and we review our past goals, and we talk about the new things coming up, and what other things we should include. So no, but I guess it's because I'm not a business major or something. I think though that because I'm not a business major, in some ways it's helped me.

I'll give you an example of when I first started and some of the distributors were doing very well. And they came up with a question like, "Are you going to reward us, like maybe reduce the price of our meals that we buy from you or what are you going to do for us if we do well?" I gave that quite a bit of thought, and I came up with the idea of something that would not only help them, but the company.

So I decided that if they reached certain levels of customers for a week and we would then reward them with local advertising. They do local advertising of their own, and we would reward them with money to do the local advertising of their choice. That would also teach them some marketing skills, and what works, what doesn't work, etc. And it could even be different in some communities, but I wanted them to kind of be educated in that too.

So we set up a plan – when they're up to 30 customers, we have some water bottles with the Seattle Sutton Healthy Eating name on it, we gave them water bottles, two dozen I think it was. They could treat their clients to those or whatever, and then if they reached 40 clients, they would receive five of our watches, which they could advertise and give to anybody. So they could either give it to their cousin, their watches or they could use it as a goal for weight loss people when they lose their 25 pounds, they could give them their watches or whatever. Then, if they hit 50 count, they will get $2,000 worth of advertising. Then 60 count, they got $3,000 more, etc., all the way up to $10,000. That gave us the ability to promote the distributors that were doing well in a way that kept everything simple. We sell to all distributors at the same cost.

KCM: Simple and fair.

SS:     Right, exactly. But this gave us the ability to really help promote those that are doing well. So I give that instead of sending them to Las Vegas for a weekend. They would be away from their phones. So I didn't want to give them a trip to Vegas, for sure.

KCM: In your book, I have stars and underlines in that section because I love that idea. It benefits them and it benefits you, everybody wins.

SS:     Well, business-wise, it's better than just giving them a check for $2,000. In order to use that bonus, they send her the invoice and the copy of the check paying for the advertising. But that's good because if you just gave that money to them as a bonus, it wouldn't be building the business. This way we know that it's building their business and our business.

KCM: Your interests are aligned, that's a good idea. So currently as you mentioned, we're in some tough economic times, heading toward 10 percent national unemployment, and so I know that must have had some impact on the sales. So what things are you doing now to weather the storm?

SS:     If a customer is worried about losing a job or even having lost a job, it's going to impact our business, and it has, but yet, I think it probably hasn't as much as with bad weight loss programs because we're in the health business. Customers value the health part of purchasing our meals. And we actually have physicians now and registered dieticians that recommend us. Some physicians are even writing a prescription go on Seattle Sutton's meals. So I think that our business hasn't been affected as much as a lot of businesses.

Yes, but generally speaking, I think as a business, you have to keep on top of that, and you have to have a plan as to what your course of action is going to be. The only time a business ever fails is when they run out of money. So you've got to be sure you don't run out of money. And I have a philosophy to that, I think it's from my dad, who really loved business, and of course, he only had two years of high school. My mother did all the bookkeeping for him. So it showed me that this can be done even if you don't have that higher education. You've got to pay your bills.

I think that I almost discharged one of our distributors once because I had a call from a telephone company who was telling me that that distributor did not pay their phone bills. And actually, we have it in our operating manual that what they do reflects on all other distributors too, and possibly franchisees, therefore, they must pay their bills or they can't be a distributor. That was about 3:00 in the afternoon, I gave that distributor until 5:00 that day to get that bill paid, and they did. It's just my philosophy. We have no debts, but part of it was because I built it slowly. We pay our bills promptly. And we have no outstanding debts and no loans.

KCM: I worked in a hotel for 10 years owned by a family. Even though they kept putting on additions and so forth, they were always very conservative about financing and never got themselves into too much debt. They never took on investors. So they built it slowly, but steadily, they didn't try and build it overnight.

SS:     Yes. I get calls all the time, people either want to buy my business, which now that I have these 14 grandchildren, nine are in college right now that are interested in possibly joining the company, it's not for sale. I tell them up front, it's not for sale, why should it be?

KCM: What are some tips for people on working with family members?

SS:     Oh, yes. Well, I think it all started with our advice or when our children got married, we gave them one bit of advice, "You're going to have problems, but we don't want to hear about it." Honestly, now they've been married – the first one got married in 1980, and then they all followed very quickly. We, still to this day, have not ever had any of our five children or their spouses complain to us about each other. I think that that just carried over to our grandchildren too.

You have to, as a business owner, or starting a business, or developing a relationship, you have to let people know what's important to you and what you expect. I can't imagine if they put me in the middle and complained about each other. It would be not be any fun, and right now, it's so much fun. And I can already tell that the two cousins that have joined the company that they're never going to have a problem, or at least I won't know about it, they're going to work it out.

KCM: I remember that story about you losing the buildings with little notice.

SS:     That's right, this is another important business lesson. If you deal with somebody in business, it's important that, if it does have to end, to end it on at a good relationship, especially in a small community. I have never said a bad word about that landlord. We're still good friends with him. Even the people that purchased my business, I really never had any harsh words with them.

KCM: Are there any questions that I should've asked but didn't?

SS:     I'm trying to think of what else we do that might be a little different. You did a good job. You brought out everything.

KCM: Thank you so much. I really appreciate it.

## Chapter 19

# A Summary of Big Ideas from the Entrepreneurs Profiled

*Few men during their lifetime come anywhere near exhausting the resources dwelling within them. There are deep wells of strength that are never used.*

– Richard Byrd

I occasionally encounter skepticism when I recommend to aspiring entrepreneurs that they seek out and study success models. One concern is "survivorship bias," the possibility that the successful ones may have just been lucky and others who did the same things may have gone out of business. Another is the tendency for successful people to be "revisionist historians," recalling their experiences in a more favorable light than was really the case.

As a scientist, I can't simply dismiss these concerns out of hand. However, unlike medical interventions where we can run clinical trials, randomly assigning one group to receive the intervention and another to a placebo, evaluating the factors associated with entrepreneurial success and failure must rely on other types of evidence. In this book I have tried to provide practical ideas that can be applied in the real business world. I have not attempted to present theoretical and empirical background to support these approaches, although this has been done in some of the books listed in the bibliography and in published studies cited by those authors. However, over more than 20 years of studying small business owners, I have become very adept at predicting which ones are likely to do well and which ones will fail. Each time I encounter a new small business, I rate it on the degree to which it is aligned with the principles summarized in this book, particularly the elements of SLEEC (sales/marketing quality and my assessment of their efforts to generate employee and customer loyalty and engagement).

I have had a particularly good record with restaurants, which are some of the easiest businesses to evaluate because customer service and marketing can be readily evaluated. In one shopping center close to our home that contains about 18 restaurants ranging from fast food to higher-end casual dining, my record has been 100% for predicting which establishments will last longer than 2 years. In the 9 years that we have lived in the area, I have counted 26 restaurants. In each of the 8 cases of a restaurant closure, I had put the establishment on my "likely to fail" list after visiting once or twice. In one instance, three separate establishments have occupied the same space, all of which have failed. Location certainly cannot be the culprit, since this spot has two restaurants adjacent to one another, one of which has been thriving for the entire 9 years.

This experience is just one of many that have led me to conclude that small business success is rarely a matter of luck. Instead, successful entrepreneurship results from learning and practicing a set of skills. Peter Drucker famously said:

> "Because the purpose of business is to create a customer, the business enterprise has two – and only two – basic functions: marketing and innovation. Marketing and innovation produce results; all the rest are costs."

Successful entrepreneurs constantly search for innovative ways to market their products and services to new and existing customers, to enhance customer and employee loyalty, and to improve their competitive position by being better than their competition on one or more of the drivers of purchase decisions: time (speed), price (relative to expectations), quality (product and service), convenience and risk.

The entrepreneurs profiled in Section 2 of this book have all been very successful or, for those earlier in the process, are applying the success principles outlined. Below are a few of the themes (big ideas) emphasized by one or more of those profiled.

**Owning a Business is not a 9 to 5 Endeavor**
Seattle Sutton would set her alarm in order to wake up in the middle of the night to answer telephone calls when a commercial for her company was running. In her book, Doris Christopher recounts having to give up various activities she enjoyed such as playing bridge and pinochle with friends in order to have enough time for her family and the business. When we met, Anthony Curtis talked about driving to the office early in the morning, before the sun came up.

Successful entrepreneurs behave like optimists. They have tenacity. They are willing to put in the hard work and the long hours, to make the necessary sacrifices, because they believe that doing so will lead to success. However, hard work alone is not enough. Successful entrepreneurs channel their efforts toward those things that are most important. To paraphrase Peter Drucker, they make sure that the right things are getting done in the two basic functions – marketing and innovation.

**The Importance of Integrity**
Every one of the entrepreneurs profiled puts a high value on honesty and integrity. They have been able to develop high levels of trust with their customers and employees. Trust is never given freely, it has to be earned. The easiest way to earn trust is to deserve it. Successful entrepreneurs always work hard to do the right things for their customers and employees. They treat them fairly, tell the truth (especially in advertising) and try to offer good value for the prices they charge. The entrepreneurs profiled also refuse to use high pressure or misleading sales tactics.

Bill Child fixed washing machines that were sold by the manufacturer with defective parts, wiping out nearly a full year of profits. When the manufacturer refused to do the right thing by Bill's customers by properly fixing the machines, he stepped up and did so at a time when he could not easily afford to do so. The payoff was earning the trust and loyalty of hundreds of customers.

**Find a Niche**
Many successful businesses have been launched to fill a gap in the marketplace. Anthony Curtis launched a company to sell a newsletter and books about Las Vegas. Doris Christopher recognized that kitchen utensils would sell better if they were demonstrated because people would not recognize how a particular tool could be used to save time or to quickly prepare tasty meals. By using an in-home demonstration model, she was able to more clearly convey the benefits of using The Pampered Chef's products in a comfortable, fun and pressure-free atmosphere.

**Marketing is Essential**
You may have the world's best product or service, but you will not be successful unless you get the word out to potential customers. All of the entrepreneurs profiled are aggressive (but truthful) marketers. Anthony Curtis said during his interview that they do not market aggressively and rely mostly on media appearances to get the word out about their products. He did not mention that the Las Vegas Advisor web site generates more than 100,000 unique visitors per month and 3 million page views. They have features such as Question of the Day, Today's News, message boards and blogs that attract many visitors. In addition, Huntington Press is largely a wholesaler for books, so other companies such as Amazon, Barnes and Noble and various independent bookstores and web sites provide marketing for them. While I believe that Anthony could enhance his sales by employing more marketing methods, I would still classify him as an aggressive marketer.

Many companies spend too much time and energy trying to obtain new customers and not enough on strengthening and deepening their relationships with existing customers. I once heard a marketing consultant discuss a survey in which people who had expressed very high or extremely high satisfaction with a company were called and asked the name of the company that provided the service several months later. A majority could not remember the name of the company they used. How many restaurants have you visited in the last three months? How many of these establishments made any attempt to get your contact information so that they could keep in touch?

## Customer Service Must be Top-Notch

All of the entrepreneurs profiled go to great lengths to provide exceptional customer service and to make things right when a customer has experienced a frustration or inadequate service. Vlado Lenoch said it well when he said "If a customer is on the verge of leaving, it's like a 20 alarm fire." They work hard to keep customers happy because they understand how much more expensive it is to obtain a new one than to keep existing customers happy.

Rose Hanbury emphasized the importance of eliciting feedback from customers to find out what they would like that is not being offered. This led to the creation of nightlights with themes they had not considered, such as Asian Indian artwork. Many existing customers would be happy to offer suggestions for how you might improve your interactions with them, such as by offering a product or service you currently are not providing, or improving some aspect of your business they find frustrating (for example, a web site shopping cart or an automated telephone tree). However, most will not go to the effort to offer these suggestions unless you elicit their feedback.

## Hire Well and Keep Employee Turnover Low

In small organizations every person counts and, as a small business owner, you cannot afford weak links. It is usually a good investment to pay a bit more to hire the best candidates. With proper training and experience, employee value and productivity per unit of time will generally grow faster than payroll. I like to say that our company has high turnover during the first three to

---

six months – when we weed out the individuals who do not perform or do not buy into our mission and values – and low turnover thereafter. Research shows that the two factors that predicted profitability across many industries were low employee turnover and low customer defection.

The same companies that have happy, loyal customers tend to have happy, loyal employees. Like customer loyalty, employee loyalty has to be earned. This results when employees feel they are treated equitably, have opportunities for achievement (advancement as well as knowledge and skill development) and a sense of camaraderie (team spirit). In Chapter 9, I used the acronym EATS to describe the elements that contribute to employee satisfaction: Equity, Achievement and Team Spirit. Vlado Lenoch reports that their average employee tenure is 8 to 10 years. I can attest to this, as during a recent visit to the hotel at which I worked 20 years ago, I was surprised at how many familiar faces I encountered. It is not a coincidence that their properties have been successful.

One critical aspect of maintaining low turnover is to be sure that your business is run as a meritocracy. All employees should receive regular, candid feedback, and expectations regarding what constitutes adequate performance should be clear. Good performance should be rewarded with money, recognition and training. Employees should receive feedback and instructions for improvement when performance is inadequate or behavior is unacceptable. Failure to do these things will cause the best performers to look elsewhere for employment. In addition, the poor performers are likely to stay, producing a double dose of downgrading in your staff.

**Be Patient – Success Does Not Happen Overnight**
Television shows, magazines and newspapers are filled with stories about people who made it big in a short time. While these are always interesting, they are the exception, not the rule. For every Michael Dell or Bill Gates who succeeds on an enormous scale in a short time there are thousands of small business owners who succeed, but on a smaller scale and over a longer period.

Building a business takes time, in part because it takes time to establish relationships with customers through repeated favorable interactions. While there are many things that can be done to speed up the growth process, particularly with regard to marketing, it is important not to grow so fast that your systems cannot keep up, leading to poor service and frustrations for employees and customers. In her book, Doris Christopher describes a difficult decision they had to make at The Pampered Chef in 1990. The company had grown so quickly that they had to temporarily put recruitment of new Kitchen Consultants on hold and establish an early order cut-off date (November 2$^{nd}$) in order to guarantee pre-Christmas delivery. They felt that this was the right thing to do for the long-term health of the company.

**Systems are Important**
Seattle Sutton and Doris Christopher both have businesses that have been able to expand dramatically because they developed simple processes and procedures that could be replicated. When asked about business books that she found influential, Seattle cited one by Ray Kroc (*Grinding it Out, The Making of McDonald's*), who was responsible for spearheading the expansion of McDonald's Corporation. The business and its main systems were actually created by Richard and Maurice McDonald in San Bernardino, California, who then partnered with Ray Kroc to expand and grow the concept.

Author and consultant Michael Gerber has written a series of books based on the concept of The E-Myth, which is short for the entrepreneurial myth. The central idea is that most businesses fail, or at least fail to reach their potential, because they are not systematized and their successful operation revolves around the owner. Systems and procedures have not been set up to allow major aspects of the business to run without his or her direct involvement. As a result, the more successful the business becomes, the more stretched the owner becomes, leading to overwork, burnout and frustration. His solution is to advise business owners to organize and systematize their businesses as if they were planning to franchise. This involves thinking through each step in the process of providing whatever product or service the business delivers and committing each to paper. Then sufficient time, energy and resources are committed to training staff on how to implement these steps.

By developing formal processes and procedures, translating them to concrete steps and checklists, then training staff on how to implement these, the business owner creates several advantages. First, this helps to set clear expectations for each employee's role. If the goals and steps necessary to achieve those goals are clearly laid out in writing, this helps to prevent ambiguity regarding expectations and whether results obtained are consistent with expectations. Second, the written materials provide a resource for staff to use as a reference when the owner or manager is not available, which helps them to work independently. However, management is required to ensure that people really use these tools. Staff members should be referred to the training manual to look up the answers to questions. Systems should be in place to ensure that checklists are really used in practice. This will help to avoid preventable mistakes that occur when people attempt to complete a process without referring to a formal checklist. Such checklists are used almost universally when the consequences of failure are enormous. Even after flying for 20 years, a pilot will complete a checklist before taking off.

### Simpler is Often Better
McDonald's and many other businesses that have been able to expand dramatically have systems that help to ensure consistency. The experience one has at a McDonald's, Starbucks or Subway shop is going to be similar and familiar whether the interaction takes place in Boise, Idaho or Elkhart, Indiana. Among the drivers of purchase decisions (time, price, quality, convenience and risk), these three businesses have somewhat different propositions, but the consistency they provide helps to reduce the risk. I travel a great deal and often eat at chain restaurants in destination cities because I know what to expect. I am not sure what my experience is going to be like if I go to an unfamiliar deli or sandwich shop, so the risk of having a bad experience is higher.

While it is not always possible to fully systematize businesses that employ knowledge workers such as lawyers, physicians, engineers, etc. There are always aspects of the business that can be systematized, which will help to maintain consistency and provide a better match between customer expectations and the product or service delivered.

Simplicity can also have important cost advantages. Seattle Sutton offers only two options, a 1200 or a 2000 calorie diet plan with a five-week rotating menu. At one point she sold the original business and later restarted under a new name after the entrepreneur she sold the business to was unsuccessful. The new owner had made changes to offer greater variety and more options. While this greater flexibility very likely had some marketing advantages, it also increased costs and the risk of making costly errors. By keeping the systems simple and limiting options, Seattle had been able to keep costs and errors to a minimum.

Our family has cable television and the cable company offers a large variety of options. During the time we have lived in our home, we have had to upgrade equipment every few years. Various options require different types of equipment and a single home with multiple televisions may require two or three types of cable boxes. If you order service that includes video recording, one type of cable box is necessary and if you have certain channels in your package the basic cable box does not carry these. On multiple occasions we have had equipment updates, only to discover later that an option in our package, for which we were paying a monthly fee, no longer worked after the new equipment was installed. This necessitated additional service calls, which were inconvenient. Also, if we wanted to get credit for the service we had paid for but was unavailable for part of a month due to the cable company's error, this would require a call during business hours that would take as long as 15-20 minutes after considering the time spent wading through a telephone answering tree, time on hold, etc. This complexity resulted in additional costs for the cable company due to errors and frustration on the part of the customer (our family).

Contrast this approach with that taken by Southwest Airlines. They have the distinction of being one of the only US-based airlines that has shown consistent profitability over a period of decades. They use a single model of airplane (the Boeing 737) and do not offer their passengers multiple classes of seating. Rather than using a hub and spoke system, they fly multiple short, quick trips into and out of the secondary airports of major markets. As a result, they maintain high utilization rates for their airplanes, which spend a smaller fraction of time on the ground than for any other major airline. They offer basic, no frills transportation and, by keeping their systems simple and streamlined, are able to maintain a low cost structure (despite having a predominantly unionized workforce) and are therefore able to maintain profitability while charging lower prices than other major airlines.

If you own a small business, it pays to regularly review your systems with an eye toward simplification. Ask customers and staff what can be done to make your processes simpler and easier to use. Doing so will often contribute to greater satisfaction for both groups. In the end this can translate into lower costs, greater customer and staff engagement, and higher profits.

**Stick to Your Knitting**
This is really just a restatement of Warren Buffett's circle of competence idea. Each of the entrepreneurs profiled has resisted the temptation to diversify into other industries where they lacked the necessary skill and experience to compete effectively. They stuck with what they knew how to do well. This does not mean that they did not experiment with new offerings. For instance, Rose Blumkin's Nebraska Furniture Mart and Bill Child's RC Willey stores expanded beyond furniture and appliances to include electronics and other items for the home in their retail stores.

Many large companies have run into trouble when they made acquisitions in new and unfamiliar businesses. It is certainly possible to successfully pursue acquisitions in new areas, but the risk is greater. I once worked for people who had been very successful in growing a health information technology business, but made many mistakes when they tried to expand into the clinical research business. Often these mistakes were avoidable and better options would have been obvious to people with more experience in the field with a better understanding of the organization dynamics of pharmaceutical companies.

The astute reader may be wondering if the author is making a mistake by trying to operate in too many businesses at once. My wife and I own a residential property management company, a clinical research company and we are now moving into publishing and consulting (on a very limited basis) with small business owners. In addition, I write medical textbooks and teach part of a board review course in Clinical Lipidology. I have to admit that I am spread more thinly than might be ideal, but I have passion for all of these areas and I have been reasonably astute at picking managers who can operate business units without a lot of direct management from me. I understand the risk associated with not sticking to my knitting, but hope that I can make it work anyway. My advice to other entrepreneurs is to think long and hard about any move that is not a logical extension to your core area of expertise.

**Finance Conservatively**
Many entrepreneurs feel frustrated at the rate of growth they can generate by relying on reinvestment of profits and look for debt or equity financing to enhance growth. I have very little personal experience with equity financing. I have had an ownership interest in two businesses in which I had partners other than my wife. In one case I closed the company, essentially subsuming its activities into my main business (Provident Clinical Research & Consulting, Inc.). In the other case I ended up buying out my partner. The old maxim applies – business partnerships are like marriage, but without the sex, and more likely to end in divorce.

I also worked for two companies that had venture capital financing. My impression was that management was constantly making short-term oriented decisions in an attempt to keep the investors happy. The investors wanted to see fast, uninterrupted growth. Not surprisingly, this short-term thinking led to poor long-term performance.

If your goal is to make an enormous fortune by starting the next Starbucks or Dell Computers and you are willing to risk losing control of the business, selling equity to investors in order to accelerate growth is likely to be the only way to make that happen. My orientation is to accept slower growth in exchange for complete control. I am much more concerned with the potential downside risk than I am with the possibility of becoming a billionaire, so I am not able to offer any useful guidance to the entrepreneur who wants to sell an equity interest to investors.

All of the entrepreneurs profiled in this book kept control of their businesses themselves or in partnership with family members. All started their businesses with fairly modest initial investments and grew mainly through cash flow and without excessive use of debt. Part of the art of entrepreneurship is skillful use of debt. To borrow an analogy from real estate expert Jack Reed, leverage [debt] is like the accelerator in a car. It can help you get to your destination more quickly, but not necessarily more safely.

Debt can be a very useful tool when used conservatively. Bill Child took on debt to build stores. The Lenoch family used debt to acquire or build motel and hotel properties. Doris Christopher, Rose Hanbury and Annette Norwood borrowed funds to make initial investments in products to sell and, in Annette's case, furnishings for a retail shop in which to do business.

The key is not to take on so much debt that a downturn in business would be likely to make it impossible to maintain debt service. This is largely a matter of thinking through "worst case" scenarios and having contingency plans for the inevitable rough spots. Often this means arranging for credit when it is not needed so that funds are available during tough times. Ironically, the ability to obtain credit, or credit on favorable terms, is greatest when one doesn't need it and lowest when one does. You don't want to be shopping for raincoats as a hurricane is bearing down. Buy your raincoats when the skies are clear and the forecast for more of the same.

**Hire Good Advisors**

A piece of advice to those who are just starting out as business owners that came up repeatedly in my interviews was to have a good lawyer and a good accountant. The importance of getting good advice regarding taxes, employment laws and contracts cannot be overstated. These professionals can help you decide what form your business should take (sole proprietorship, S-corporation, C-corporation, LLC, etc.) and how to operate in such a way that you protect your personal assets and don't run afoul of tax or employment regulations.

The tax laws in particular are ridiculously complex. Warren Buffett points out that the US tax code has more pages than the bible, but unlike the bible, almost every line of tax code has some special interest group defending the status quo or lobbying congress to have it changed. We use multiple attorneys in our businesses and, because we operate in two states, we have at least one attorney and one accountant in each state to deal with issues that our advisors in the other state cannot or will not handle because licensing laws require that the work be done by a party licensed in that state.

*Chapter 20*

# Big Ideas on Success for the Small Business Owner – A Refresher

*A vision is a clearly-articulated, results-oriented picture of a future you intend to create. It is a dream with direction.*
— Jesse Stoner Zemel

The previous chapters have covered what I believe are some of the most important concepts for entrepreneurial success, as well as profiles of business owners who have applied these principles in their businesses. This final chapter provides an overview of key concepts from Section 1, which, along with Chapter 19, will serve as a useful tool for quickly refreshing your memory about the big ideas presented in this book.

I wish each of you good health, wealth and happiness! Please visit us at www.TippingTheOdds.com to share your feedback and stories about the results you experienced when applying these concepts and strategies.

### Chapter 1: Learning to be a Successful Entrepreneur
- Only 31% of new businesses survive 7 years. Studying success models will help you to tip the odds in your favor.
- Seek out and study people (success models) who have already accomplished what you would like to do.
- Learn their strategies and mistakes they made along the way, then copy their strategies, minus the mistakes.

**Chapter 2:  Loyalty, the Key to Running a SLEEC Business**
- SLEEC = Sales/marketing + Loyal, Engaged Employees and Customers
- You must have effective marketing and sales efforts to succeed.  You can have the best product or service in the world and fail if you don't actively work at informing potential customers that you exist and how they can benefit from your offerings.
- Loyal, engaged customers will purchase more often, in larger amounts and provide referrals.
- Loyal, engaged employees will produce more and be less likely to seek work elsewhere, lowering the expenses associated with recruitment, hiring, and training new staff.
- Profits are the life-blood of a company, but the focus of the successful entrepreneur will always be on creating long-term value through trust and loyalty rather than short-term profits.  In the long-run, profits follow from value creation.
- It costs more to obtain a new customer that it does to entice a happy customer to return.
- Don't be afraid to walk away from toxic relationships.

**Chapter 3:  Attitudes and Habits of Successful Entrepreneurs**
Successful entrepreneurs consistently show the following characteristics:
- They have high integrity.  They work hard to tell the truth, keep their promises and treat customers and employees fairly and with respect.
- They behave like optimists.  They have persistence and tenacity.  When they encounter a road block they find a way to go around, over or under it.  They do not give up easily.  They believe that if they do the right things, good results will follow eventually.
- They realize that success does not happen overnight.  They are willing to sacrifice and delay gratification in the short-term in order to achieve long-term success.  They have enough passion for what they do to stay motivated in the face of inevitable short-term setbacks.

- They make an effort to know their personal strengths and weaknesses. They engineer their work so that they can focus on the things they are best at and get assistance with what they are not through delegation, outsourcing or partnering.
- They realize that it is impossible to please everyone. They don't allow criticism from others to knock them off course.
- They set short-term, intermediate-term and long-term goals for the activities required to generate success and reward themselves and their staff for achieving those milestones.
- They ensure that the right things get done, even those that are tedious and difficult.
- They reward good performance among staff members with MRT – money, recognition and training.
- Finally, successful entrepreneurs recognize that we live in the information age and that significant time should be invested in study to continually upgrade knowledge and skills.

### Chapter 4: The PARETO Principle – Using 80/20 Thinking to Achieve More with Less Effort

- A large percentage of the results in business (about 80%) are produced by a small percentage of the inputs (about 20%).
- Typically, the top 20% of entrepreneurs will account for 80% of business successes; the top 20% of employees will generate 80% of productivity; the top 20% of customers will generate 80% of the profits, etc.
- Systems should be in place to segment your staff, your customers and your products and services into those that are the most productive (top 20%) and least productive (bottom 10-20%). The greatest return on your time and energy will be from identifying those vital few staff members, customers and products or services that are responsible for a majority of your profits and productivity, then applying strategies to enhance your efforts in these areas.
- Engineer your work so that you are able to spend most (80%) of your time on
  - (1) high value tasks,
  - (2) activities you find enjoyable and fulfilling,

- o (3) strategic planning.
- High value tasks are those you can do better than anyone else that are also key to the success of the business.
- It is essential that you work into your routine some time to spend on activities that you find enjoyable and fulfilling. Failure to do this is likely to contribute to burnout and loss of enthusiasm.
- As a business owner, you need to spend a significant amount of time on strategic planning. You must set aside time to analyze metrics such as profit by type of customer, results from marketing efforts, etc. in order to keep the business moving toward your long-term goals. If you are spending all of your time working "in the business" you won't be able to devote adequate time to working "on the business."

## Chapter 5:  Avoiding Common Mistakes that Lead to Business Failure

Consulting and accounting firms have done business "autopsies" to identify the characteristics that lead to business failure. These characteristics include:

- Lack of Direction. Many entrepreneurs launch a business without specific goals and metrics for assessing their progress toward these goals. A business plan is simply a method for formalizing your goals, timelines for achieving them, and strategies for accomplishing the steps required to meet the goals.
- Insufficient Sales. Good marketing and sales efforts will get the attention of potential customers, generate interest and desire and move them to action. Failure to invest adequately in high quality marketing and sales efforts to bring in new customers and to sell more to existing customers is perhaps the most common reason for business failure.
- Poor Quality: Customers will generally return to make repeat purchases if they feel they have received good value. Price and quality are related. If a customer receives quality below what is expected for the price, defection is likely.

- Greed and Impatience. Owners who try to charge too much for the quality of product or service they deliver will soon find themselves struggling. Customers will be willing to pay more if they trust that they will receive good value. Trust is built over time through favorable interactions. It is better to price a bit low at first in order to increase the number of customers and build trust. Prices can be raised gradually after relationships have been built. Impatience and greed can cause a business owner to fail by driving its owner to take too much risk.
- Poor Cost Control: Poor cost control increases risk.
- Insufficient Working Capital: It is a common myth that large amounts of money are needed to start a business. However, a business needs a steady stream of sales to generate cash flow. Without cash flow, your business will die. It is critical to manage cash flow and to keep reserves of cash and credit available for the inevitable times when the market is soft. If in a cash flow crunch, take action! Get invoices out quickly, collect money from those who owe, renegotiate contract terms, use secondary or tertiary sources of credit you have secured ahead of time, minimize expenses.

## Chapter 6: A Few Big Ideas about Marketing and Sales

- The purpose of a business is to obtain and keep profitable customers.
- You must let potential customers know you exist. The four elements of marketing/sales performance are: lead generation, lead conversion, initial sale value and residual customer value from repeat sales and referrals.
- The only way to be sure about cost effectiveness is to set up systems to track responses to each of your marketing efforts so that you can assess the return on investment for each marketing strategy employed. This will allow you to track cost per sale and return on investment.
- Try many strategies on a small scale. Ramp up those that produce a good return on investment and eliminate those that do not after sufficient experimentation to determine that changing the copy does not improve the results.

- No matter what media are used (web sites, e-mail, social networking sites, newspapers, radio, television, etc.), your advertising should convey benefits associated with the use of your product or service.
- Narrow your focus. A great deal of money is wasted each year on advertising that is not targeted to an audience that has greater than average likelihood of being receptive to the message.
- You need to make a compelling offer in order to get people interested enough to learn more about your product or service.
- Do not stretch the truth. Maintain high quality products and services so that you can feel good about the benefits that you truly deliver to your customers or clients and describe them truthfully in your marketing.
- Offering a strong guarantee will almost certainly enhance your sales.
- Obtain testimonials from happy customers or clients.
- Never sell anything that you don't believe in, even if you could do so profitably.

## Chapter 7: Maximizing Lifetime Customer Value
- A common mistake that small business owners make is not working hard at maintaining and deepening their relationships with their existing customers and potential customers after an initial contact.
- There are many ways to stay in touch with your customers and potential customers:
  - One of the simplest is to send a thank you of some sort after a sale, particularly a first sale. For regular customers, be sure to send an acknowledgement at least once per year thanking the customers for their business.
  - Send out a short newsletter on a regular basis. This is costly and time consuming. However, the return on investment is nearly always positive and the cost can be minimized by using e-mail as a method of delivery.

- For certain types of businesses, a blog or new articles posted regularly on a web site is an excellent way to give your customers a reason to visit and take an active part in maintaining their relationship with you. This can serve as a low-cost method of advertising. An e-mail announcement can go out each time a new article is posted and new media (e.g., Facebook™ and Twitter™) can also help to inform customers of new developments.
- Happy customers will recommend your businesses to their friends, colleagues and relatives. You can enhance this process by actively requesting referrals from your happy customers.
- Rekindle relationships with former customers who have not recently purchased from you. Many business owners fail to do so.
- Respond quickly if you learn of a problem. An unhappy customer can frequently be converted to a "raving fan" if the situation is handled correctly.
- A database of people with whom your business has made contact and started relationships is an enormously valuable asset. This includes customers/clients, vendors and related businesses. It costs much more to make a sale to a stranger than it does to make a sale to someone with whom you have already transacted.

## Chapter 8: Managing Your Business in a Way that Builds Customer Equity

- Customers make a buying decision based on time, price, service/product quality, convenience and risk. Every interaction with a customer will build or destroy equity. Building equity does not happen by chance.
- Your job as a business owner is to set your customers' expectations, and then consistently meet or exceed these, so that your customers feel they are receiving good value.
- Your marketing and sales process will help to define your implied promises and your operations will determine how well you deliver on those promises.

- Customer feedback will provide valuable insights to help you improve. It may help identify a problem employee or ways to improve your systems to reduce customer frustration.
- A simple and convenient customer satisfaction survey will result in more people taking the time to complete it. In addition, you will be more likely to take the time to tabulate and analyze the results of a simple survey.
- Fred Reichheld of Bain and Co. makes a compelling case for asking one particular question. *How likely would you be to recommend [your company name] to a friend or colleague? Please circle your answer below.* The scale is 0 to 10. 0 = not likely at all  10 = extremely likely
- Only scores of 9 or 10 are adequate. Reichheld and colleagues define customers who provide scores in this range as *promoters*. Those who provide ratings of 7 or 8 are *passively satisfied* customers and those at 6 or below are *detractors*.
- Their studies showed promoters accounted for more than 80% of referrals. Detractors were responsible for 80% of negative word of mouth comments.
- Your goals should be to maximize the number of promoters and move passively satisfied into the promoter category.
- Some detractors are worth working with to see if they can be moved up the scale. Some need to "fired" because they are a poor fit for your business.
- Include a section on your customer feedback tool for comments and suggestions. For positive comments, ask the customer for permission to use his or her statement as a testimonial. For negative comments, assess whether this is an opportunity to salvage a damaged relationship.
- Make your values and expectations clear to your employees. CEOs Jamie Dimon and Bill Harrison put together a list of values and behaviors when Bank One and JP Morgan Chase banks merged.
    - o  Give customers a good, fair deal. Great customer relationships take time. Do not try to maximize

short-term profits at the expense of building those enduring relationships.

- o Never let profit center conflicts get in the way of doing what is right for the customer.
- o Always look for ways to make it easier to do business with us.
- o Don't forget to say thank you.
- Have an energizing mission statement. A mission statement conveys what you hope to accomplish if your business is successful.
- If you do not provide explicit instructions for staff on how to interact with your customers, you are not likely to get good results. You must follow this training with ongoing feedback and accountability.
- Remember that the way you interact with your employees will be reflected in the way they interact with your customers.
- You need ways to objectively measure compliance with your systems. What gets measured gets done, and what gets measured can be managed.
- Empower your staff to make it right for the customer. You want your staff members to direct their energy and intelligence toward doing everything they can to build equity with your customers through both word and deed.

## Chapter 9: Management that Promotes Employee Engagement and Enthusiasm

- Engaged and enthusiastic employees are more productive, stay longer, and business units with higher proportions of engaged employees are more profitable.
- David Sirota of Sirota Consulting uses four broad categories to describe employee morale: enthusiasm, satisfaction, neutrality and anger.
- Sirota and colleagues assert that there are three major sets of goals that are most important to people at work. In order of importance, they are: equity, achievement and camaraderie. Regular evaluation of employee satisfaction in a way that provides feedback to management on their

performance in these areas is critical in order to ensure these needs are being met.

- o We like to use the term "team spirit" in place of camaraderie, which produces the convenient acronym EATS (Equity, Achievement, Team Spirit).
- Equity is the degree to which the employees feel fairly treated. Greater equity ratings are produced by companies where employees feel that management truly cares about their well-being, treats them with respect, and provides compensation and benefits that are at least in line with industry norms.
- A sense of achievement results when people find the work they do a challenging use of their intelligence and abilities, when they are able to acquire new knowledge and skills, and when they feel pride in the importance of their role, as well as the overall mission of the company. Feelings of achievement are enhanced by recognition for performance, including advancement within the organization.
- Employees spend a large percentage of their time in the workplace and need to feel a sense of teamwork and community, i.e., camaraderie or team spirit. The most productive business units are characterized by groups of people who agree with the company's mission and values, enjoy interacting with one another, and report a spirit of teamwork and cooperation both within and across business units.
- Jack Welch at General Electric used the 4Es of Leadership to evaluate managers. The four parameters are:
    - o Has *Energy*: drive to succeed; embraces change; in constant motion toward goals and makes things happen rather than waiting for things to happen.
    - o *Energizes* others: ability to motivate others to perform; sharing credit and owning blame.
    - o Possesses *Edge:* competitive spirit; ability to make difficult decisions and take action when needed.
    - o *Executes*: performs consistently and delivers results.

- Technical skills are not enough to be a good manager. Being a good manager requires a set of talents and skills that allow one to motivate others to high levels of performance.
- Mission and values must be known by employees at all levels and everyone needs to be held accountable for living up to the stated values. Employees should receive regular, candid feedback on their performance. Managers should elicit feedback about how the employees feel about teamwork and camaraderie in the organization.
- Reward performance and withhold rewards from those who do not perform, to the point of termination if necessary. The best and the brightest are attracted to companies that are run as meritocracies and developing such a reputation will help you to get the best players in the field.
- Remember, one of the best aspects of owning a business is the ability to choose who you will work with each day. Toxic relationships should be terminated, whether with employees or customers.

## Chapter 10: Leveraging Individual Strengths and Building Teams with Complementary Strengths
- In general, employees will get the most pleasure and satisfaction when they are allowed to do what they do best on a daily basis.
- Better results are obtained by helping employees develop their strengths than by working to improve weaknesses.
- Individuals often have a difficult time accurately assessing their own strengths, so it is usually helpful to implement structured systems for assessing strengths and working with staff members to further develop their individual talents.

## Chapter 11: Preparing for and Managing Through Recessions and Other Crises
- There will be disappointments and crises in your business. Do not put yourself in a position where everything must work perfectly for your business to stay solvent.

- Use leverage (debt) sparingly and be willing to accept a slower, but safer rate of growth in revenues and profits.
- Be fearful when others are greedy and greedy when others are fearful. Economic downturns often bring with them the best opportunities for those who are prepared.
- During a recession, invest in ways that will make your business stronger during the rebound. In order to be in a position to invest heavily during the down segment of a business cycle, the business owner must manage conservatively during the up-portion of the cycle. This means developing cash reserves and avoiding excessive leverage.
- Weak or overleveraged competitors will go out of business during a downturn, which will allow you to build market share and emerge stronger when things turn around.
- Emphasize training and other ways of upgrading of knowledge and skills during the downturns.
- Control expenses at all times. The time to start controlling expenses is not during a downturn in the business cycle.
- Cut staff as a last resort. If you manage conservatively, the need to downsize will be rare. When layoffs are unavoidable, morale after the cuts will be strongly influenced by how you handle the layoffs. Treating people in a caring way and communicating regularly and candidly will minimize the damage.
- Obtain disability and life insurance.
  - Lifetime risk of experiencing disability of at least 90 days during a career ranges from 20-35% depending on age, sex and health issues. Don't let a disability of a few months force you to close your business.
  - Obtain inexpensive term life insurance policies for yourself, your spouse and any key employees whose deaths could significantly impair your business.

# Chapter 12: Big Ideas from Warren Buffett, Charlie Munger and Berkshire Hathaway

- Doing what you love with people you like, trust, and admire, will have a tremendous positive impact on your quality of life.
- Have heroes who display qualities you admire and wish to emulate, but don't follow them blindly.
- Set an example. If you don't behave with integrity and treat people with respect you cannot expect that your employees will do so with your customers.
- Devote significant time to self-education. Study business successes and failures, including your own.
- Understand that your returns on investments depend, in large part, on the price you pay. When buying a business, real estate, a stock or a bond, insist on a margin of safety a discount to a conservative estimate of the current discounted value of future cash flows.
- Think independently. You are neither right nor wrong because the crowd disagrees with you. You are right when your data and reasoning are sound. Grow only when it makes economic sense. Don't follow the crowd over a cliff (avoid the "institutional imperative").
- It is not critical to have a large circle of competence, but is critical to know where the perimeter lies and to stay within the circle.
- Only accept risks that you can properly evaluate, and avoid risks that threaten solvency.
- Turnarounds rarely turn, whether people or struggling businesses.
- When attempting to persuade, appeal to self-interest, not reason. For managers in your business, align your interests with theirs. An insufficient number of saints are available to staff a business.
- Hire people with integrity, intelligence, and energy. Of the three, integrity is the most important.
- You can't do a good deal with a bad person. Choose clients as you would friends.

- A reputation is built on years and years of integrity and hard work, but can be destroyed in a few minutes by a single misdeed.
- Understand the time value of money and the money value of time.
  - The most productive people are those who figure out how to spend much of their time on high value activities and less on low value activities.
  - Partner with people who have circles of competence complimentary to your own.
- Recognize your mistakes, admit them, and learn from them.
- Focus on what is important and knowable. Much of the financial news is noise and the main value of economic forecasters seems mainly to be to make fortune tellers look good.
- When approaching problems, a solution can often be found by inverting the problem. This is a useful mental habit.
- Work on your written and oral communication skills. Many entrepreneurs underestimate the importance of clear and compelling communication for business success.

## Acknowledgments

I am indebted to many people who assisted directly or indirectly with the creation of this book. First and foremost, I want to thank my wife (Cathy), our son (Miles) and my stepdaughter (Sarah) who put up with my absences during many weekends and evenings while I was writing.

Special thanks are due to Theresa Tardi for help with editing and far too many other issues to list. Several of our Provident Clinical Research & Consulting, Inc. staff members and consultants provided assistance with various activities, particularly Tia Rains, Denise Umporowicz, Tracey Resuali and Mitchell Silverman.

Sarah Sellergren, Phillip Anderson and Mark Morrison assisted with the creation and refinement of the cover art. April Stevens from Seattle Sutton's Healthy Eating provided invaluable assistance with coordination of my visit to the company headquarters and obtaining permissions from individuals mentioned in Seattle's interview.

A number of people read draft copies of this book and provided valuable input, including Jeffrey J. Fox; Richard Koch, Dan Kennedy; Drs. William Harris and David Mark; Roger Farley; Gloria Tiwari; Steve Vivian and David Sklansky. From Berkshire Hathaway, Bill Child (RC Willey), Ron Blumkin (Nebraska Furniture Mart) and Warren Buffett kindly provided input regarding the accuracy of the sections that dealt with their companies. I sent a copy to Charlie Munger, but it happened to arrive just days before his wife died, so he could hardly have been expected to respond. I extend my condolences to him and his family.

Finally, I am grateful to the entrepreneurs who allowed me to interview and profile them: Vlado Lenoch (William Tell Banquets), Rose Hanbury (Night Light Designs), Anthony Curtis (Huntington Press), Annette Norwood (Posh Salon), and Seattle Sutton (Seattle Sutton's Healthy Eating).

*Appendix A*

# Recommended Authors and Selected Titles

*Drive thy business, or it will drive thee.*

– Benjamin Franklin
(Writing as Poor Richard)

The amount of information published every year about business and entrepreneurship is enormous and often overwhelming. After years of study, I still regularly come across useful concepts that are completely new to me. Below is a list of authors and selected titles that I have found to be particularly helpful. I have purposely limited the list to books and did not include any academic research papers or other less accessible sources. This is by no means a comprehensive list of useful business books. However, I can guarantee that reading any of these will be well worth the time and effort. If there are books you have found especially helpful, please feel free to contact me with your recommendation through our web site at www.TippingTheOdds.com.

### *Jack and Suzy Welch - General Electric*
Perhaps the best business book I have ever read is *Winning* by former General Electric CEO Jack Welch and his wife Suzy, who is a former Harvard Business Review Editor. I can't recommend this book enough. I also enjoyed *Winning, the Answers*, which was a follow-up written after Jack and Suzy toured the world, visiting various organizations and business schools. The follow-up has answers to some of the best and most commonly asked questions they heard while on this multinational tour.

### Howard Schultz – Starbucks

Howard Schultz was not the founder of Starbucks, but like Ray Kroc, who did not found McDonald's, but spearheaded its growth and transformation into a household name, Schultz created what we know today as the Starbucks concept – the coffeehouse with a welcoming atmosphere where people go to relax and enjoy the luxury of Italian-style coffee beverages. After reading his book *Pour Your Heart Into It*, I bought Starbucks stock because I felt that he operated the company according to the SLEEC principles I had learned were excellent predictors of business success. I sold much of my stock some time after Schultz stepped down as CEO, in part because the price had risen to a point where I thought that the company would need near perfect performance to avoid a major decline in price.

I wish I had sold all of it at that time because the price was more than $40 per share. I got a painful surprise when the price cratered, eventually dropping below my initial purchase price of about $9 per share during the crash of late 2008 to 2009. At that price I thought Starbucks was a bargain and I bought more shares. Also, Schultz had returned to take over the CEO role again, refocusing the company on its core values of customer service and maintaining a unique and welcoming atmosphere. He shut down many poorly performing stores and slashed the growth projections. I am happy to report that the overall return on Starbucks shares has been quite positive, despite my holding some shares through a peak to trough drop of more than 75%.

### Paul Orfalea – Kinko's Copy Shops

Paul Orfalea founded Kinko's Copy Shops when he was a college student. From the humble beginning of a single, small store in a college town, he grew the business to more than 1400 stores and eventually sold it to FedEx for more than $1 billion. After acquiring the company, FedEx raised prices significantly and reversed many of the policies (for example, 24-hour operation) that had been responsible for Kinko's success, which Orfalea outlined in his book *Copy This*! Because of the way FedEx reports its numbers it is difficult to tell how successful they have been with the copy shop division, but I suspect that it is no longer as successful as it was before the sale.

### *Fred DeLuca - Subway*

Just as Paul Orfalea founded Kinko's while in college, Fred DeLuca founded Subway, the sandwich shop company, when he was starting college. In his book *Start Small, Finish Big*, he tells the story of how Subway was started to provide him with a part-time job while he was in school. The idea for the company started with his partner and family friend Pete Buck. Fred sought council from Buck, his parents' good friend, about how to make some money while in school. Buck was a successful scientist and it just happened that he had read an article about an entrepreneur who had opened 32 sandwich shops in 10 years. He suggested that the two of them could be partners and they opened their first shop almost simultaneously with Fred's starting college in 1965. Pete Buck put up $1,000 in seed money and Subway was born. As of this writing in November of 2009, the Subway.com web site says that the chain has 31,949 stores in 91 countries. This is roughly the same number of stores McDonald's has around the world.

I particularly enjoyed *Start Small, Finish Big* because it includes stories of other entrepreneurs who started businesses with very little initial capital and turned them into successful enterprises, including Paul Orfalea, founder of Kinko's. In the book DeLuca outlines the 15 key lessons he learned that helped him "finish big" with Subway. This book is both useful and inspiring and I recommend it to any aspiring entrepreneur.

### *Ray Kroc – McDonald's Corporation*

The late Ray Kroc found inspiration in the form of a hamburger shop operated by the McDonald brothers (Mac and Dick) in San Bernardino, CA. In 1954, at the age of 52, Kroc decided to go into business with the McDonald brothers to launch what is now, arguably, the most successful restaurant chain in history. In his book *Grinding It Out: The Making of McDonald's*, Kroc describes his life and the trials and tribulations involved in growing the McDonald's corporation. The book is loaded with fascinating details about the hurdles Kroc and his team encountered and overcame during McDonald's amazing growth. Throughout the book, Kroc emphasizes the core values that have been central to the success of the McDonald's chain: *quality, service, cleanliness* and *value.*

### Fred Reichheld – Bain and Company
In his excellent books *The Loyalty Effect, Loyalty Rules!*, and *The Ultimate Question: Driving Good Profits and True Growth*, Fred Reichheld of Bain and Company outlines his research findings regarding what he terms the Loyalty Business Model which is described in detail in Chapter 2 of this book.

### Jeffrey J. Fox – Fox & Company
Jeffrey J. Fox has written many very practical books on various aspects of business management and success. His firm is a premier provider of marketing consultation services. Two of my favorite Fox books are *How to Make Big Money in Your Own Small Business* and *How to be a Fierce Competitor*. His books are short enough to be read in an evening, but packed with useful information.

### Brian Tracy – Brian Tracy International
Brian Tracy is a success guru who says that his personal mission is to help people to achieve their personal and business goals faster and easier than they ever imagined. While I am often reluctant to recommend "success coaches," I have been reading and listening to Brian Tracy's materials for years and have found them to be quite helpful. I particularly recommend his book *Eat That Frog!* (on time management) and *The 100 Absolutely Unbreakable Laws of Business Success.*

### Peter Drucker – Father of the Modern Discipline of Business Management
Peter Drucker was a business consultant, academic and the author of dozens of books on management and leadership. He is credited with being the inventor of the discipline of professional management and the ideas and concepts that he outlined in his books on the topic have influenced countless executives and business owners since the 1940s. I am continually amazed at how

many useful concepts and strategies about business had their origins in the mind of Peter Drucker, including many of those promoted in recent business books by other authors.

For those not familiar with Drucker's books, I recommend starting with *The Daily Drucker: 365 Days of Insight and Motivation for Getting the Right Things Done* (co-written with Joseph Maciariello), which is a compilation of his key ideas taken from his many books and articles. I also particularly like Drucker's book *The Effective Executive: The Definitive Guide to Getting the Right Things Done* and one of the many books about Drucker called *Inside Drucker's Brain* by Jeffrey A. Krames, which I provides a useful overview of key Drucker concepts.

### *Dan Kennedy – Marketing and Business Consultant*
I believe that Dan Kennedy's books are some of the best and most clearly written available on the subject of marketing for the small business owner. I have also read academically oriented texts that say many of the same things, but in a less clear and interesting manner. Although I don't agree with all of Mr. Kennedy's viewpoints, and some of his marketing methods make me uncomfortable, I generally find his books and other materials to be of tremendous value. I have probably learned more about marketing from his products than any other individual. In addition to the books listed above, his book *No BS Business Success* (the latest edition is called *No BS Business Success in the New Economy*) on the mindsets and habits of successful entrepreneurs is a classic.

### *Jim Collins – Business Researcher and Consultant*
Jim Collins is the author or co-author of several excellent books based on research conducted by him and his team of business students. The Collins team has conducted several years-long studies aimed at systematically identifying and analyzing factors associated with business success and failure. I particularly liked *Good to Great: Why Some Companies Make the Leap and Others Don't*, which reports their findings from a study of Fortune 500 companies that transitioned from good results to great results and then maintained great results (defined as stock returns three times

those of the general market) for at least 15 years. These good-to-great companies were compared with two sets of comparison companies: 1) a matched set in the same industry that showed no leap from good-to-great during the same period, and 2) a group that made a short-term shift from good-to-great, but did not maintain the trajectory.

### The Gallup Organization (Several Authors)

When people hear about a Gallup poll, many think of election-related opinion polls that are so often reported on news programs. What is less well known outside of the business community is that The Gallup Organization has a business unit called Gallup Consulting which has conducted interviews and surveys of literally millions of employees and managers. They have developed objective methods to evaluate employee engagement and provided compelling research-based evidence to support their assertion that managers can be taught skills that will help them to create a culture that encourages engagement. They have also shown that business units and companies that have high levels of employee engagement are more likely to have better outcomes, including lower employee turnover, enhanced customer satisfaction and greater profitability. I strongly recommend *First, Break All the Rules: What the World's Greatest Managers Do Differently* by Marcus Buckingham and Curt Coffman (who have both since left Gallup), as well as other books published by them and their Gallup colleagues.

### David Sirota – Sirota Consulting

Another group that has long been involved in the study of employee morale and attitudes is Sirota Survey Intelligence. Their model for organizational effectiveness is outlined in the excellent book *The Enthusiastic Employee: How Companies Profit by Giving Workers What they Want* by David Sirota, Loius A. Mischkind and Michael I. Meltzer.

### Richard Koch – Entrepreneur

Richard Koch is the author of several books, including three focusing on how to apply the PARETO principle (80/20 rule) in business and life. My favorites are *The 80/20 Principle* and *The*

*80/20 Individual.*  Koch has made a number of extremely successful personal private equity investments, including Filofax, Plymouth Gin, and Betfair.  He is also the co-founder of the LEK Consulting, a management consulting firm.

### Books about Warren Buffett, Charlie Munger, Berkshire Hathaway and its Subsidiaries

Many good books have been written about Warren Buffett, Charlie Munger and Berkshire Hathaway's operating managers. A few of my favorites are listed here and more are included in the bibliography.

1. *The Essays of Warren Buffett: Lessons for Corporate America* by Warren Buffett, selected, arranged and introduced by Lawrence Cunningham.  This is a collection of excerpts from Warren's letters to shareholders arranged by topic.
2. *The Real Warren Buffett: Managing Capital, Leading People* by James O'Loughlin.  This is a favorite of mine because it was the first to provide an in-depth analysis of Warren's approach to management.
3. *Poor Charlie's Almanack: The Wit and Wisdom of Charles T. Munger*, edited by Peter D. Kaufman.  This large, coffee-table style book is modeled after Ben Franklin's *Poor Richard's Almanack*.  The authors describe the book as "a survey of Charles T. Munger:  his approach to learning, decision making, investing, his speeches, his "zingers" and more."  While Warren gets most of the attention and press coverage, Charlie's influence on Warren and Berkshire Hathaway's success should not be underestimated and I believe that one can learn just as much valuable insight from studying his views and actions as from studying Warren's.
4. *The Snowball: Warren Buffett and the Business of Life* by Alice Schroeder.  This book is a biography of Warren for which he cooperated, giving Schroeder unprecedented access to himself as well as his family, friends and business associates.

5. *The Warren Buffett CEO: Secrets from the Berkshire Hathaway Managers* by Robert P. Miles. This book profiles 20 of Berkshire Hathaway's operating managers. I consider this a "must read" for any serious entrepreneur.

6. *Warren Buffett Speaks: Wit and Wisdom from the World's Greatest Investor* by Janet Lowe. This is a book of Warren's quotes and aphorisms organized by category with stories and descriptions by the author to add context. I especially enjoyed the audio book version.

7. *Damn Right! Behind the Scenes with Berkshire Hathaway Billionaire Charlie Munger* by Janet Lowe. This is a biography of Charlie for which the subject provided access to himself, family, friends and business associates.

8. *How to Build a Business Warren Buffett Would Buy: The RC Willey Story* by Jeff Benedict. In 2009 while attending the Berkshire Hathaway annual meeting I purchased a copy of this book. I started reading it on the plane ride home on Sunday, and first thing Monday morning I asked my assistant to order a copy for every member of our management team. The book is mostly the story of Bill Child, who, at age 22, took over a 600 square foot retail appliance store in 1954 when his father-in-law (RC Willey) died after a short bout with pancreatic cancer and built the business into large, successful operation that was acquired by Berkshire Hathaway in 1995.

9. *The Pampered Chef: The Story of One of America's Most Beloved Companies* by Doris Christopher. Warren Buffett wrote the foreword to this book in which he says that the book has a lot to teach anyone reaching for the American dream. He advises the aspiring entrepreneur to read it, then read it again. I could not agree more. I think Doris Christopher and her husband Jay are terrific success models.

10. *Pleased But Not Satisfied* by D.L. Sokol. David L. Sokol is the CEO of MidAmerican Energy, one of the largest Berkshire subsidiaries. He is often mentioned as a potential successor to Warren Buffett as Chairman of Berkshire Hathaway, and his qualifications for this role will be clear to those who read his book.

*Appendix B*

# Bibliography

A complete bibliography for this book may be found at our web site: www.TippingTheOdds.com.

**About the Author**

Kevin C. Maki, PhD is the founder and Chief Science Officer of Provident Clinical Research & Consulting, Inc., a company specializing in the design and conduct of clinical research on food and pharmaceutical products. In addition to being an expert in the prevention and management of coronary heart disease, he has spent more than 25 years studying the factors associated with entrepreneurial success. He is the author or co-author of five books and hundreds of articles on topics ranging from entrepreneurship and to preventive medicine.

# Index

maintaining contact with,
45–46, 81–83
maximizing lifetime value
of, 284–85
nurturing relationships
with, 87–88, 268–69
referrals, 84–85
Customers, repeat
and happy employees, 13
and PARETO Principle,
38
economics of, 15–17
rewards programs for, 83
Customer service
importance of, 269
training in, 96

Davidson, Michael, 119–20
Debt, 276
Delegation, 118
Dimon, Jamie, 94
Disability insurance, 131–32
Dow, Herbert H., 130
Downsizing, 54–55, 105, 131
Drucker, Peter, 7, 33, 103,
123, 266, 267
Dweck, Carol, 121
EATS, 270, 288
Edison, Thomas, 25
Effort, 121
Emotional intelligence, 110–
11
Employees
and Petero Principle, 37–
38
bad, walking away from,
18
choosing, 134–35
downsizing, 54–55, 131

engaged. *See* engagement,
employee
feedback for, 270
happy, 13, 270
hiring, 269–70
integrity in, 98
need of to buy into values,
111
number of, 50
rewarding. *See* MRT
E-Myth, 271–72
Engagement, employee. *See
also* management
achievement, 106–7, 288
and flexibility, 105–6
and loyalty, 14
and morale, 102–3
camaraderie, 107–8, 288
equity, 104–6, 288
goals for, 103–8
importance of, 100
praise *vs.* criticism, 113–
14
studies of, 101
Envy, 152
Equity, employee, 104–6,
288
Example, setting, 33, 136
Expectations
and communication, 151
and customer equity, 89–
91, 93–95
and success, 22–23
Expenses. *See* cost control

Failure, business
and cash flow, 52–55
and cost control, 50–52
and greed, 48–49

---

Kroc, Ray, 77–78, 271

Mistakes
avoiding obsessing over, 152
learning from, 137–38
Money, 147. *See also* MRT
Morale, employee, 102–3
MRT (money, recognition, and training), 29, 37, 50, 55, 106–7, 112, 270, 281, 289
Munger, Charlie, 4, 6, 32, 134–52, 291–92

Nebraska Furniture Mart, 156–58
Negativity, 32
Newsletters, 82
Niche, finding, 268
Night Light Designs, 187–204
Norwood, Annette, 233–43

Optimism, 22–23, 280
Orfalea, Paul, 78–79
Overhead, 50. *See also* cost control

Packaging, 76–78
Pampered Chef, 162–67
Patience, 280
PARETO Principle, 281–82
and customers, 38–39
and employees, 37–38
and products/services, 39
and sales/marketing, 59
and time management, 39–41
at GE, 37
explanation of, 35–36

Performance appraisal, 111–13
Persistence, 23–25, 157–58, 280
Polish, Joe, 61
Posh Salon and Color Bar, 233–43
Practice, 122
Praise, 113–14, 121
Predictions, 149–50
Price
and repeat customers, 16
and trust, 48
relationship to quality, 46–48
*vs.* value, 16
Problems
fixing, 86–87, 97–98
inverting, 150
Profitability and payroll expenses, 11–12
Provident Clinical Research & Consulting, Inc., 9

Quality, relationship to price, 46–48

Rath, Tom, 113
Reading, 136
Recessions
cost control during, 130–31
investing during, 130
managing through, 128–31, 289–90
preparing for, 127–28, 128–30
training during, 130
Recognition. *See* MRT